The
UNITED STATES
and
NORTHEAST
ASIA

The
UNITED STATES
and
NORTHEAST
ASIA

Edited by
Robert H. Puckett
Indiana State University

Nelson-Hall Publishers / Chicago

Project Editor: Rachel Schick
Cover Art: "Mountain Winds are Soft" by Nancy Fortunato

Library of Congress Cataloging-in-Publication Data

The United States and northeast Asia / edited by Robert H. Puckett.
    p.   cm.
  Includes bibliographical references and index.
  ISBN 0-8304-1279-4
  1. East Asia—Relations—United States. 2. United States—
Relations—East Asia. 3. East Asia—Relations—Russia (Federation).
4. Russia (Federation)—Relations—East Asia. I. Puckett, Robert
H.
  DS518.8.U586 1993
303.48¾27305—dc20   92-38565
                                                   CIP

Manufactured in the United States of America

10 9 8 7 6 5 4 4 2 1

™ The paper used in this book meets the
minimum requirements of American
National Standard for Information
Sciences—Permanence of Paper for
Printed Library Materials, ANSI
Z39.48-1984.

To my parents
and
Barbara and Sarah

CONTENTS

vii

INTRODUCTION

The United States faces a decade of transition in Northeast Asia, after the end of the Cold War and the momentous internal changes occurring in the former Soviet Union. Now there is an opportunity to shape a security structure for the region that includes the Commonwealth of Independent States, China, the United States, Japan, and South Korea, and/or a comprehensive arms control regime for Northeast Asia. Such approaches could create a consensus on the reunification of Korea, thus ending the last major Cold War crisis point.

Peaceful change in Northeast Asia will have to be based upon a broad political and strategic understanding among China, the former Soviet Union, and America as well as a strong U.S.–Japanese partnership and progress toward reunification of Korea. But there is no escaping the fact that this post-Cold War period of transition will be filled with anxiety, hazards, and challenges.

The eleven original essays in this volume analyze the trends emerging in Northeast Asia from a variety of perspectives. The contributors discuss the increasingly multipolar balance of power, potential interstate as well as internal conflicts, and the role of the United States in the period of transition toward security structures based on enhanced regional self-reliance.

Jimmy W. Wheeler surveys Japanese foreign and security policies in regard to the former Soviet Union, China, Korea, and the United States in "Japan's Security Role in the Post-Cold War Era." He argues convincingly that Japanese leaders believe that Asia is potentially an unstable region and that the end of the Cold

War has ushered in a period of transition which will be filled with great uncertainty and risk. In particular, Northeast Asia contains the last major Cold War crisis point—Korea—and has the highest levels of military readiness between American and Russian forces. As Japan continues to be involved in major economic and security issues affecting the world, its neighbors will perceive Japan's role as less threatening and more balanced if it is in a strong partnership with the United States.

In "Japan's Strategic Options," Martin E. Weinstein analyzes the current foreign policy debate in Japan by surveying the various positions of Japanese writers, publicists, government leaders, and foreign policy officials. He then discusses three very different scenarios for the future. Weinstein emphasizes that, "It is difficult to conceive of a future international environment in which the United States would gain substantial, lasting benefits by ending its alliance with Japan."

Robert S. Wood provides a thought-provoking analysis of the "new world order" and American national security strategy in "Naval Power in the Pacific in the Post-Cold War Era." He demonstrates that the naval buildup in the Pacific results from a "heightened sense of independence and the loosening in the geopolitical configuration that the end of the Cold War has generated." In the transitional period after the Cold War, peace and stability in Asia and the Pacific will depend upon a generalized understanding between the United States, the former Soviet Union, and China as well as solid U.S.–Japanese relations. Wood also stresses the importance of the presence of the U.S. Fleet in the Pacific to enhance the "stability of expectations" of nations in the region.

"An American Perspective on Security and Tension Reduction in the North Pacific," by Sheldon W. Simon, is an overview of East Asian security arrangements in a period of growing superpower détente. He proposes that in this transitional stage, Japan and South Korea will play more independent roles in an increasingly multipolar balance of power in Asia. Simon argues that, ". . . an immediate dissolution of security arrangements could create disorder and instability, precipitating conflicts among other states in Asia. Rather, dependence upon the United States as the prime security guarantor and market must be gradually altered as new security arrangements are forged and markets diversified."

Robert H. Puckett, in "Japan's Role in Regional and Global Security," argues that Northeast Asia is bound to be inherently unstable unless there is enhanced regional cooperation as well as a comprehensive arms control regime. America's medium-term role in the area will be as a balancer of power; and Japan will intensify its efforts in foreign aid, investment, and technology transfer. Japan, as the world's first "peace superpower," could contribute to a space-based global defense system in the post-Cold War era.

Stephen Blank, in "Moscow, Seoul, and Soviet Strategy in the Asia–Pacific Region," stresses the Russian objective of becoming an active dialogue partner in coping with security issues in Northeast Asia. As the internal political balance within the Soviet Union evolves, its security strategy will become less confrontational, but perhaps more unpredictable.

David Arase provides very useful historical background of Japanese policy toward North and South Korea, in "Japanese Policy Toward the Two Koreas in a Changing Security Environment." Arase stresses the importance of Japan's current equidistant, mediating role in the Korean peace process. That function could be expanded by Japan using its economic resources to enhance regional conflict resolution. The author concludes that, ". . . events in Northeast Asia have developed in such a way as to present Japan with an opportunity to enter into the ongoing process of ending the Cold War in Northeast Asia while strengthening ties with both Koreas."

In "U.S. Forces in Korea and Inter-Korean Arms Control Talks," Tae-Hwan Kwak presents his own timetable for a three-stage reduction of American military forces from South Korea. He contends that the U.S. troop reduction and withdrawal issue should be used as a political bargaining chip in arms control and peace negotiations with North Korea.

Many Americans see Northeast Asia as a key source of the perplexing new economic challenges confronting the United States in the post-Cold War era, according to Edward A. Olsen, in "Economic Frictions and Alliance Cohesion in Northeast Asia." Olsen argues that the former Soviet Union does not pose a credible threat to United States interests in Asia; and there are no other nations which threaten such interests, either. He maintains that economic competition with allies will become much more crucial to the United States than security issues. Olsen contends that Japan appears nervous that America will place greater emphasis on economic issues in ways that might damage alliance cohesiveness.

The United States, Japan, and South Korea have become increasingly interdependent in regard to access to goods and services as well as in security cooperation, according to Robert W. Beckstead, in "The United States' Economic Interdependence with Japan and the Republic of Korea." Beckstead provides a thorough analysis of the issue of protectionism versus free trade; economic growth patterns of America, Japan, and South Korea; direct foreign investment among the three nations; and the nature of economic interdependence among them.

R. Christopher Perry, in "American Themes Regarding Japan: The Persian Gulf Case," analyzes U.S. media treatment of Japanese internationalism and the proper "role" of Japan in international relations. As Perry argues, Japan often becomes a symbol of other concerns in domestic American politics. Also, media coverage ranges from "Japan-bashing" to internationalists' views of U.S.–Japan cooperation.

Japan's Security Role in the Post-Cold War Era

Jimmy W. Wheeler[1]

Introduction

The 1990s will be a critical transformative period for Japan. Fundamental pressures for change face the nation across a broad range of domestic and foreign issues. The country's demographics, its wealth, its global economic reach, and the expectations of its population are beginning to challenge the traditional political consensus that has produced perhaps the most impressive example of economic modernization in the twentieth century, a close political and security relationship with the United States, and more than thirty years of uninterrupted rule by the Liberal Democratic Party (LDP). Such fundamental domestic political and social changes will necessarily affect Japan's evolving role in the Pacific and the world, its policy responses to foreign and security concerns, and the health of its relationship with the United States.

The ultimate shape of the Japanese vision of their nation's international role that will emerge from the evolving domestic political debate remains unclear. Nevertheless, some responses to the basic forces to which Japanese society must adapt already are reasonably clear, and others are subject to informed speculation. Of course, this emerging international vision also will be influenced strongly by the domestic social, political, and economic challenges that the leadership will undoubtedly face in the

1

decade ahead. Moreover, Japan's policy vision will develop in a global fishbowl—Japan has become too important for outsiders to ignore. This paper will seek to assess the likely implications of these various trends for Japanese foreign and defense policy, particularly as it affects Japan's policies toward the Asia–Pacific region.

The analysis begins with a brief assessment of the 1990s context, Japan's current role in the world, and of the major international challenges with which it must deal. This is followed by a discussion of trends in domestic politics affecting foreign and defense policy. These various elements are then brought together to analyze some of the difficult foreign and defense policy choices being forced on the leadership. The final section projects the most likely outcomes, draws defense and foreign policy implications for Japan, and assesses some possible policy directions.

Uncertainty in the Midst of Change: Japan's Regional and Global Roles

The 1990s Context

The breathtaking political, security, social, and economic changes of the past decade pose fundamental policy challenges to all countries, but especially to Japan. The great ideological divides that have so dominated the post-World War II world are fast fading toward pragmatism and a narrow pursuit of national self-interest. The bipolar confrontation that defined alliances and lay as a backdrop to world affairs is slowly and erratically becoming a multipolar competition. As the perceived risk of global war abates and security increasingly becomes defined in regional and/ or economic terms, superpower ability to control regional events declines, old alliance structures weaken or are transformed, and the political, military, and economic leverage of regional powers rise.

Perhaps nowhere are the impacts of these great changes more ambiguous than in Northeast Asia. In most of Asia, the breakdown of bipolarity has occurred more rapidly than in many other parts of the globe. Yet, Northeast Asia contains the last major Cold War crisis point—the potential for conflict in Korea—and one of the highest levels of military readiness—between U.S.–

Japanese forces on the one hand and Soviet (now Russian) forces on the other. As the global superpower rivalry is being transformed, and as regional states increasingly pursue their own ambitions, old historical antagonisms reemerge and new regional rivalries are born, reshaping Asian political and security dynamics.

Economics has been a key force in creating this new environment. Ultimately, it was the economic success of the West that drove reform in the Soviet bloc. Gorbachev, forced to recognize economic failure, had to reduce Soviet military activity, seek to tap into the free world's economic dynamism, and shift the political competition with the West toward greater reliance on low-cost diplomatic initiatives.

Asia has been the showcase for the success of capitalism, becoming the most economically dynamic region of the world. No major corporation can now succeed without an Asia strategy, whether defensive or offensive. Economic policymakers in every major and most smaller nations face daily concerns about the yen exchange rate, Tokyo and Hong Kong interest rates, and financial decisions made by Taiwanese and Japanese central banks. Trade within the region is growing faster than extra-regional trade, raising concerns about the emergence of an Asian trade bloc focused on Japan.

Japan, without question, has star billing in this Asian drama. However, the strongest economic dynamism has already shifted to the "four tigers" (Hong Kong, Singapore, South Korea, and Taiwan) and beyond (notably Thailand). Moreover, from Japan's point of view, the trends toward a North American free trade area and the plans for Europe 1992, combined with strong protectionist reactions to Japan's success, present a potentially hostile international trading regime. Thus, Japan's new prominence already faces global competition, even as it is a major beneficiary from regional growth.

The political transformation of Asia is as equally impressive as the economic change. As U.S.–Soviet tensions eased, there was improvement in Sino–Soviet and Soviet–Japanese relations. Vietnam has withdrawn from Cambodia and is seeking to improve relations with the rest of the world. Various countries are dealing with the challenge of developing democratic systems. New leaders are emerging, less bound by the emotional and policy burdens of World War II, independence struggles, and challenges of internal conflict and nation building. This creates new directions and

3

new constraints on these nations' foreign and security policies.

In the 1990s, as all of the new and accelerating changes interact, the Asian political environment will become highly fluid. State behavior will become much less predictable, and the opportunities for new alliances, major policy innovation, and confrontation rise sharply. For Japan and the United States, in particular, the possibility of great change forces reconsideration of what have been quite successful policy strategies.

A rapidly changing economic and political environment leads directly to a new security landscape. Tensions have eased between the components of the former Soviet Union and both Japan and China. The former Soviet Republics have eased their confrontational policies toward American friends in Asia, notably the Association of Southeast Asia Nations (ASEAN) and South Korea, and are seeking acceptance in the region as legitimate political and economic players. The decline in Soviet/Russian military activity in the region is raising regional and domestic pressures to scale back the American presence as well, even though military forces arrayed against vital American interests have changed only marginally. These pressures intensify existing trends leading toward a reduction of the U.S. military presence in Asia, including the confrontational Philippines bases negotiations; the sometimes rocky relationship with allies over burden sharing, bases, and other issues; and growing Congressional efforts to cut the defense budget.

This decline in superpower presence and military confrontation appears to many to signify a great reduction in the risk of war. It is most certainly a reduction in the risk of superpower conflict. But the reality is that as the superpowers reduce their military presence, the regional powers are expanding and modernizing their own military capabilities. Some of these states clearly see improved military capabilities as necessary to assert their own regional power objectives. Neighbors are forced to respond in kind, in order to protect their own interests. This is already well advanced in the Middle East, and, of course, Korea. What is new in Asia is a region-wide military buildup that will result in the development of significant capabilities by the end of the 1990s. The most serious concerns for regional stability are the blue water naval forces being developed by China and India.

If the reduction of superpower tension also reduces American presence and willingness to help manage regional events, and thereby encourages regional powers to assert their own national interests, the risk of regional political confrontation and limited armed conflicts of varying intensity could very well increase in the 1990s.

America faces a situation in which long-term forces are challenging its presence and policy approach in Asia, even as its political, strategic, and economic interests in the region are rising. Continued global interests in the context of declining relative power will force the United States to develop more complex, cooperative mechanisms to deal with an increasingly fluid, multipolar environment. America's mobilization of international support in the Iraq–Kuwait crisis may be prototypical of 1990's crisis-response patterns.

Similarly, long-term forces are creating an Asia and indeed a world that require Japan to take actions that help protect not only narrow commercial interests, but the broader interests of Japanese friends and allies. Japan cannot and should not continue to depend upon the United States to manage and direct such actions. Japan is too rich and has too many of its own specific interests for a dependency relationship not to generate growing friction and resentment on both sides. However, Japan has not yet developed either the vision or the institutional structure for dealing with many political and security challenges without relying upon strong U.S. leadership and its security umbrella. Thus, fundamental forces are pushing Japan toward redefining its role in the region and world in the 1990s.

Japan's Changing Roles

That Japan has become an important regional and global player is obvious to all. Also obvious is Japan's struggle to define the current and future dimensions of this relatively new international role. The challenge, of course, is that this effort must contend both with enormous global change and fundamental domestic restructuring.

Among the many global changes, five stand out.[2] First, Japan's economic interests have become worldwide, extremely complex, and more dependent upon an active government role in the international community. Secondly, trade and investment frictions have intensified with virtually all of its major trading partners. Thirdly, the European Community's 1992 plans and the U.S.–Canada Free Trade Agreement raise the specter of the emergence of inward-looking trade blocs that might seek to exclude Japan.[3] Fourthly, Japan faces intense, if often contradictory, external pressures to take on greater political, diplomatic, and security responsibilities, especially from the United States. Finally, the collapse of the Soviet empire, with its sharply different impacts in Europe and Asia, has imbued the whole process of identifying Japan's emerging interests, threats, and future roles with a much greater sense of urgency.

Until recent years, Japan's global and regional roles have been almost entirely economic—indeed commercial—in nature. Economic progress has been the overriding goal and driving force behind Japanese policymaking, both domestic and foreign, for most of the four-and-a-half decades since the end of World War II. Most other policy areas, especially foreign and defense policy, took secondary roles.[4] While the United States served as Japan's sponsor in the world community, its guarantor of non-aggressive behavior with neighbors in Asia, and its shield from major external threats, and Japan's economy remained modest-sized in global terms, Japan could tie external policy reactively to that of the United States and devote most of its attention to economic gain. However, Japan's awesome economic success has made that strategy untenable.

Economic Dimensions of Japan's Global and Regional Roles[5]

Although, as the Japanese so often tell us, Japan is "a small island nation with no natural resources," its gross national product has grown five-fold since 1963, increasing its share of gross world product to more than 13 percent in 1988. Japan now is the second largest economy in the world after the United States ($2.4 trillion versus $4.5 trillion in 1987), the second largest exporter (since 1988), and the largest creditor nation (since 1986). In 1988 Japan passed the United States as the largest provider of overseas development assistance (ODA). Japanese firms also have become major sources of foreign direct investment worldwide, pushing Japan into fourth rank after the United States, the U.K., and West Germany in 1988. The largest banks in the world are now Japanese, and corporate Japan has an increasingly global presence.

Table 1.1 • Trade Dependency: 1988 (Percent of GNP)

	Exports	Imports
Japan	9.3	6.6
United States	6.6	9.4
West Germany	26.8	20.7
United Kingdom	17.8	23.2

Source: *Japan 1990: An International Comparison* (Tokyo Kieixai Koho Center, 1990).

Regionally, the economic might of Japan is even more pronounced. Japan's economic role in Asia, with the exception of the immediate post-World War II years, always has been large and has rapidly strengthened.[6] The most striking changes have been in finance, foreign investment, and official development assistance—where the Japanese expanded dramatically throughout the 1980s—and in the rapid growth of manufactured imports in just the past few years.

The magnitude of Japan's involvement in regional and world economies highlights its stake in continued global economic growth and stability, as well as the world's stake in a Japan that integrates smoothly into international economic institutions, negotiations, and practices. Economic forces produce several important implications for foreign and security policy concerns.

Compared to other major nations' histories, the current magnitude of Japan's involvement with the world economy occurred over an extremely short time span. The mindset of the domestic leadership and the institutional framework within which it works simply could not adjust rapidly enough. This adjustment problem was intensified by the relative lack of experience caused by its largely passive acquiescence to American policy leadership for most of the post-World War II period, the lack of a domestic vision or consensus to guide policymaking, and its relatively low trade share in domestic output and consumption—lower than any other major industrial country except the United States (table 1.1).[7]

The shocks and instability of the 1970s and the acceleration of economic interdependence of the 1980s have initiated fundamental changes in Japan's domestic perceptions about the rest of the world, which in turn are supporting the development of new

7

external policies, both more global and more proactive. Indeed, the 1980s saw an intense, but so far only partially successful, effort to come to terms with the large gap between Japan's economic and political power, presence, and roles.

Japan's growing global economic reach is forcing the creation of a more complex global foreign policy, though it remains strongly economics-focused. Major new issues of policy concern now include: economic cooperation among the industrial states, overall macroeconomic management of key international challenges (such as Third World debt and integrating the former Soviet-bloc states into the international system), and the functioning of multilateral economic organizations (GATT, IMF, IBRD, ADB, etc.).[8] Economic assistance has become a favored foreign policy tool, especially within the Pacific. Indeed, some 63 percent (1988) of Japan's bilateral aid goes to Asia, providing over half of total aid flows to the nations of East and Southeast Asia.[9] Japan also has supported various forms of regional cooperation, including those organized in the private sector and as a "Dialogue Partner" in the ASEAN summits. Most recently, the Asia–Pacific Economic Cooperation Conference (APEC) process, initiated by Prime Minister Hawke of Australia in 1989, has received the most attention.[10] Moreover, among the multilateral organizations in which Japan has sought a greater role, the ADB was a principal objective.

Besides clear economic self-interest, many other forces have slowly been creating a growing acceptance of the need for an expanded global role. Three of the most important are an understandable pride in the nation's economic achievements, a growing sense of nationalism, and a United States that is less willing to represent and protect Japanese interests on the global stage. Particularly in the 1980s, the Japanese government has sought a higher international policy profile, and has taken a variety of initiatives to achieve that profile. Nonetheless, Japan's global political and security roles have remained highly circumscribed.

Political and Security Dimensions of Japan's Global and Regional Roles

There is a great public reluctance in Japan to become heavily engaged in global political, diplomatic, and security issues. Indeed,

Iraq's invasion of Kuwait served to point out the systemic problems that Japan faces in dealing with global threats, even when vital national interests are at stake.[11] Even so, the longer-term question must be explored. Can a nation with the economic and technological strength of Japan remain a purely regional and commercial power, without taking on global and political/security roles? If, as this chapter contends, the answer is "no," then one must ask, when and in what specific ways will the Japanese seek to convert their potential into actual political power?[12] This section reviews Japan's evolving political and security roles, and explores areas for which a more proactive posture may and, in some cases, must be developed.

Until recently, Japan's role in the world has been that of a commercial democracy, operating largely outside major global political and security developments.[13] Until the late 1960s, Japanese foreign policy was essentially submerged within American policy. Japan's leadership chose to tie foreign and security policy to the United States and concentrate on economic progress. Indeed, Japan's leadership recognized early in the post-World War II period that economic progress was the basis for national strength. The Cold War and the invasion of South Korea only served to reinforce the decision to abide by American leadership, despite the lack of domestic political unanimity on this choice. Such a relationship achieved several key foreign policy and security concerns simultaneously.[14]

- It accelerated reintegration into the global economy and international relations under American tutelage.
- It provided a "cost-effective" security arrangement that insured protection against all major threats without itself presenting any threat to Japan's neighbors.
- It helped commit the United States to supporting Japan's long-term economic goals.

The costs, of course, were linking the nation tightly to America foreign and security leadership, accepting a permanent American military presence, and acquiescing to the need to rearm in concert with broad U.S. requirements. However, with two major exceptions, American regional foreign and security policy concerns were highly compatible with those of Japan.

The first exception was the American effort to isolate China.[15] Even here, where they had great policy reservations,

Japan formally adopted the U.S. position. However, Japan also pursued an informal China diplomacy, and carefully balanced its formal policy by trading simultaneously with Taiwan and the mainland.[16]

The second exception was America's early efforts to include Japan as an active participant in its regional political and security affairs, especially its containment policy. Although Japan's conservative leadership held no sympathy with communists at home or abroad and maintained strong historical suspicion of the Russians, fear of being pulled into an Asian conflict cut broadly across the political spectrum. At no time was this made more public than during the short but intense domestic political turmoil over the 1960 revision of the bilateral security treaty with the United States. Throughout these early formative years, Japan's leadership skillfully managed the bilateral relationship not only to limit their actual security role to self-defense, but to convince the American leadership it was their most appropriate role.[17]

By separating politics and security from economics in its external relations, Japan was able to pursue a foreign commercial policy and achieve important diplomatic gains that may not have been possible with a more active political and security involvement. Examples include: the 1964 successful American sponsorship of Japan for membership in the OECD; Japan's hosting of the Olympic Games in the same year; normalization of relations between Japan and South Korea in 1965 under strong U.S. guidance; and reentry into regular commercial relations with most non–communist Pacific states throughout the 1960s.

The end of the 1960s, however, marked the beginning of what proved to be a period of severe challenge to the assumptions of this rather unusual policy arrangement. Besides the economic shocks and instability, the Japanese faced serious concern about a number of regional political trends: American involvement in Vietnam (first fear of being drawn in, then fear of the consequences of American failure); the Sino–Soviet split; recurring threats of American pullback from Asia (the precipitous American withdrawal from Vietnam, Nixon's one division drawdown of U.S. forces in Korea, and the Carter Administration announcement of a planned withdrawal of all ground forces from Korea); the increasing perception of the United States as an unreliable ally; and the rapid growth of Soviet forces in East Asia.

These trends initiated a broad domestic debate on Japanese foreign and security policy, a debate that in many respects remains unresolved today. Several strands stand out in this internal debate on foreign and security policy. One of the older and, for many years, more powerful was an idealistic vision of demonstrating to the world that "a modern industrial nation could expand without arming itself and that nation states could engage in mutually beneficial relations in a peaceful international order."[18] As articulated by such public policy positions as "security without armaments," the various versions of this vision have held strong emotional appeal for the Japanese people, and have heavily influenced policy thinking. The power of this vision has weakened, although it retains an important role in the platforms of some opposition groups, most notably the Japanese Socialist Party (JSP). Nonetheless, such attitudes have deep roots in Japan's postwar social character.

In the 1960s, the concept of an omnidirectional foreign policy emerged, building in part on this idealist vision, in part on the decision to enshrine economic progress as the policy goal against which all other policy must be tested, and, not inconsequentially, on the need to minimize the increase in perceived threats to Japan's security. Proponents took the position that Japan should rely almost exclusively upon economic exchanges as a means of establishing the nation's international relations across as wide a political and ideological spectrum as possible. It was perceived by many of its supporters as a non-threatening foreign policy that could use economic means to both reduce threats to Japan and promote worldwide peace. To the extent that it came to be accepted that Japan must play a larger world role, such a nonideological policy basis catered strongly to the great Japanese reluctance to become politically involved. With the growing perception of external risk in the 1970s, and a reduction in the perceived reliability of the United States, Japan tried to diversify its relations with as many nations as possible. In general, this approach was kept consistent with its overall bilateral relationship with the United States. However, in one case Japan sharply split with the American policy—it joined the West Europeans in taking a pro-Arab stance after 1973.

Outsiders saw this policy approach as highly mercantilistic and opportunistic. Japan could take advantage of events and trends without taking any national political stand. Moreover, even to some of its Japanese proponents, it became clear that such a policy could only work explicitly in the context of the special security relationship with the United States. Over time, support for the purist position weakened as it became increasingly obvious that growing economic power was inconsistent with avoidance of political involvement. Even so, an omnidirectional bias and a strong preference for the use of economic interaction remain fundamental characteristics of Japanese foreign policy.

A third, and less historically prominent, strand in the web of Japanese foreign and security thinking might be called pragmatic nationalism. Typically, proponents accept that Japan has regional and global interests requiring protection. Moreover, from their perspective, the realities of the modern world also require that Japan more explicitly align itself with nations holding long-term interests most consistent with those of Japan, and take on greater responsibilities in helping those friends maintain stability, peace, and economic vitality in Asia and the world. In general, supporters of this view tend to believe that Japan has a strong stake in helping to promote greater democracy and free markets. The 1980s saw far greater attention and respect given to this view. Prime Minister Nakasone (1982–1987), in particular, can be pointed to as crystalizing and promoting this position.

Insular nationalism perhaps best characterizes the fourth major stand in the debate over Japan's external role. Some of its basic propositions are not, in and of themselves, unreasonable. Proponents see the development of Japanese foreign and security policy, and of Japan's external role since World War II, as unnatural and unhealthy. In general, they seek a Japan whose political and security roles are commensurate with its economic power. These propositions are reasonably consistent with those of the pragmatic nationalists above. However, the remaining basic positions become far more extreme. Some spokesmen for this view see, or at least express, limited common interest with the Western democracies. Others seem to believe in the inevitable emergence of a fundamental divergence of interest with the West, for which Japan must prepare. The most extreme groups see a militarized, even nuclear-armed, Japan.

Although the extreme views are rejected by most of the population, clear signs of growing nationalism give the insular nationalists a rising potential impact. Even a few years ago, the now well-known Shintaro Ishihara, member of the Diet and coauthor of *The Japan That Can Say 'No,'* with Sony Chairman Akio Morita, would have been largely ignored. Today his aggressive, nationalistic stance is attracting considerable support among younger Japanese.[19] The growing nationalism reflected in this support comes from a variety of sources: quite understandable pride in the nation's economic and technological progress, defensiveness about the disruption to Japan's cohesive society from foreign influences, and reaction to persistent and rising economic confrontation, all intensified by the arrogance and insensitivity that characterize a highly insular and cohesive culture.

Pragmatic nationalism is now the basis for declaratory policy, but in fact none of these strands are dominant today in Japanese policymaking. Indeed, it is difficult to fit most individuals and groups rigidly into one of these positions. All of these various strands are components of the mainstream debate on Japanese foreign and security policy. The leadership, and even individuals, seem to adopt positions that reflect any or all of these strands based on current needs.

It was out of this background that Japan's concept of comprehensive security emerged. The 1980 "Report on Comprehensive National Security," prepared by a study group established by Prime Minister Ohira Masayoshi, became the basic guidance for Japanese external policy.[20] Although the term "comprehensive security" has fallen from favor, the analysis presented in this report and its recommendations have guided policy formation more or less strongly for all governments since 1980.

Using the terminology from above, this report may be best described as the bible of the pragmatic nationalists. It wove together various aspects of the domestic, foreign, and security policy debate, and presented, at least in general terms, a policy framework for a more active external policy that dealt with many of the pressing concerns. Several points stand out. It explicitly expressed the belief that the United States was "no longer able to provide its allies and friends with nearly full security." It further recognized that Japan had done little to promote the peaceful world it had publicly advocated, relying instead upon others.

The report went on to advocate Japanese policy action on three levels: "efforts to turn the overall international environment into a favorable one; self-reliant efforts to cope with threats; and as intermediary efforts, efforts to create a favorable international environment within limited scope while protecting security in solidarity with countries sharing the same ideals and interests.''

One of the more important implications was the rejection of omnidirectional policy as a guiding principle and the recommendation that Japan's security was best preserved by explicitly linking national policy with its friends and allies.

Another important change was the elevation of priority given to national defense. Comprehensive security was expressed as a policy framework to protect Japan against all forms of external threat, using whatever economic, diplomatic, and defense instruments were most appropriate.[21] No guidance was provided on how the appropriate balance was to be made, but in principle, national defense was elevated to equal status with economic and diplomatic policy. Although in practice national security receives lower status, this policy change was fundamental to the enhanced role and budgets of the Japanese Self Defense Force during the 1980s.

A variety of initiatives were taken under the umbrella of this new doctrine. As noted above, Japan was most aggressive in economic diplomacy, international economic policy management, and providing economic assistance to developing countries.[22]

Japan's political and security initiatives under this new umbrella remain highly circumscribed by Western standards, but, by Japanese standards, policymakers have been quite daring. The basic trends have included:

- A more active and comprehensive use of Japan's participation in the annual economic summits to express and pursue Japanese views on major policy issues of the day.[23]
- An explicit effort to be Asia's spokesperson in various advanced country fora, most notably the summits and the OECD.
- An expansion of economic assistance in total and outside Asia, and of the share targeted on political and strategic objectives important to the West as a whole.[24]
- A more-or-less sustained effort to enhance Japan's relationships with all countries in Asia, expressed initially with the Fukuda Doctrine (August 1977).[25]
- Provision of support for a wide variety of initiatives to promote a Pacific community.

- Greater cooperation in joint Western political actions, such as boycott of the Soviet Olympics, other Soviet sanctions, sanctions against Vietnam, diplomatic pressure on China, etc.—though in some cases reluctantly.
- Agreement to expand its role in sea-lane protection and surveillance out to 1,000 nautical miles.
- Expanded participation in joint military exercises with American forces.
- A positive role in seeking a solution to the Cambodia quagmire, by supporting ASEAN initiatives, offering economic support to help insure the success of the agreement that has emerged, and, more controversially, hosting a meeting of the competing parties in 1990, in an effort to restart the stalled peace process.[26]
- A growing willingness to pursue an independent policy path on important international issues. For example, Prime Minister Toshiki Kaifu took a strong stance on China and the Soviet Union at the 1990 Houston summit that was respectively more accommodating and far less accommodating than either the North American or European participants.

These basic foreign and security policy trends are some of the more noticeable, but are only part of a broader diplomatic engagement worldwide. Clearly, policymakers have accepted that Japan must adopt a more global policy approach. It is increasingly recognized that an economics-only foreign policy is inadequate. Moreover, the vital link between peace and stability, especially in Asia, and Japanese well-being are becoming accepted. This, in turn, is leading to the very slow acceptance that Japan must take actions to enhance such peace and stability. However, except regarding the nation's economic stake, Japan has yet to develop an international outlook among its political leadership, much less a shared domestic vision of Japan's role in the world to guide policy. Iraq's invasion of Kuwait revealed that even in a crisis with great potential impact on Japan, neither the political process nor the polity as yet has truly accepted international political and security responsibilities.

To the extent that a Japanese external role is accepted, the consensus is that it should build primarily upon economic leverage and aid. Indeed, consistently since the early 1980s, Japan has responded to American pressures for increased security burden sharing in Asia with proposals for expanded economic support of countries and initiatives that have great strategic interest to both nations.

Although Japan has been willing to challenge U.S. policy on some important issues, including Arab–Israeli policy, the Iran–Iraq war, and the treatment of China, Japan has consistently supported most U.S. policy positions. One major long-term Japanese policy objective has been to keep the United States actively engaged in Northeast Asia. There remains a deep-seated perception that an Asia without a strong American presence would be potentially threatening to Japan.[27] Despite all the various changes and initiatives noted above, the bilateral relationship with the United States remains Japan's single most important foreign policy issue.

As the 1990s begin, global events are changing so rapidly that Japan will be forced to continually respond in ways that challenge the slowly evolving domestic consensus on foreign and security policy. The greatest challenge is to the U.S.–Japan relationship. Though neither side seems willing to face up to this challenge, economic, political, and security trends appear to present two rather stark alternatives for the 1990s. The positive alternative is that both nations begin to come to grips with their respective domestic problems and start a fundamental reassessment and rebuilding of the U.S.–Japan bilateral relationship to take advantage of the great mutual interests and complementary strengths. The negative alternative is a continuation of current trends, in which there is a cumulative deterioration of the relationship, rising nationalism on both sides, declining gains from economic exchange, a reduced U.S. presence in Asia, and concomitantly, higher regional tension and greater potential risk of instability and conflict. However the U.S.–Japan relationship evolves, it will shape, to a large extent, Japan's responses to the many other global challenges with which it must deal. Because of its importance, the challenge of managing the bilateral relationship will be returned to below.

Japanese Foreign and Security Policy: The Domestic Political Dimension

Outside observers have watched the recent convulsions in Japanese domestic politics with both concern and amusement.

Amusement always seems to accompany the antics of high ranking officials embroiled in scandal. But the concern was over what this turmoil might mean for Japanese foreign and domestic policy, since either large policy changes or policy immobility could have important global and regional impacts. Intensifying this concern is the insular nature of Japanese politics and leadership. Foreign affairs generally have limited impact on the domestic political process, and the foreign impact of domestic affairs even less.

This insular character reflects several aspects of Japan's post-World War II development, some of which were noted above. Despite its reliance on the international economy, Japan's trade share in gross national product is lower than any of the advanced nations except the United States. Until recently, only small numbers of Japanese traveled or lived abroad, and those who did have extensive foreign contact were often viewed with suspicion. Culturally, Japan has a strong self-image of uniqueness, and comparatively few foreigners have sought to learn the very difficult Japanese language, its history and culture. Geographically, Japan has been isolated from countries of similar levels of economic power and development. Combined with the natural historical suspicions of its lesser developed neighbors, this geographic isolation prevented the development of comparably widespread business, social, education, and other relationships that came to bind the countries within and among Western Europe and North America.

Foreign Policy Issues in Domestic Politics

How have domestic politics influenced foreign and defense policy? With a few important exceptions, through most of the postwar period foreign and defense policy has been left to a small handful of experts in the ministries. The few times when foreign and security policy became issues of high politics, however, have had profound impacts on Japanese policymaking.

First was the intense controversy over and following the San Francisco Peace Treaty and the U.S.–Japan Security Treaty, both signed on September 8, 1951. Indeed, 1945 to the early 1960s was a period of great volatility in party politics, in part centered on matters of Japan's external relations. The intense ideological struggle between the socialists and the conservatives continued until the early 1960s, when the two party framework began to fracture into a multiparty system. The fracturing was mainly on the left. The great controversy over the revision of the security treaty in 1960, and the failure of the socialists to significantly affect the outcome, contributed to already strong splits in the socialist party. By adopting many of the concerns of the left, including carefully managing the inevitable tensions between the strong support for Japan's "Peace Constitution" and by the comprehensive U.S.–Japan alliance enshrined in the Mutual Security Treaty, and by concentrating almost totally on economic progress, Japan's leadership made great strides in eliminating confrontational ideological struggle from the center stage of domestic political debate.

A strong and ideologically intransigent opposition remained, however, Periodically during the 1960s and 1970s this opposition managed to force important foreign policy and security concessions from an internally divided LDP.[28] At the height of the Vietnam War (strongly opposed by the Japanese left and only ambivalently supported by the conservatives), when it became known that Japanese firms were providing important weapons components for systems used to prosecute the air war against North Vietnam, strong protests forced the government of Prime Minister Sato Eisakuin in 1968 to adopt an arms export ban and propound the three nonnuclear principles (no possession, no production, and no introduction into Japan)—both of which subsequently became fundamental policy constraints.

Adoption of Japan's one percent of GNP limit on defense spending has a similar history. In the mid-1970s, antimilitary forces in Japanese politics had become quite strong. Moreover, strong links between the government of Prime Minister Miki and the opposition parties were an important part of the prime minister's leverage within the LDP. Signs of opposition to Japan's National Defense Program Outline for the years after fiscal 1977 led the prime minister to look for ways to ease its passage without weakening his complex and highly disparate support base. The one percent limit and the ratification of the nuclear nonproliferation treaty in the same year became important parts of that effort. Indeed, the limit was announced by Self Defense Agency Chief Sakata Michita before the Diet while defending the defense program against opposition criticism—only six weeks before what was expected to be a crucial election in 1976.

Another case is the attribution of the sharp electoral losses by the LDP in the December 1983 election to Prime Minister Yasuhiro Nakasone's aggressive foreign policy and outspoken hawkish behavior. After the prime minister toned down his public position for two-and-a-half years, the LDP came back with its biggest-ever victory in the July 1986 election.[29] The political message seen by the LDP leadership was strong and clear. Do not reach too far, too fast. The Japanese polity continues to tightly constrain foreign and defense policy initiative.

Major Participants in Japanese Foreign and Defense Policymaking

That Japanese foreign and defense policy responds so readily to opposition and popular pressures flies in the face of some of the fashionable claims about Japanese politics. In particular, the interaction of the various major policy players is generally misunderstood outside Japan.

Policymaking in Japan is usually described as a triumvirate of the LDP, big business, and the bureaucracy, with the latter having preeminence. Although this may be a useful breakdown for many purposes, in fact, the process has always been far more complex and is becoming even more so. Indeed, it would be impossible to explain such examples as the one percent defense spending limit in this framework.

In general, however, foreign policy has far fewer participants than other policy areas, and has been left largely to the bureaucracy, especially the Foreign Ministry, to manage. The strength of the bureaucracy has been enhanced by the limited number of domestic politicians or interest groups with a strong perceived self-interest in foreign policy outcomes, the resulting low profile that foreign issues normally take in the domestic political debate, and a prime minister and Cabinet whose tenures in office have been very short in recent years. The Ministry of Foreign Affairs plays the central coordinating role in Japan's foreign and defense process.[30] It acquired stature and power during and after the Occupation, as it came to be the primary organ for managing relations with the United States. With essentially all external issues subordinated to the bilateral relationship, the Foreign Ministry became the key player. Moreover, since defense was a core part of the bilateral relationship, defense policy became the responsibility of the North American Bureau, while the Defense Agency was primarily in charge of military operations. By international standards the Ministry's budgets and staff are small, and it lacks a strong domestic power base that can be used to support its policy initiatives. Much of its power comes from its position as coordinator of conflicting interests on most issues of external policy.

As Japan's international interests have grown, this central coordinating role has been challenged by a variety of other ministries, especially the Ministry of International Trade and Industry (MITI) over trade and other economic policy issues. MITI's involvement in dealing with American trade frictions, in particular, challenged a central Foreign Ministry policy role and priority. Many other aspects of international relations now influence the policy debate and create strong demands on Foreign Ministry expertise and focus. Interministerial conflicts over turf, and the expanding internationalization of Japan now require the Ministry to explain to and involve a broad range of Japanese people and organizations on many foreign issues.

Japanese industrial might, the close relationship between the government and business sectors on many levels, and the enormous appetite for campaign funds by the political process often give a perception of strong business influence on the policy process. Business issues clearly receive priority concern in the policy process. But on many issues, business remains but one voice among many, especially if there is no strong consensus. Even when a strong consensus exists, business may not win. In the late 1960s, when economic priorities were higher than today, a strong business consensus existed around the notion of making Japan the "Arsenal of Democracy" for the United States. This did not stop adoption of Japan's arms export ban. Business similarly opposed the one percent limit on defense spending.

Because of the reliance of Japan on economic exchanges as foreign policy levers, the government must determine what the private sector might be willing, or induced, to undertake. Japan's promises to help the Eastern European countries to succeed can only be fulfilled if they can design a package that private firms will agree to join, which in turn assures a commercial cast to both policies and aid. Much of Japanese foreign policy has this commercial character, even that which was designed with more strategic objectives in mind.

Through the mid-1960s, the Diet mainly served to rubber-stamp LDP policies and bureaucratic initiatives. Thereafter, it became an increasingly important policymaking forum. With the economic growth slowdown after the first oil shock, Japan faced difficult domestic policy trade-offs. The bureaucracy could not and, by standards of most democracies, should not make large programmatic changes. Political bargaining became more important and increasingly institutionalized. As a result, during the past two decades, but especially in the 1980s, both the Diet and the prime minister have enhanced their power in general, including over foreign and defense policymaking. The effectiveness of the prime minister's office on foreign and defense policy concerns, however, has depended very much upon the individual prime minister, and his own factional power. For example, Prime Minister Nakasone reorganized the Cabinet Secretariat in 1986, greatly strengthening its crises management functions and its overall coordination capabilities. Yet, Prime Minister Kaifu chose not to engage this process in response to Iraq's invasion of Kuwait.[31] By standards of Western democracies, the prime minister is weak and the role of the Diet in policymaking limited. In part, this reflects the highly factionalized parties and the structure of the electoral process that focuses on party and patronage almost to the exclusion of issues.[32]

Important recent changes include much stronger use of personal diplomacy by all recent prime ministers, and Prime Minister Ohira's introduction of the use of outside advisory commissions, deliberately chosen to deal with bureaucratic and party barriers to important policy changes. Nakasone used such commissions quite effectively, notably on defense and international economic policy. Both of these mechanisms have proved useful in stimulating change in situations where intense factional differences or interministerial turf barriers have led to political immobility. The relative weakness of the prime ministership in Japan suggests that such leadership can probably only occur in crisis situations, or under other circumstances in which the imperative for action is beyond the bureaucracy's capabilities.[33]

Current and Future Challenges

Japanese domestic politics face important pressures for adjustment and change. The tensions between these pressures and the great systemic rigidities could have strong impacts on foreign and defense policy. Although the number of participants in formulating policy has expanded, the Japanese political system remains highly insular. Not surprisingly, foreign and defense policy suffers from constraints imposed by higher priority domestic interests.[34] In particular, solutions to domestic problems often will not consider foreign concerns or impacts.

At the same time as external forces are requiring creative response, so too are domestic forces, producing a strong political competition for attention and resources. Dealing with a more politicized domestic environment also has become more difficult. Domestic politics have become more pluralistic. Opposition parties are attempting to shed some of their more extreme policy positions and compete for the center. The loss of an LDP majority in the upper house of the Diet increased both the opposition influence on policy and the possibility of acquiring greater future influence. The prime minister and the LDP (with varying degrees of internal enthusiasm) are pushing for political reform, reflecting public reaction to the recent scandals. Yet, no one is confident that they really understand all of the implications of the proposed reforms, and the various parties and factions within parties are seeking to protect themselves. If reform is adopted, and at least some aspects probably will be, political campaigns should become more issue oriented. Growing wealth and growing power of politicians will continue to reduce the power of the bureaucracy. Finally, all of this will occur in the context of a generational change in Japan's leadership and voting population. The emerging new leaders have grown up in a postwar, post recovery world. Their interests, concerns, and goals necessarily differ from the older generation, and they have a self-confidence, even arrogance, that may well make domestic and foreign policymaking somewhat more competitive.

Creating a global political and security role not only requires that Japan's domestic political process overcome the great reluctance to change policy and produce a reasonably clear international vision, but also that such a vision be developed concurrently with the dramatic reformulation of the global visions of Japan's friends and allies, and of its major potential adversaries.[35]

There are no good role models for Japan to follow in developing its foreign policy vision. The Cold War, at least in its traditional form, is over. Japan's own historical examples are clearly to be avoided. And past European and North American experience offers limited examples to draw from. Perhaps more than the other advanced states, Japan must build an international vision from scratch.

Japan's domestic political system makes such development difficult. Foreign and defense policy are no longer under control of a relatively small elite. Many more interests must be consulted. Moreover, the process itself lacks a locus for policy initiative and strong leadership. In addition, despite the recent frictions and tensions, Japan's policies, fundamentally, have succeeded. There is a great reluctance to change the policies that contributed to past success. It is always difficult to make fundamental changes in policy without a perception of crisis—and, except sporadically on trade issues, such a perception does not exist.[36]

Japanese Foreign and Security Policy: Major Challenges and Future Prospects

The previous two sections pointed to some of the basic foreign and domestic challenges that face Japan as it slowly adapts its policies and practices to more accurately reflect its global economic and technological importance. In some ways, Japan's role at the beginning of the 1990s ranks with that of the United States, the E.C., or the Soviet Union. Japan is now a critical player in global economic management, and indirectly, it is indispensable in supporting America's superpower status. Yet its bases of power are relatively soft—economic performance, adaptability, ties with the United States, etc. Further, Japanese leaders and the interests that they represent have been unwilling, and sometimes unable, to accept and deal with the implications of their nation's global reach. The 1990s will produce ever greater pressures on Japan to take on responsibilities, deal with economic frictions, and make foreign and security policy choices that may raise difficult domestic political tensions. This section will analyze the interaction of foreign and domestic challenges as they apply to specific foreign and security policy issues with which Japan must deal in the 1990s.

Basic Management Issues

Japanese foreign and security policy continues to be anchored to the relationship with the United States. Although economic and other frictions persist, core political and security aspects of the relationship remain healthy, at least for now. It is clear, however, that long-term tensions will force a fundamental rethinking of the bilateral relationship during this next decade.

The changing Soviet threat offers special challenges to Japanese foreign and defense policy. The broad consensus that has supported American containment policy and the alliance with the United States as a shield against the Soviets will weaken as this view becomes a less and less adequate strategic concept. Moreover, the importance of the security relationship to American policymakers (especially in Congress) is declining, and provides a weakening counter to other types of policy friction. Like it or not, security is no longer America's touchstone in the bilateral relationship, and security, economic, and other issues will become inexorably linked.

In light of the changes in the Soviet Union, policymakers and the informed public seem to recognize that some drawdown of American forces in the Pacific is reasonable. However, there is a strong fear that the United States will cut its regional presence without accounting for the significant differences between European and Asian strategic realities.[37] From the perspective of many Japanese, the threat of Soviet forces has not changed, even if the assessment about the potential use of those forces has improved considerably. There has been no reduction in threat comparable to the implications of the Soviet loss of Eastern Europe for NATO. Moreover, even with a greatly reduced threat of superpower conflict, Asia remains potentially volatile. Without a strong American presence, this potential volatility could seriously threaten Japanese interests. Thus, at least for the main policymaking elite, retaining a strong bilateral security relationship has high priority.

Although perceptions of the state of the former Soviet Union have not swung so widely in Japan in any way comparable to the United States and Western Europe, changes in the Soviet Union and East Europe are being used by the political opposition to challenge LDP policies and Japan's Mutual Security Treaty with the United States. This opposition is from the traditional, and still large, peace constituency and, increasingly, from the more aggressive and vocal insular nationalists. Among other factors, this opposition has clearly contributed to slowing the rapid growth of defense spending.[38] The prime minister has even forced the Foreign Ministry and the Defense Agency to alter the way it referred to the Soviet threat in its 1990 Defense White Paper.[39]

Thus, changes in the Soviet Union and the various and quite different perceptions of how this affects the threat to Japan intensify the basic medium- to long-term management challenge to Japanese external policy—that of developing, in conjunction with the U.S., a foreign/defense policy assessment that supports the American presence, the Mutual Security Treaty, and an acceptable level of Japanese military capability, all focused far less exclusively on the Soviet threat. This requires the leadership to develop a vision of Japanese security interests and a strategy for its implementation.

General Threat Perception

Several themes provide the backdrop for Japanese assessment of the threats that they face, some of which were noted above. The most important is a broad sense of vulnerability. Although economic success has reduced the extreme sense of vulnerability of earlier years, the Japanese perceive themselves as highly susceptible to external threat. Most concern about external threat is economic in nature—e.g., oil, exchange rates, access to markets, sources of supply for critical goods.

Due to the great importance of the bilateral relationship, trends and events in the United States loom large in perceptions of threat. Two recent trends are of particular note: concern about a precipitous American withdrawal from Northeast Asia, mentioned above; and the rising adversarial rhetoric and negative public perception of Japan among Americans (e.g., Japan replacing the Soviet Union as America's number one threat). These only add to the older perception that the United States was becoming an unreliable ally whose demands could never be met. Regardless of the merit of any specific issue, or indeed of the rapidly changing global environment, the constant battling with the United States and its increasingly acrimonious nature creates a threatening atmosphere in which compromise is difficult to achieve.

These problems with the United States are especially troubling because there is a broad sense in Japan that Asia is potentially an unstable region and that the end of the Cold War is a period of transition with great inherent uncertainty and risk. Takakazu Kuriyama, Vice Minister of Foreign Affairs, argues that the end of the Cold War implies a reduction of the "peace management capabilities" of both the United States and the USSR, as nationalism, formerly held in check by ideology, reemerges as a major threat to stability. He advocates the development of a broader system to help maintain peace, within which Japan would have an unspecified but significant role.[40] It is only in this broad context of uneasiness and vulnerability that Japanese reactions to specific threats can be assessed.

Specific Threats[41]

The USSR: Enduring Threat or Amicable Neighbor?

Since Gorbachev's Vladivostok speech in 1986, and in light of the great changes sweeping the former Soviet Union, intense speculation has focused on the possibility of resolving the last of the big questions left over from World War II—a peace treaty and the territorial dispute between Japan and Russia. Except for some unrealized enthusiasm about Siberian resource development in the 1970s, Russo–Japanese relations have been remarkably poor since the end of the last century.[42] Several elements contribute to this state of affairs:

- The historical relationship between the neighboring countries.
- A generally harsh, hostile, and unsophisticated Soviet policy approach towards Japan.
- Soviet intransigence on the four southern Kurile islands under dispute, matched by Japanese unwillingness to improve relations without dealing with the islands dispute.
- A dramatic increase in the Soviet, now Russian, military power arrayed against Japan since the mid-1970s.

Gorbachev's ascent to power signaled the emergence of a far more sophisticated approach to Japanese policy (indeed, to Asia policy in general) that has continued under Yeltsin. Personnel in both the Moscow foreign policy apparatus and in Tokyo have been replaced. The harsh rhetoric has been toned down, to be replaced by a variety of real and potential economic incentives. A variety of official and "unofficial" links between the two countries have been enhanced, such as expanded mutual official exchanges, the establishment of friendship societies, and limited permission for visits to grave sites in the Kuriles. Indeed, the Gorbachev Tokyo visit in 1991 was meant to signal a potential breakthrough in the relationship.

The potential implications of enhanced relations between Japan and the states of the former Soviet Union are significant, but the stakes and risks of various possible agreements are highly asymmetrical. The perceived threat clearly has decreased, and in the future will be highly sensitive to any realization of some of the possible improvements in Russo–Japanese relations currently under discussion. What are the stakes and possible compromises?

For the Russians, improved Japanese relations have several important dimensions. The basic driving force is economic. Whatever form of leadership finally emerges in Russia and the other Republics after the failed coup of August 1991, they desperately need some economic successes. Japan is the largest and most sophisticated economy in Asia, and is among the highest ranked globally by virtually any measure of economic leadership. Thus, in terms of trade, technology, capital, finance, management skills, etc., Japan has far more to offer than any other nation in the Pacific. Besides the potential direct economic benefits, improved relations with Japan offer a variety of broader regional benefits. In many ways, Japan could be the Soviet key to Asia. For example, Japanese trading companies could play central roles in coordinating Soviet Pacific trade. On a more political level, Japan would be less prone to oppose a growing regional economic presence for the Russians if there were a lower level of mutual hostility and suspicion.

Other major Soviet goals will persist even with the fragmentation of the Union, including the traditional objectives of: (1) weakening Japan–American ties and thereby reducing American influence in the region; (2) preventing the growth of the Japanese military and Japanese nationalism, while supporting domestic forces for passivism and neutralism; (3) minimizing any Sino–Japanese rapprochement aimed against Russia; and (4) reducing the military forces arrayed against the Russian Far East. The main factors that seem to have changed are the priority given to economics, an implicit rejection of Lenin's view that improving Russo–Japanese relations required U.S.–Japan hostility, and, perhaps most importantly, recognition of the abject failure of past Soviet policy towards Japan. These objectives are unlikely to change even with a great devolution of power to the Republics, though priorities certainly will.

What do the Soviets have to offer in return for gains in some or all of these objectives? Access to raw materials and energy products have been among the most prominent incentives dangled. Of course, the Japanese would have to provide the capital and the expertise, and bear most of the development risk. Since the peak raw material supply fears of the 1970s, Japanese firms and government officials have become increasingly sophisticated and cautious about raw materials. "Limits to growth" fears of catastrophic shortages proved to be unfounded. Japanese sources of supply are now far more diversified than in the 1970s. And the economy itself is transforming towards higher technology products and services which require a smaller volume of imported raw materials. With its near 100 percent import dependency, Japan remains highly concerned about raw materials, but it will no longer jump into high risk, high cost projects without careful analysis.

Other economic incentives include reduced investment barriers in a broad array of industries, possible creation of a Russian Far East free trade zone, improved deals on fishing rights, and many others. Many of the incentives are similar to those offered to all foreign firms, and those that are targeted mainly toward Japan seem to fall short of similar efforts focused on Western Europe and the United States.

What else can the Soviet Republics offer Japan? Already, they have reduced confrontation, hostility, and threat seen by Japan—mostly indirectly. These actions include: reduction in superpower tensions; collapse of the Soviet empire; devolution of power to the Republics; the general pullback from its aggressive global posture; improved relations with China; growing Soviet willingness to cooperate with other nations on important issues (the Iraq–Kuwait crisis, for example); the establishment of formal diplomatic relations with South Korea; and the greatly improved Russo–Japanese dialogue. As yet, however, there has been no decrease in the military forces facing Japan. Indeed, current trends point to continued improvement in their quality.[43] Nor has Japan seen any real moves on resolving the territorial dispute over the Northern islands—mostly rhetoric and high hopes. The Gorbachev failure to offer some sort of island compromise during his Tokyo visit was a particular disappointment to his Japanese hosts. Events since August 1991 have yet to produce concrete steps on the islands.

What is Japan's stake in improving its relations with the former Soviet Republics? Overall, the immediate gains are small and the potential costs fairly high. Economic relations are now limited and there will not be much in the way of significant markets, or new sources of supply any time soon. There is considerable enthusiasm about the long-term economic potential of dynamically expanding trade links across the Sea of Japan, among Japan, Russia, the two Koreas, and potentially, even China (if it can negotiate access rights and develop the port and other required facilities on the Tumen River). Little gain is likely in the 1990s, even if events are all favorable.[44] Nonetheless, the potential is large enough to represent a goal well worth seeking.

Politically, Japan's major gain would be return of the Northern territories. At present, Japan's position is that their return is a prior condition for better relations on all fronts. If Japan persists in this position, compromise may be blocked. However, if it is merely a negotiating position, the Russians may, finally, be willing to talk. Without some sort of compromise, Russo–Japanese relations will continue to stagnate. The importance of the islands far exceeds their political symbolism. For example, the four islands claimed by Tokyo have an area larger than Rhode Island and Delaware together, though they have not been economically exploited to any significant degree. The marine resources in the area have become vital to the Soviet fishing industry. More important, however, is their strategic location. Control of these islands eases the Russian task of protecting access to the Sea of Okhotsk, the sanctuary for the Pacific Fleet's nuclear forces.

Considerable attention is being given to the possible dimensions of a compromise solution. Most of these discussions focus on some sort of joint development arrangement, agreement to exclude the islands and surrounding waters from military use, and eventual Japanese sovereignty over at least two, if not all four of the disputed islands.

In return, many of these proposals also require Japan to give up all claim to Southern Sakhalin, which Japan captured in the Russo–Japanese War and lost back to Soviet forces in 1945 along with the disputed Kuriles. The Russians also want the Japanese to open the flood gates on economic aid, trade, capital, and technology. Many Japanese rather naively think that economic support is all that they want.[45]

What else they want remains a matter of considerable dispute. Indeed, now that the interests of the Russian Republic weigh more heavily than those of any other republic, goals are even less clear. Even so, it seems unlikely that the Russia military leadership would be satisfied only with a guarantee of a non-militarized zone around the disputed islands, particularly in light of the pressures to open Vladivostok to foreign visitors, shipping, and investment. Any Soviet/Russian offer almost certainly will be linked to a major arms control initiative. Arms control, especially naval arms control, has been a high Soviet priority, and a compromise solution on the Northern territories offers an extremely powerful opportunity for linkage. Moreover, it helps the Russian government content with internal opposition and strengthens the negotiating position vis à vis Japan. This strength comes from putting the Japanese leadership into a difficult position with most opposition parties, possible strong public opinion, and even within the LDP. Indeed, the Japanese leadership remains sensitive about the Soviet use of the U.S.–Soviet INF Agreement in December 1987 to stir up opposition to U.S. bases in Japan. Arms control, no matter how unbalanced, is good political fodder, especially with the current weakness of Japanese leadership.

In a climate of difficult U.S.–Japan relations, opening a major rift over arms control may be a fight that the Japanese would prefer, but may be unable, to avoid. If forced to deal with arms control, it appears that the Japanese would attempt to avoid regional negotiations and shift to some sort of global framework. But if a regional Conventional Forces in Europe analogue were to develop, the Japanese almost certainly would seek tough matching constraints on Russian ground and air forces, not just focus on the Russian interest in a naval agreement.[46]

Improved Japanese–Russian relations mostly benefit Moscow. Even a compromise on the Northern territories, unless it is largely on Japanese terms, gives Japan few material gains and potentially creates significant domestic political problems for managing its security relationship with the United States. Even so, relations between Japan and Russia have been so poor for so long that considerable unrealized potential for improvement exists. How much of this potential is realized will depend very much on the dynamics over the next year or so. If the Russians deliberately stir up security problems between Japan and the United States, if the Russians prove unwilling to deal openly on the territorial dispute, or if the Japanese are intransigent on their position of prior return, then few or no gains will be made.[47]

China: Risk of Instability

Japan views China with some ambivalence, which China returns in full measure. Historical antagonism, memories of World War II, economic potential, mutual concerns about each other's regional aspirations, and geographical proximity all complicate the bilateral relationship. Though not often discussed publicly, many in Japan view China, not the former Soviet Union, as Japan's major long-term threat.

The potential threat from China takes several forms. In the very long-term there is an explicit but usually unspecified fear that an economically developed China could easily have competing interests with Japan. In the shorter-term there is some concern about Chinese aspirations in the South China Sea, its long-term rivalry with Vietnam, and the possible expansion of the Sino–Indian competition into Southeast Asia. Each of these dimensions of Chinese regional competition raise potential risks of conflict and instability in Southeast Asia which, in turn, threaten Japanese economic interests (markets, sources of supply, and vital sea lanes of communication to the Indian Ocean and the Persian Gulf). The more pressing concern is about the highly uncertain risks posed by instability within China. Instability poses less of a direct military threat than it does a threat to regional stability, which would present Japan with some difficult choices regarding refugees, military assistance, possible use of force, etc.

31

As Japanese policymakers review these risks, they must also walk a fine line among the West (mainly the United States), China, and Russia. Well into the 1980s, China sought to create an anti-Soviet character to its relationship with Japan, an effort Japanese largely resisted.[48] Similarly, China supported Japan's military buildup, in conjunction with the United States, as a counter to the growth in Soviet forces. However, Japan resisted Chinese efforts to develop a degree of military cooperation and acquire military assistance.[49] Indeed, Japan did not care for U.S. efforts to help modernize Chinese forces. Japan clearly sees a stronger, more modern Chinese military as potentially detrimental to long-term national interests.

Japanese leaders tend to see an economically developing China as the best defense against domestic instability and longer-term regional conflicts of interest. Japan has contributed heavily to Chinese economic development, and at the 1990 industrial country summit, gained agreement or at least acquiescence to Japan's return to a more open China policy. Needless to say, strong domestic commercial interests also support a more open China policy, but in this case commercial interests support Japanese perceptions of strategic interest. Of course, Japanese objectives of using economic linkages to restrain potential Chinese threats are sometimes seen by the Chinese as efforts to dominate China.

Korea: The Last Cold War Hot Spot

Korea has always been vital to Japanese strategic interests. China and Japan competed for control of Korea off and on for centuries. This competition intensified in the late 1870s, when Japan forced Korea into an unequal treaty, opening the country to Japanese trade. This led to the Sino–Japanese War of 1895, in which China was soundly beaten. About this same time the expanding Russian empire began to be seen as a regional challenge, eventually resulting in the Russo–Japanese War of 1904, which Russia lost. In both cases, rights to Korea were fundamental to Japanese interests. Finally in 1910, Japan annexed Korea as a full-fledged colony, where it stayed until Japan's defeat in World War II. Since then, Korea has been a focal point where U.S., Soviet, Chinese, and Japanese interests all come together.[50]

Japan is greatly concerned about the potential threat from renewed conflict between the divided Koreas. Its economic and, indirectly, its security support (through its hosting of U.S. forces in Japan) for South Korea in part reflects this concern. However, Japan has felt constrained in taking any proactive role in helping to reduce tensions on the peninsula—the bitter history of occupation and Japan's immense role in the Korean economy made them very sensitive to greater involvement. Indeed, it has only been in the 1980s that regular visits of military personnel have become common. Relations with North Korea have been much more strained, managed indirectly through political party and other unofficial contacts, though this is slowly changing.

Besides the obvious concerns about the implications of possible conflict on the peninsula, some Japanese are beginning to openly discuss the long-term fears of a nuclear-armed Korea.[51] Several, not very well developed, scenarios serve as the basis for this fear, but the most common is: North Korea develops or nearly develops the capability to build nuclear devices. It may or may not actually build weapons before political events lead to a reunification in which the North is absorbed (the Germany model), at which point, Korea keeps this nuclear capability. What happens next in this scenario is never made explicit, but some at least infer that Japan may have to revise its own anti-nuclear stance. Others seem to be saying that only a continued strong American presence can prevent this from happening.

Such longer-term and not very widespread fears, in fact, seem to reflect more general unease about trends and events next door, in the context of Japan's own history. As both China and Russia develop closer economic and political relations with South Korea, Japanese long-term concerns about the future of Korea rise commensurately. After all, control over Korea was central to earlier wars with both of these powers. Despite Japan's great economic role, the natural Korean antipathy towards Japan limits Japanese influence on Korean political events and places barriers to close cooperation. For now, American interests and presence help tie Japan and Korea closely together. Longer term, however, Korea could well become the locus of competition among China, Russia, and Japan.

Instability and Conflict in Southeast Asia[52]

Southeast Asia has been an area of considerable concern to Japan since early in this century, first as a target of colonial domination and now as a valuable partner in an increasingly complex interrelationship. In the late 1970s, when Japan began taking cautious foreign policy initiatives, Southeast Asia was one of its first priorities. Japan's objectives in the region are reasonably straightforward:

- Access to raw materials and energy products.
- Access to expanding regional markets for manufactured products, and for investment sites.
- Access and freedom of transit to the vital sea-lanes around and through the region, with a special priority given to oil from the Gulf after the early 1970s.
- Prevention of any potentially hostile power from acquiring regional dominance.

Thus, peace and stability within and among regional states are important objectives. Both regional fears and self-imposed constraints have limited Japan's actions to pursue these objectives. Mainly, Japan has supported American initiatives or those of ASEAN. Japanese policy initiatives have been mainly economic in nature or implemented through economic means. For example, Japan has long recognized Indonesia's strategic importance—all major straits between the Pacific and Indian Oceans lie through or adjacent to Indonesian waters—and has taken a leadership role in providing that country with economic assistance. Similarly, Japan has sharply expanded its assistance to the Philippines, in large part because of its strategic importance to the United States and its location, even though the Philippines is much less economically important to Japan than some of the other ASEAN states.

A key factor in Japan's assessment of the threat to its interests in Southeast Asia is a continued American military presence in the region. The loss of American bases in the Philippines thus creates uncertainty about how longer-term problems might be dealt with. In particular, Japan is concerned about possible Chinese assertiveness in the South China Sea, or the spillover efforts of a Chinese–Vietnamese or Sino–Indian conflict. In response, Japan is actively seeking close bilateral relations with all countries in the region, promoting an active U.S. role, slowly increasing its participation in political affairs, and supporting economic development. It has yet to begin providing security assistance, although slowly it is beginning to consult with some countries on political and security matters. A regular, broad-based consultative process has not yet developed, however.

Whether Japan would ever take a direct Southeast Asian security role is uncertain, but highly unlikely in the 1990s. Besides the great political impediments, both in Japan and among most Southeast Asian states, the possibility of strong direct threats to Japanese interests remains limited. Economic development is reducing the risk of political instability among the ASEAN members, in which Japan's greatest economic interests reside. Moreover, except for a spillover from a war among the coastal states (or between China and India), the sea-lanes vital to Japan are unlikely to be disrupted or blocked. Thus, any security role for Japan in the next decade would most likely be indirect.[53]

Middle East Instability: A Threat to Japan's Industrial Lifeline

As noted above, Middle East policy is one of the few major policy areas in which Japan split from the United States, taking a pro-Arab stance in the 1970s. Since that time, Japan diversified sources of oil supply away from the Middle East, pursued broad-based diplomatic initiatives to develop closer relations with all regional states, sharply expanded economic assistance to the region, and tried to avoid taking controversial foreign policy positions.

For example, during the Iran–Iraq war, Japan maintained strict neutrality, traded equally with both, resisted strong diplomatic efforts to take sides (including from the United States to support its pro-Iraq stance), and attempted to play a facilitating role between the combatants. Japan pursued a variety of largely unsuccessful initiatives at the United Nations and the summit meetings of the advanced nations, both to limit the conflict and bring it to an end, including financial support of U.N. mediation efforts. Despite these efforts, Japan had limited ability to influence the course of events. Moreover, political reality also required that Japan support and share the cost of U.S. and other navies' escort operations in the Gulf.[54] Even though these facilitation efforts failed, Japan has expanded its independent political role in the Middle East, and has become an increasingly well-accepted intermediary.

Iraq's invasion of Kuwait presented Japanese leaders with a far more difficult set of choices than did the Iran–Iraq war. It directly challenged the even-handed strategy developed earlier. Japanese citizens and assets were at risk. A strong international consensus required that Japan contribute, but at a pace that the domestic system was unable to deal with. Moreover, it raised all of the domestic challenges and debates over security that have been argued about since the end of World War II. What does the constitution permit? What is in Japan's best interest? What are Japan's international obligations in this situation? Domestically, who should be involved in the decision over Japan's involvement? All of these questions and more became topics of grave concern. The result was a policy response that the rest of the world saw as typically Japanese—run from responsibility, cave in under outside pressure, but only in a small way, then cave in again more responsibly, but with great anguish and resistance, well after antagonism and resentment had risen on all sides.

The final package, in fact, was not a bad response under the constraints faced by Japan. If it had been organized promptly and presented with a sense of purpose and common cause, rather than slowly, with a great show of domestic angst, and only after offering an initial pittance, this response could well have contributed to the perception that, perhaps, Japan was going to carve out a new role for itself in world affairs. Unfortunately, just the reverse was true.

The internationalists in Japan, as well as those who recognize Japan's growing global responsibilities, are rightly embarrassed by this policy fiasco. They claim it will not happen again. Only time will tell if Japan can correct the systemic problems that interfere with its ability to respond to foreign crises of this sort.

What are the main lessons of this policy failure?[55] The most general lesson is that with a relatively weak prime minister, Japan's policy system goes into gridlock in a crisis. There is no institutionalized crisis management mechanism in place that automatically gears up to support and promote fast response on issues that require a more global approach and cut across political and ministerial authorities. Moreover, "Japan has no system whereby it could cooperate with the United Nations to contribute to peace."[56]

Apparently, Mr. Kaifu relied mainly on a small group of advisors with limited political vision, and could not or did not attempt to impose his leadership on the Cabinet. This permitted the ministries to largely pursue their own, highly competitive interests. The Defense Agency was cut out of the process by the Foreign Ministry, while reportedly the Ministry never informed the prime minister about messages from Tokyo's U.S. Ambassador concerning Washington's growing outrage over Japan's dithering.[57]

Prime Minister Kaifu chose not to take an aggressive stance, partly to distance himself from the behavior of some of his predecessors—most importantly Mr. Nakasone, whose style was very unpopular within the party—and because of his own factional weakness within the party. A more serious failing, however, was his choice not to use the mechanism set up by Mr. Nakasone in the prime minister's office to bring all of the key players together and manage crises.[58]

In the resulting policy free-for-all, the Finance Ministry, under Mr. Rhutaro Hashimoto, aggressively resisted any spending initiatives. Of course, resisting spending increases is an implicit part of any finance minister's job, but it proved to be a particularly serious problem in this case. The Finance Ministry is perhaps the most powerful of the ministries, and strongly influences policy in the absence of leadership. Further, Mr. Hashimoto was a contender for Mr. Kaifu's job, and would not be adverse to seeing some pressure on the prime minister.

Finally, the good relationship developed between Mr. Kaifu and President Bush became enmeshed in domestic politics. He was seen as giving in to American demands too easily. The fact that the prime minister offered explicit support to President Bush, before consulting his own party or the Diet, created widespread outrage. Not only did the various factional power brokers feel obligated to demonstrate how dependent his tenure was on their good graces, they also recognized how difficult it was going to be to get any security support package past the Socialists in the Diet, without a great deal of quiet horse-trading with the centrist opposition parties.

The key point of this lengthy discursion into the Japanese response to the Iraq–Kuwait crisis is to highlight how far Japan must yet come to develop its own internal political and institutional processes before it can deal with a situation clearly threatening national interests, especially if that situation occurs in a region that had been targeted for special attention for a decade and a half. This crisis may well prove to be the stimulus for the LDP to finally face up to the task of designing in law and in interpretation of existing law at least some specific authorities to cooperate in operations for "common defense." The crisis did lead to explicit consideration of a U.N. peace cooperation law designed to improve Japan's ability to respond to international crises. Although the proposed legislation did not pass, something very like this proposal could well become law during the next several years. Such legislation would be a major political step. It would authorize sending noncombatant members of the SDF to trouble spots under the United Nations' flag and other means of cooperation.[59] Already, Japan has sent minesweepers to help clear the Gulf, following cessation of hostilities.

U.S.–Japan Relations: Stress and Reassessment

Basic Characteristics

Relations with the United States remain a critical Japanese policy focus. Indeed, despite the growing trade frictions and political acrimony, mutual interdependence deepened in the 1980s. In the economic arena, investment, joint ventures, technology sharing arrangements, and other business activities have grown in parallel to the strong trade relationship.[60] Barring major policy-induced shocks, trends towards expanding economic interdependence will continue to strengthen in the 1990s.

In political areas, the United States and Japan have found strong common ground in dealing with Europe in the GATT negotiations and on resisting the introduction of new barriers to outsiders as the E.C. integrates. Similar common interests have emerged in dealing with Cambodia, Third World debt, and many other areas. On security issues, Japan has expanded its forces in conjunction with U.S. interests, enhanced common security objectives with targeted economic aid, and contributed financially to various security operations (sea-lane protection during the Iran–Iraq war, the Iraq–Kuwait crisis, refugee programs, etc.).

In any balance-sheet assessment of the bilateral relationship, Japan still needs the United States more than vice versa. But the interdependence is so great that, to modify somewhat one of former Ambassador Mansfield's favorite statements, Japan and the United States are each other's single most important bilateral relationship. Japan serves a number of vital roles for the United States: a good friend with many common interests, a powerful economic partner, a critical forward base to support American global and regional security interests, and an increasingly critical source of political and financial support for important American policy objectives, among others. Analogously, the United States serves many vital roles for Japan: a good friend with many common interests, a powerful economic partner and a critical market, a security umbrella against direct and indirect threats to which the Self Defense Forces cannot respond, a key ally in dealing with Western Europe, a buffer in Japan's dealings with its neighbors, and a regional stabilizer.

The latter two roles are more important to Japan than usually credited. Memories of World War II remain strong, and are revived and strengthened by Japan's now immense regional economic presence. Although generational change, Japan's nonaggressive stance, and the growing confidence and economic well-being across Asia are slowly reducing fear of Japan, most regional states still desire an American presence to guarantee Japan's continued good behavior. Moreover, they also simply want to balance Japan's economic strength. The inevitable expansion of Japanese political and security involvement in the region during the 1990s will be far less threatening and stimulate fewer potentially destabilizing responses if it develops in the context of a cooperative partnership with the United States.

The Japanese leadership recognizes their neighbors' fears. They are also concerned about the medium and long-term trends, noted above, which are increasing the potential for regional tension and conflict. This is the basis for a strong perception among the conservative leadership that without a strong American partnership and presence, the region could change in ways that threaten Japanese interests—changes against which Japan has a limited number of desirable policy options. This perception is not shared by much of the domestic political opposition, nor by some of the insular nationalists in the LDP. These risks also are not well understood in public debate.

In the complex environment of the 1990s, Japan and the United States will continue to find broad common political and security interests, especially in Asia. Increasingly, they will find unilateral action inappropriate, and both countries will find a growing need for cooperative actions. Need cannot always be effected in action, however.

Challenges to the Relationship

Continued trends toward greater interdependence do not imply a smooth, happy relationship. Indeed, strong trends also point to growing bilateral frictions, emerging from growing frustration over trade issues, rising tension over various technology-related issues, greater pressure from the U.S. Congress for burden sharing (especially after Japan's slow response to the Iraq–Kuwait crisis), and the inevitable mistakes and improper reactions on both sides. As discussed above, perhaps the major challenge to the bilateral relationship is to find ways of managing these frictions and preventing cumulative deterioration, rising acrimony, resurgent nationalism, and great losses in the potential mutual benefits from cooperation.

Fundamental differences in political, social and bureaucratic systems between the two countries have contributed to the development of strong negative, counterproductive dynamics in the bilateral relationship. The Japanese negotiating style has led to a broadly-held perception in the United States that success is only possible with tactics of threat and confrontation. Further, because large policy change is so difficult to make in the Japanese system, various domestic groups have quietly sought to bring in outside pressure to help achieve their own ends. In light of the confusion about American foreign, defense, and economic policy priorities of the past decade, it is not surprising that the bilateral dialogue has increasingly become an exercise in growing nationalistic pugilism on the American side, echoed by a rising nationalistic backlash in Japan.

Security has been the core of the U.S.–Japan relationship. The SDF are structured primarily to repulse small scale attacks on the Japanese homeland.[61] Dealing with any more serious aggression depends upon American support—including the U.S. nuclear umbrella. Further, by renouncing the use of force to resolve disputes with other countries, any failure of diplomacy that results in out-of-area, indirect, or potential violence against Japanese interests has left Japan dependent upon others—in practice the United States. As long as key elements of national survival remain linked to the United States, Japanese policy must continue to give primacy in international relations to the bilateral relationship.

As the perceived threat has declined, the priority that kept most defense issues separate from the periodically intense economic and political frictions has fallen. The political crisis over the joint development agreement for the Japanese advanced fighter plane (FSX) points to the degree to which the U.S. government has lost the ability to keep defense and other issues in separate channels, and provides an example of some of the difficult issues that both governments will have to manage as they redefine all aspects of the bilateral relationship over the next decade.

Despite the broad regional aspects of the security relationship, most policy arguments, public justifications, and indeed, security planning has focused on the Soviet Union. It was, after all, the most overwhelming threat. Nonetheless, shifting policy and planning to the broader regional objectives now requires both a major strategic review and a wide public debate on national security, which unfortunately is and will remain contentious. Without a distinct threat to focus attention, defense, in general, drops sharply as a subject of national policy concern in both the United States and Japan.

As a result, various Japanese foreign policy and security challenges that must be faced and dealt with over the next decade will necessarily become entangled with intense domestic politics and the ongoing, probably confrontational, redefinition of U.S.–Japan relations.

Defense Budgets

Japanese defense budgets rose rapidly in the 1980s, in excess of 5 percent annually after 1982. Contributing to this growth was the strong recommendation for expansion of Japanese forces in the 1980 "Report on Comprehensive National Security," the growing Soviet forces around Japan, the Soviet invasion of Afghanistan, other aggressive Soviet behavior, and strong American political pressure. With this more hostile environment, Prime Minister Nakasone was able to force some difficult political choices to be made. Indeed, in 1987, the government had to scrap the one percent of GNP ceiling on defense spending in order to accommodate military build-up plans.[62] The excess was small, but the political and psychological symbolism were important.[63]

Defense spending has grown more rapidly than almost any other budget category. Current spending levels are roughly on par with the United Kingdom, and over the past decade Japan has acquired the most modern non-nuclear military in Asia. Over 90 percent of its arms are produced domestically, though much of its leading edge equipment depends upon components from the United States or is produced under license. In the last several years significant research and development has been devoted to applying Japan's civilian technologies, especially in electronics, to the production of high technology arms.

The change in the international political climate is having a profound effect on Japanese defense budget planning. Although the conservative leadership of Japan and the general population remain more suspicious and wary of Russia than many other countries, recent events are forcing a reassessment. Moreover, announced American military cuts in Asia stimulated calls for corresponding Japanese cuts by opposition parties and others.[64] The heady budget growth of the 1980s not only will stop, but the SDF will face a struggle to keep real resources constant.

Defense budgets have always been a residual in Japanese budget negotiations, with the Ministry of Finance having more influence than the Defense Agency.[65] Indeed, the Ministry of Foreign Affairs handles most defense budget negotiations. With growing domestic claims on government budget resources and continued budget deficits, the decline in the perception of external threat dramatically weakens the defense case. Efforts to convince the Japanese to take on large new roles thus will encounter much stronger budget competition than for most of the past decade. Simply asking Japan to spend more will not be enough. Indeed, it will probably become important for the United States and Japan to raise the degree of cooperative long-term planning at the service-to-service level and follow this planning with selective high level American political support for SDF programs and plans. This will be particularly important in helping the MSDF achieve its cooperative sea control goals with the U.S. Seventh Fleet.

Burden Sharing

Budgets, of course, will affect the debate over burden sharing. There is fairly widespread support behind the current proposal for Japan to pay all yen-based costs of the American military presence, lifting its share from about 40 percent to about 50 percent of the support costs of American forces in Japan—far beyond that of any other ally.[66] However, there is very limited domestic backing that could be mobilized for a large expansion of that share, such as to 75 percent, as proposed by Richard D. Fisher at the Heritage Foundation.[67] Indeed, U.S. forces begin looking very much like mercenaries at those levels of support.[68] Moving away from arguing over budget share towards developing a strategy for joint and cooperative activities and programs under a burden-sharing umbrella is perhaps the only viable strategy for managing political pressures of the 1990s.

SDF Roles and Missions

Japanese and many Americans interpret burden sharing more broadly than just spending to support U.S. forces. Shifting defense roles to Japanese forces, of course, has been a major component of this debate. It has also been controversial. The United States and others want Japan to take on greater defense responsibilities, but at the same time they express great fear of a rearmed Japan. Similar contradictions exist within Japan. Some in Japan advocate unarmed neutrality. Others see the need for Self Defense Forces, but with no role beyond that of defending the homeland against invasion. The growing support role for the SDF in helping to achieve mutual U.S.–Japanese regional objectives raises intense domestic controversy. As long as the Soviet threat remained clear and immediate, the Japanese had come to accept the need for the SDF buildup of the 1980s, the growing operational cooperation between Japanese and American forces, and the adoption of expanded SDF roles and missions.

The most well known, but as yet unrealized, new mission was the adoption of expanded sea-lane protection responsibility out to 1000 nautical miles.[69] Another mission desired by the United States and largely accepted as reasonable by the conservative leadership included the ability to mine and otherwise blockade the straits of Tsushima, Tsugaru, and Soya connecting the Sea of Japan with the Pacific, thus denying Soviet transit to and from its bases in eastern Siberia. A third mission was the establishment of an effective air defense screen for the home islands and part of the Sea of Japan that could inflict heavy losses on Soviet tactical fighters and long range bombers (including the Backfire), and support the joint U.S.–Japanese task of sea control.[70] Though none of these missions are explicitly incorporated in the Mid-Term Defense Program, adopted on September 18, 1985, the specific plans implemented suggested an evolutionary shift towards their achievement.[71]

These expanding missions required substantial changes in planning, forces, and training. Planning had to evolve away from a purely passive alliance towards that of an active alliance with the United States. The principal means used were coordinated defense planning, joint strategic and tactical studies, expanded consultation, and joint training with American forces.[72] The degree of service-to-service cooperation and consultation has grown remarkably over the past decade. Except for some of the joint exercises, such as Japanese participation in the large U.S.-led multinational Naval exercise, RIMPAC, this trend has been largely outside political debate and controversy in both Japan and the United States. Considerable effort also was devoted to ensuring a significant degree of compatibility between American and Japanese equipment. This indirectly has caused some political problems since it has led to American pressures, especially from Congress, to purchase off-the-shelf equipment. At the same time as expanding its military cooperation with U.S. forces, the SDF began exploring various other options such as directly supporting United Nations peacekeeping activities.

To take on new roles, Japan had to increase defense spending (breaking the one percent barrier, as discussed above). Procurement focused mainly on enhancing quality, rather than quantity of forces. Major improvements have been achieved. Even so, compared to the Soviet threat that had built up, Japanese improvements were glacial. Some experts question whether Japan could "defend against a limited invasion without immediately available outside assistance," much less control the sea-lanes around Japan.[73] Nonetheless, the political justifications for extending defense of the sea-lanes out to 1000 miles (which became the symbol for all expanded roles and missions in the public debate) represented a fundamental shift in the nation's policy outlook towards greater regional responsibilities. The leadership has developed a consensus around a steady defense buildup. Further, except for the Communist Party, the main opposition parties came around to accepting the need for the SDF, though they did not necessarily accept a growing regional role, nor the need for cooperation with U.N. peacekeeping operations, especially the Japan Socialist Party.

Recent events have challenged this hard won consensus. Japan's defense and foreign policy establishment largely recognizes that the SDF cannot yet meet its self-defense goals, even with the elimination of Soviet regional aggressiveness. They and many Americans involved in defense affairs see a wide range for enhanced Japanese military roles that still maintain their defensive configuration.

Such expanded roles included many specific dimensions, rarely discussed but important, such as wide area surveillance, air defense, and antisubmarine warfare (ASW) capability, among others. Properly linked with U.S. forces, these enhancements to Japanese forces could improve regional deterrence and stability. These capabilities cannot be realized with existing or planned equipment. Hardware would have to be procured, the SDF would require some reorganization, more extensive cooperation and joint operations would have to be planned and exercised, and the conceptions about defense (including the legal institutions) would require revision.[74] Yet, the new Medium-Term Defense Plan suggests a considerable scale back on acquisition of the ability to achieve the 1000 mile sea-lane defense goal.[75]

With the JSP coming out strongly in favor of a smaller SDF, focused narrowly on defense of the islands, the LDP has a major struggle on its hands to expand SDF capabilities at all.[76] Progress has been made, but in the current threat environment, further progress will require much more explicit mission definitions and will face far greater political and budgetary opposition. Shifting the context of the security relationship towards a more comprehensive, regional framework, and then defining appropriate capabilities and missions for Japanese and American forces, respectively, will present major challenges to both countries and will necessarily require much closer service-to-service cooperation than heretofore.

Due to the recent events in the Gulf, Japanese forces could and indeed probably will gain some authority for unarmed participation in United Nations peacekeeping operations. Even here great domestic opposition exists.[77] Except for a U.N. role, virtually no other direct military role away from the home islands seems possible over the next decade.

Economic Assistance

Economic assistance has long been a preferred offset to Japan's relatively low total defense spending. As discussed above, its magnitude has grown, it is less commercially based, and is increasingly targeted on countries and activities of strategic concern. To the extent that Japan has become involved in regional or global political/security affairs, it has usually had an assistance dimension (e.g., financial support of U.N. initiatives during the Iran–Iraq war, promises of support for a Cambodian peace process, etc.). Nonetheless, Japan's aid processes have not worked well. There is no central control administration, and no set of basic principles to guide policymakers. Disbursements always lag commitments. Moreover, the highly commercial character of Japanese aid has raised considerable resentment among recipients and in the United States. There is a strong perception that such aid is not burden sharing, but rather disguised subsidies for Japanese corporate expansion into Third World markets.[78]

A major internal review of Japanese aid has been under way for some time. Every ministry, various political organizations, and the major business groups have been preparing position papers and alternative policy strategies. The Japanese leadership sees aid as a principal means of foreign policy implementation around which they can build a broad consensus. Indeed, one of Japan's fundamental security objectives has been "the promotion of a politically stable and economically viable Asia."[79] Thus, they are seeking to make some sort of order out of the current process so it can function relatively efficiently, and be used to respond to a wide range of economic, political, and security concerns without stirring up major domestic controversy. One key problem is dealing with interministerial turf conflicts. Another challenge is dealing with the domestic political opposition to explicitly incorporating strategic objectives into aid policy. Japanese leaders will no longer be able to tell Americans one thing and its domestic population another. An important issue also under consideration is the American suggestion to formally cooperate on some aid programs, to the extent of joint staffing. The reaction by some Japanese has been rather cool. "Now the Americans want to spend our money, too.''[80] The complex tensions reflected in the American suggestion and the Japanese reaction expressed by this comment will not be easy to resolve.

Many in the United States and some in Japan clearly do not see past Japanese aid policy as reflecting a responsible contribution to political and security burden sharing. Indeed, some do not even see it as contributing significantly to economic progress. Others see the rapid expansion of aid in recent years as a major political breakthrough, and the lack of organization and effectiveness an inevitable result of limited experience and inadequate administrative structures, compounded by the rapid budget growth itself. Nonetheless, for economic assistance to be seen as a legitimate component of political and security burden sharing, Japan and the United States will have to explicitly agree, in as specific terms as possible, on their common interests and detail how their respective expenditures and other initiatives support those interests.[81] Only explicit policies can help offset accusations of deceit on the one hand and resentment over foreign pressures on the other.

Japanese will continue to view aid as a key burden-sharing device. Once Japan faces up to the domestic political challenge of more clearly defining political and security objectives, aid will become a more efficient foreign policy tool, and it will become easier for the Japanese to respond to explicit security related challenges quickly.

High Technology Development

Another area of explicit burden-sharing effort that will become more important, and also far more controversial, is cooperative high technology R&D and production. The Japanese have a great deal to offer in electronics, synthetic materials, manufacturing processes, communications, and many other fields. Yet, there is no area more politically explosive. It lies at the intersection of economic, political, and security leadership.

Reasonable Americans and Japanese recognize that much more cooperation in technology is both necessary and inevitable throughout the 1990s. Indeed, the official policy infrastructure has been building for several years. Based on the 1960 revision of the Treaty of Mutual Security and Cooperation, these various elements include:[82]

47

- The 1983 Exchange of Notes on the Transfer of Japanese Military Technologies.
- The 1984 Report of the Defense Science Board Task Force on Industry-to-Industry International Armaments Cooperation.
- The 1988 U.S.–Japan Science and Technology Cooperation Agreement.

At present, the Japanese government permits the foreign transfer of military technology only to the United States. With some exceptions, progress in implementing a reverse flow of military and dual-use technology has been very slow. The three main programs tested under these new agreements have been the portable KEIKO surface-to-air missile, the FSX support fighter, and the Strategic Defense Initiative (SDI). KEIKO was noncontroversial and set a good precedent. The FSX proved to be highly controversial and also did not represent true codevelopment. Participation in the research phase of SDI is perhaps a much better case of the reverse transfer process. Two binational industrial consortia are conducting research on missile defenses that could well result in collaboration in their production.

Following the controversy over the FSX, nobody is quite sure how to manage anything big without unleashing intense controversy. The confrontation over the joint production of the FSX has made Japan wary of joint programs. Indeed, few in the United States realize how angry Japanese became about the American actions.[83] However, like aid, development of high technology offers an issue around which a Japanese political consensus potentially can be built. Reportedly, Japanese defense and other government officials are open to a variety of smaller codevelopment projects.[84] For example, on September 28, 1990, an agreement was reached to form bilateral working groups for cooperation in advanced defense technology in five areas: steel for ships and armored vehicles; ceramic-based fighting vehicle propulsion technology; ducted rocket engines; magnetic field technology; and millimeter wave/infrared hybrid seekers.[85]

The challenge to greater technology cooperation may be more serious in dealing with domestic politics in the United States than in Japan. As the FSX debate revealed, cooperative development in high technology areas raises intense concern, both legitimate and perfidious. Legitimate concerns include the possible emergence of Japan as competing arms producer, control of classified information, and stimulation of intensified commercial competition. But properly managed, the strategic benefits of growing technology cooperation tend to outweigh the potential costs.[86] After all, the United States is seeking a reverse technology flow in selected areas where Japan has something to offer. More than anything else, the U.S. side lacks the leadership required to set the priorities for cooperative technology development, negotiate effectively with the Japanese, and manage resulting programs to maximize the benefits to American producers. It is incumbent on the individual military services to identify and promote specific programs in which cooperation is likely to offer high payoff. Areas that have been raised include possible cooperation in the development of a new antisubmarine warfare frigate or a new class of diesel attack submarines.[87] An area of even higher American priority and greater potential Japanese contribution is in design of fast logistics support ships.

Arms Control[88]

Japan's participation in arms control issues began with its acceptance, after long debate, of the nuclear Non-Proliferation Treaty in 1976. But the INF treaty was the first such effort in which Japan participated so completely, and which had important potential implications for East Asia. In particular, Japan fought to prevent the shift of SS-20s from Europe to Asia. Japan has also participated in a test ban and a ban on chemical weapons, and an agreement to ban export of selected missile technologies.

Over time, Japan has slowly aligned its positions with the Western negotiating stance on most major issues. It has also tended to emphasize the importance of taking regional characteristics into account in any arms negotiation. Regional inequities are the fundamental reason why Japan has strongly opposed repeated Soviet initiatives on conventional and naval arms control.

As noted above, the next few years pose a special challenge in the arms control area. Russia almost certainly will offer some sort of starting point for negotiation on the Northern territories dispute. Such an offer almost certainly will attempt to link new arms control initiatives to the process. Arms control, especially naval arms control, has been a high Soviet priority in Asia. Russian spokespeople continue to espouse similar positions. A possible

Northern territorial deal is a potentially powerful lever to seek some of these objectives.

The preference of the conservative Japanese leadership will be to refuse to link the issues, which is also the American preference.[89] Moreover, with Russian economic needs, Japan holds a strong negotiating position. However, depending upon domestic political circumstances and upon the contents of the opening proposals, Japan may be forced to treat them seriously. The LDP holds a minority in the upper house of the Diet and is split on defense issues internally. Arms control that is not so imbalanced as previous Soviet initiatives, and also reduces American forces in Japan, could be an attractive unifying theme for Japan's fragmented opposition groups and some in the LDP. If forced to seriously consider arms control in the domestic political debate, it appears that the Japanese first would attempt to shift from a regional to a more global framework. This is critical to American interests and presence. If a regional conventional forces discussion were to emerge, the Japanese would focus on a comprehensive forces approach, rather than permitting a Russian focus only on naval arms.[90]

Although arms control issues are receiving considerable bilateral attention at the service level, especially in discussions between the U.S. Navy and the Maritime Self Defense Force, the risks of and possible counterproposals to a major regional naval arms control initiative do not appear to be a major topic in the DOD–JDA or Department of State–Ministry of Foreign Affairs consultations. It should be.

The Mutual Security Treaty and the Presence of American Forces

The security treaty received considerable attention in the Japanese media in the first half of 1990; it was the Treaty's thirtieth anniversary. All of the security concerns and debates were reexamined, and when the dust settled, nobody in the conservative leadership and few in the centrist opposition wanted to renegotiate the treaty. Vice Foreign Minister Takakazu Kuriyama, the ministry's senior bureaucrat, characterized the treaty as fulfilling three primary roles into the 1990s.[91] First, it continues to fulfill the deterrent role during the period of intense uncertainty that is accompanying the winding down of the East–West confrontation. Second, "It serves as 'a foundation for dialogue' between

Japan and other nations. In particular . . . the Soviet Union." He argues that it is the close relationship with the United States that forced the Soviets to take Japan seriously. Finally, "It provides a framework for Japan and the U.S. to effectively execute their policies in the Asia–Pacific region, both individually and in partnership." Notably, the treaty facilitates acceptance of Japan's growing political and security roles with its Asian neighbors, negates the need for Japan to rearm to the extent of posing a potential military threat to them, and helps keep an active American presence in the region. Though opposed in principle, most of the main opposition parties have accepted the treaty as necessary at least for now. Considerable media attention was devoted to the inconsistency of a Cold War military alliance document serving as the basis for the complex political, economic, security relationship that would be required in the 1990s. The prediction was that it would have to be revised. The more pragmatic foreign and defense policy practitioners felt that the treaty did not prevent the bilateral relationship from evolving into whatever the United States and Japan wanted.[92]

Similarly, many suggestions have been made by Americans to convert the treaty into an alliance with more symmetrical responsibilities. Various administrations have avoided even addressing this issue, if possible. Japan has slowly become an active alliance partner with the United States, even though the pace of change and the specific ways in which this partnership has evolved have led to significant political problems. Congress, in particular, has become highly aggressive and almost certainly would prevent a balanced renegotiation of the Mutual Security Treaty. It would be impossible to keep the whole range of trade and other frictions out of any renegotiation. Further, the strength of opposition forces in Japan would clearly make the success of any renegotiation a potentially high-risk exercise from the point of view of achieving U.S. objectives. There is far more to lose than to gain.

Both Japan and the United States benefit greatly from a strong security relationship, supported by a large American military presence. Events in the former Soviet Union and China are so uncertain that it is impossible to assume a benign outcome. Moreover, regional trends point to the risk of rising competition and potential conflict that threaten both Japanese and American interests. It is easy for the United States to both deter and manage such risks based on a strong cooperative relationship with and a presence in Japan. Relying on the American relationship is Japan's only attractive option for dealing with these risks in the medium term, and Japan will go to great lengths for its maintenance.

In the complex environment of the 1990s, Japan and the United States will continue to find broad common political and security interests, especially in Asia. Increasingly, they will find unilateral action inappropriate, and both countries will find a growing need for cooperative actions. Japan sees a partnership with the United States as an important adjunct to its growing regional and global roles; Japanese long-term interests are largely parallel to those of the United States; and a cooperative partnership greatly strengthens the likelihood of successful outcomes for both nations. Continued trends toward greater interdependence do not imply a smooth, happy relationship. Indeed, strong trends also point to growing bilateral frictions. It is incumbent on the leadership in both countries to manage to the short-term frictions in ways that do not prevent meeting longer-term national imperatives.

Dealing with the inevitable growth of bilateral frictions requires concentrated efforts to build countervailing successes. The military arena offers a variety of successful ongoing activities upon which to build closer, nonconfrontational cooperative programs. Some of the successes upon which to build are in planning and operations—notably expansion of the Japanese role in sea-lane protection and air defense. As budgets and other factors force a decline in American forces around the world, the U.S. military, especially the Seventh Fleet based in Japan, gains considerable regional flexibility from a growing ability to rely on Japanese sea-lane protection out to 1000 miles. The evolution of defense roles already accepted will be much easier for the Japanese political system to deal with than large new initiatives. Other successes to build on are industrial and technological complements to Japan's growing defense capabilities. For example, the political decisions to transfer both the P-3C Orion and AEGIS are behind us. Not only does this represent a major capability that the Japanese will use to substitute for current American activities, but also these are two major programs in which the Japanese could contribute a significant reverse technology flow—particularly in second and third tier electronics components R&D and production. American producers are already heavily dependent on Japanese products at lower tiers of production. Creating explicit joint research and coproduction agreements would recognize this dependence and seek to strengthen both countries' abilities to support these systems.

Finally, by building on existing strengths, the U.S. military can help Japan's conservative leadership to manage security affairs in the increasingly pluralistic domestic political landscape. With the changing security environment and the rising frictions in the U.S.–Japan relationship, opposition to close security relations increasingly will have opportunities to interfere with the smooth development of the relationship. Indirectly, reducing possible sources of tension and initiating strong cooperative programs greatly weakens opposition credibility with the public.

Alternative Political and Security Roles

The recent Middle East crisis brought to the fore all of the major challenges that Japan faces in defining external political and security roles. In the Japanese domestic context, much progress has been made. Declaratory policy explicitly recognizes common political and security interests with the United States and other Western states. Slowly, an independent foreign policy framework is being developed, especially regarding participation in multilateral organizations and on economic issues. Aid and other means of support for developing countries has expanded dramatically, and Japan's goals have broadened to encompass political and security concerns.[93] Japan increasingly participates, at least as an observer, or is consulted, in major political and security issues of the day. For example, Tokyo had considerable involvement in the INF Treaty negotiations.[94] Japan's Self Defense Forces have expanded rapidly and taken on a much greater role in the defense of Japan. Domestically, opposition politics have shifted toward the center, with most major parties officially accepting, at least in the short-term, the need for the alliance with the United States and the presence of American forces, and even the basic need for Self Defense Forces.

From the outside, however, an immense gap remains between Japan's economic and political/security roles, and there is a great debate over whether or not Japan even has or can acquire the qualities that would permit it to become a world leader.[95]

Common disclaimers by the Japanese themselves include: we lack the military power, we do not care for taking initiative, we lack influence, we lack the ability to deal with conflict, our neighbors are afraid of us, and we want the United States to stay the world leader, among many others. Japan's own actions give lie to this common litany. Yet, uncertainty, discomfort, and political constraints impede taking international leadership roles.

As discussed above, perhaps the key problems are the political system itself, Japan's domestic lack of leadership, and the absence of a vision or ideology to guide its foreign policy. The diffuse, fragmented political and policy structure is not conducive to producing visionary or creative foreign policy, nor to providing a strong domestic base of support for aggressive pursuit of such initiatives. Following the experiences of World War II, Japanese have a strong aversion to any ideology but economic self-interest. Narrow economic self-interest is a poor basis for world leadership. It is not clear whether Japan can develop a world view to guide policy that is not threatening to its neighbors, has a universalistic character, and has broad internal consistency. Domestic trends pointing toward a greater role of issues in the policy debate and toward a more international outlook suggest that it may be possible to at least develop broad agreement on a set of principles for policy guidance, even if a vision that might permit leadership is not possible.

An effort has been made to describe Japanese foreign policy in terms of "Peace and Prosperity."[96] Under this umbrella, it is argued that Japan should organize its policy around four objectives: (1) democracy; (2) peace; (3) industrialization of developing countries; and (4) world stability. In pursuit of these four objectives, Japan has renounced ever becoming a great military power, and has said it would use peaceful means of effecting its foreign policy.

These positions create a domestic policy confrontation whenever Japan faces the challenge of how to protect its interests in conflict-prone situations—such as the recent conflict with Iraq. Now, only its alliance with the United States provides this capability. In the 1990s, Japan will have to come to some sort of domestic agreement on participation in actions of common defense. It is likely the policy fiasco surrounding Japan's response to Iraqi aggression will force Japanese policymakers to adopt some version of the U.N. peace cooperation law as an explicit policy for participating in U.N. peacekeeping operations, beyond just money.

Another area in which Japan will expand its political and security role is as a regional partner. Although Japan quickly and forcefully turned down Thailand's request that the Japanese SDF participate in a joint exercise with the Thai military, closer political and security consultation, perhaps even limited cooperation, become increasingly attractive for several regional states.

Finally, despite development of a more independent foreign policy line and some explicit disagreements with the U.S. over specific issues, Japan will expand its direct and indirect support of U.S. political and security objectives in Asia and elsewhere. Two factors are at work here. First, Japan wants to keep the United States engaged in Northeast Asia, and more explicit support of American goals will be part of the price. Second, and perhaps most important, for now Japanese long-term interests are largely parallel to those of the United States, but Japan needs the American partnership to strengthen the likelihood of successful outcomes. To most of Asia, a growing Japanese role in political and security affairs is potentially destabilizing. A strong partnership with the United States permits Japan's role to evolve in a less threatening, balanced framework.

Notes

1. This chapter is based on "The Transformation of Japanese Foreign and Defense Policy: The Impact of Domestic Politics," a paper presented to the Midwest Conference on Asian Affairs, November 2, 1990, which summarized some of the major findings in a Hudson Institute research project with the same name supported by the U.S. Navy. This chapter represents solely the opinions and views of the author, not Hudson Institute or its clients or contributors.

2. Domestic change and impediments to Japan's ability to adjust to change are discussed on pages 16–17.

3. The usefulness of trade blocs to exclude Japan was seen as an advantage by various more or less mainstream speakers at the Federal Reserve's Annual Summer Conference held August 24–25. Japan clearly sees such attitudes as a dire threat to vital national interests. See Lana Uchitelle, "Blocs Seen Replacing Free Trade," *New York Times*, August 26, 1991, pp. C1, C4.

4. For a discussion of the primacy of economic success in the Japanese policy process, see T. Pepper, M. E. Janow, and J. W. Wheeler, *The Competition: Dealing with Japan* (New York: Praeger, 1985), chapters 2 and 3.

55

5. The issues discussed in the following paragraphs are dealt with in more detail in several sources: *Ibid*, chapters 1 and 2; Reihard Drifte, *Japan's Foreign Policy* (New York: The Royal Institute of International Affairs and Council on Foreign Relations Press, 1990), chapters 6 and 7; and Martin E. Weinstein, "Trade Problems and U.S.–Japan Security Cooperation," *The Washington Quarterly*, Vol. 11, No. 1. The data are mainly from *Japan 1990: An International Comparison* (Tokyo Keizai Koho Center, 1990). Selected values are drawn from the other sources noted.

6. The recent growth of the Japanese economic stake in Asia and some of the policy implications are analyzed in Edward J. Lincoln, "Japan's Role in Asia–Pacific Cooperation: Dimensions, Prospects, and Problems," *Journal of Northeast Asian Studies*, Vol. VIII, No. 4 (Winter 1989), pp.3–23.

7. These various political and institutional factors will be discussed in more detail throughout the chapter.

8. These acronyms stand for General Agreement on Tariffs and Trade, the International Monetary Fund, the International Bank for Reconstruction and Development (usually called the World Bank), and the Asian Development Bank.

9. See the data in Lincoln, "Japan's Role in Asia–Pacific Cooperation," pp.10–13, drawn from OECD, *Geographical Distribution of Financial Flows to Developing Countries* (Paris: OECD, 1989).

10. APEC is an informal grouping of fifteen Asia–Pacific states, set up to provide a forum for ministerial discussion on a broad range of economic issues. It is the first official mechanism designed to enhance cooperation among the Asia–Pacific states. For a brief overview of APEC's structure see "Fact Sheet: Asia–Pacific Economic Cooperation (APEC)," *U.S. Department of State Dispatch*, August 5, 1991, p. 565.

11. Recent events in the Mideast will be dealt with in some detail later in this chapter, since it is an excellent case study of Japan's political/institutional process at work.

12. This is a somewhat modified form of a question that was posed to the author by Prime Minister Lee Kwan Yew, in response to a question regarding Singapore's major future challenges. Personal interview, June 1989.

13. The next several paragraphs draw upon a brief foreign policy overview presented in "Japan and ASEAN," chapter 4 in P. L. Wood and J. W. Wheeler, *Southeast Asian Security in the 1990s*, Hudson Institute, October 1989.

14. See Drifte, *Japan's Foreign Policy*, pp.6–7, for a discussion of several of these concerns and policy goals from a somewhat different perspective.

15. Chalmers Johnson provides a perceptive review of Japanese

concerns and of some of the creative responses used to work around the American position. See his "Japanese–Chinese Relations, 1952–1982," chapter 6 in H. J. Ellison (ed.), *Japan and the Pacific Quadrille: The Major Powers in East Asia* (Boulder, CO, and London: Westview Press, 1987). See also John Quansheng Zhao, "Informal Plualism and Japanese Politics: Sino–Japanese Rapprochement Revisited," *Journal of Northeast Asian Studies*, Vol. VIII, No. 2 (Summer 1989), pp.65–83.

16. This informal, private diplomacy also offered opportunities for manipulation that the Chinese were not loath to employ.

17. Of course the U.S. leadership was not terribly difficult to convince. Memories of the Pacific war provided a powerful counterweight to anyone seeking a rearmed Japan.

18. Wood and Wheeler, *Southeast Asian Security in the 1990s*, p.111.

19. Besides the book noted in the text, many of Ishihara's views are expressed in a follow-up book, *The Japan That Still Says "No."* For a brief discussion see Konosuke Kuwabara, "Ishihara still says 'no'—and much, much else," *The Japan Economic Journal*, August 25, 1990, p.4.

20. Drifte, *Japan's Foreign Policy*, pp.29–31, provides an insightful analysis of comprehensive security, upon which this discussion is based. The quotes from the English translation of the original report are from p.29.

21. There is even a section on responding to earthquakes.

22. Examples of policy management include: joining with the U.S. in 1983 to initiate a new round of trade negotiations over the reluctance of the Europeans; active participation in developing the "Plaza Accord" on exchange rates among the group of five countries with key currency status; and a series of follow-up and related meetings.

23. Shiro Saito, *Japan at the Summit: Its Role in the Western Alliance and in Asian Pacific Cooperation* (London and New York: Routledge, 1990), provides a detailed analysis of Japanese participation in the various summits.

24. Even with this policy shift, Japan's aid remains highly focused on narrow economic gains that benefit Japanese companies; its allocation has had limited overall policy guidance; and the grant element of aid is less than that of other donors. All of these criticisms are subject to considerable internal debate and policy changes to varying degrees.

25. Wood and Wheeler, *Southeast Asian Security in the 1990s*, reviews Japanese policy initiatives in Asia, with a focus on Southeast Asia.

26. This meeting occurred in Tokyo in June 1990. Unfortunately, the Khmer Rouge refused to participate. However, the discussions and agreements among those who participated did, indeed, seem to help force the negotiating process back on track. For the purposes of this analysis,

the degree of success is virtually irrelevant. What is important was Japan's willingness to take the political initiative of hosting the meeting.

27. Certainly, this view comes through strongly in conversations with senior LDP politicians, mid-level to senior officials in the Foreign Ministry and the Defense Agency, and many others. This statement is based on interviews with a wide range of Japanese, in and out of public life, in June 1990. Though unscientific, the broad perception derived from these interviews agrees with other analyses of elite attitudes.

28. See Kent E. Calder, *Crisis and Compensation: Public Policy and Political Stability in Japan, 1944–1986* (Princeton, NJ: Princeton University Press, 1988), pp.436–38, for details on the two examples presented in this and the next paragraph.

29. This episode is discussed in Martin E. Weinstein, "Trade Problems and U.S.–Japanese Security Cooperation," *The Washington Quarterly*, Vol. 11, No. 1 (Winter 1988).

30. Much of the following discussion of the Foreign Ministry draws upon Drifte, *Japan's Foreign Policy*, pp.21–24.

31. For discussion of this choice, see Konosuke Kuwabara, "Critic Calls for Permanent Crisis Agency," *The Japan Economic Journal*, September 8, 1990, p.3, and "How Japan Missed the Boat," *The Economist*, September 22, 1990, pp.35–36.

32. Japan's multimember constituency process forces party members to compete against one another in each district, thus mitigating against any strong personal issue orientation.

33. See Hans H. Baerwald, *Party Politics in Japan* (Boston: Allen & Unwin, 1986), pp.163–68, for a discussion of the various elements in the changing balance between politicians and bureaucrats.

34. In most countries, most of the time, domestic issues have political priority. The priority of domestic issues is stronger in large and in insular countries. Japan's insularity may be one of the country's more pressing constraints on effective development of external policy over the next decade.

35. A national vision does not have to be very specific. Indeed, it probably helps not to be too specific. But, such a vision must lay out objectives in a clear enough fashion to define basic missions for all external policy programs, and provide some framework against which trade-offs can be evaluated.

36. Calder, *Crisis and Compensation*, assesses major periods of policy change in Japan. A crisis-compensation pattern is shown to be a critical dynamic for major shifts in policy direction.

37. This concern came up repeatedly in interviews with a broad cross-section of Japanese bureaucrats, politicians, and businessmen.

38. See "Japanese Defense: Back Under One Percent," *The Economist*, August 4, 1990, for an assessment of the recent defense budget debate.

39. See "Japan Reverses Policy on Soviet as a Threat," *New York Times*, September 1990, p.A8.

40. These comments were included in a major policy paper, articulating many of the government's views on important foreign and security policy issues. The untitled draft English translation was provided by the Ministry of Foreign Affairs, June 1990.

41. Although a variety of sources are used to explore Japanese threat perception, this entire discussion draws heavily on a series of interviews in Japan, conducted in June 1990.

42. For an overview of the history, see John J. Stephen, "Japanese–Soviet Relations: Patterns and Prospects," chapter 7 in Ellison, *Japan and the Pacific Quadrille*.

43. See Defense Agency, *Defense of Japan: 1989*, translated from the original White Paper by *The Japan Times, Ltd.*, chapter 2, section 2. There has been some decline in the numbers of surface ships in the Soviet fleet, mainly retirements of old equipment. However, they have been replaced with a smaller number of far more capable craft.

44. A good summary of the views and expectations about the long-term potential is provided in Clayton Jones, "East-West Thaw a Boon for Nations on the Sea of Japan," and Daniel Sneider, "Vladivostok and the Soviet Far East: Still Closed, or Open for Business," both in *The Christian Science Monitor*, September 27, 1990, pp.10–11.

45. Interviews in June 1990 found a surprisingly low level of debate about what else the Soviets might want besides economic support.

46. For a discussion of Japanese attitudes and positions on various arms control issues, see David T. Jones, "Post–INF Treaty Attitudes in East Asia," *Asian Survey*, Vol. XXX, No. 5, May 5, 1990, pp.483–87.

47. These are more difficult conditions than they might appear on the surface. Introducing a split on security issues between Japan and the United States has been a long-term priority of Soviet foreign and defense policy, one that is difficult for Russia to change. Similarly, yielding territory when regions within Russia are seeking greater power, even independence, and in the face of other important territorial disputes has to give pause to the new leadership. Finally, not only have the Japanese invested a great deal of political capital in their all or nothing position, but there is a strong domestic perception that Japan holds all of the negotiating cards, and does not need to compromise.

48. Indeed, there is an article in the 1978 Treaty of Peace and Friendship, in which both countries pledge to oppose an unspecified hegemony, that all knew referred to the Soviet Union.

49. Drifte, *Japan's Foreign Policy*, pp.51–52.

50. This complex history is summarized in R. Mark Bean, *Cooperative Security in Northeast Asia* (Washington, DC: National Defense University, 1990), chapter 2.

51. A nuclear-armed Korea came up several times in interviews in response to a line of inquiry about long-term threats to Japan.

52. Wood and Wheeler, *Southeast Asian Security in the 1990s*, chapter 4, discusses the relationship between Japan and Southeast Asia in some detail.

53. For a discussion of possible Japanese security roles, see Muthiah Alagappa, "Japan's Political and Security Role in the Asia–Pacific Region," *Contemporary Southeast Asia*, Vol. 10, No. 1, June 1988, pp. 17–54.

54. Reportedly, Prime Minister Nakasone was willing to consider sending a minesweeping force to support the Gulf effort, but was blocked by strong domestic opposition, including within his own LDP.

55. See "How Japan Missed the Boat," *The Economist*, September 22, 1990, pp. 35–36.

56. Quote from Mr. Kaifu's September 27 speech, reported in Steven R. Weisman, "Kaifu Outlines His Proposal For Unarmed Japanese in Gulf," *New York Times*, September 28, 1990, p. A4.

57. See "How Japan Missed the Boat."

58. See Foreign Broadcast Information Service, *Daily Report: East Asia*, 90–168, August 29, 1990, p. 8, which reports Chief Cabinet Secretary Misoji Sakamoto's comments on the limited scope of this crisis office.

59. For some discussion of the failed legislation, see for example a speech by Foreign Minister Taro Nakayama to the U.N. General Assembly session on September 25, 1990, reported in "Nakayama Calls for Revision of UN Charter," Foreign Broadcast Information Service, *Daily Report: East Asia,* 90–187, September 26, 1990, p. 2, and in "Nakayama Vows Close Contact on Noncombatants," ibid, p. 3.

60. These various investments and other business links are also slowly acting to help reduce the huge American trade deficits.

61. A description of basic security policy and the respective roles of Japanese and American forces can be found in the annual White Paper on Defense. See Defense Agency, *Defense of Japan*, parts II and III.

62. If calculated according to NATO practices, Japanese defense spending is closer to two percent of GNP.

63. Defense Agency, *Defense of Japan*, pp. 166–173.

64. Interviews, June 1990.

65. Calder, *Crises and Compensation*, chapter 10, assesses the process by which defense budgets are negotiated. This analysis highlights the weakness of the domestic defense constituency.

66. This support came up clearly in interviews. See also "Government Plans Revision of U.S. Bases Pact," and "More on Pact," both in Foreign Broadcast Information Service, *Daily Report: East Asia*, 90–193, October 4, 1990, pp. 5–6.

67. Richard D. Fisher, "How to Improve the U.S.–Japan Security Alliance," *Backgrounder*, Asian Studies Center, The Heritage Foundation, September 26, 1990.

68. This attitude was expressed in interviews with senior U.S. officers in Japan as well as many Japanese.

69. This decision was made in 1981 by then Prime Minister Zenko Suzuki.

70. For an early discussion of the difficulty faced by Japan of even considering these expanded missions, see Paul Keal, "Japan and International Security in the Region," in T. B. Millar (ed.), *International Security in the Southeast Asian and Southwest Pacific Region* (Australia: University of Queensland, 1983), pp.92–113, especially pp.95–101.

71. Defense Agency, "On the Mid-Term Defense Program," *Defense of Japan*, pp.268–272.

72. For a brief discussion see Sam K. Lee, "United States–Japan Security Relations: A Need for Realism," *Comparative Strategy*, Vol. 9, No. 2 (1990), pp.85–99. This enhanced cooperation was developed under the "Guidelines for Japan–U.S. Defense Cooperation," adopted in 1978. See Defense Agency, *Defense of Japan*, for an English translation of the guidelines.

73. Lee, "United States–Japan Security Relations," p.91.

74. See Seizaburo Sato and Yuji Suzuki, "A New Stage of the United States–Japan Alliance," chapter 1 in John H. Making and Donald C. Hellmann (eds), *Sharing World Leadership? A New Era for America and Japan* (Washington, D.C.: American Enterprise Institute, 1989).

75. For a highly critical view of the draft Japanese plans, see Hank Gafney Jr., "Japan Still Avoids its Share of the Work," *Defense News*, October 8, 1990, pp.23–24.

76. All the opposition parties criticized the 1990 *White Paper on Defense* approved by the Cabinet on September 18. See "Opposition Parties Critical of Defense Paper," Foreign Broadcast Information Service, *Daily Report: East Asia*, 90–183, September 20, 1990, p.11. For the new JSP position accepting the SDF, but only if cut to minimal, purely defensive capabilities, see "JSP Report on Smaller SDF, Restrictions," and "JSP Supports SDF, Two-Stage Reform," both in Foreign Broadcast Information Service *Daily Report: East Asia*, 90–188, September 27, 1990, pp.4–5.

77. For example, see "JSP Against Using Defense Forces," Foreign Broadcast Information Service, *Daily Report: East Asia*, 90–195, October 9, 1990, p.3.

78. For example, see Bryan T. Johnson, "Japanese Foreign Aid: Defending America's Interests," *Backgrounder*, Heritage Foundation, January 30, 1990.

79. Gregory P. Corning, "U.S.–Japan Security Cooperation in the

1990s: The Promise of High Tech Defense," *Asian Survey*, Vol. XXIX, No. 3, March 1989, p.272.

80. Interview, June 1990. Several academics and government officials expressed similar views.

81. Kenneth P. Pyle argues that only by making the strategic aspects of aid explicit will expanded aid be seen in America as a contribution to burden sharing. See his "The Burden of Japanese History and the Politics of Burden Sharing," chapter 2 in Making and Hellmann, *Sharing World Leadership?*, pp.72–75.

82. Corning, "U.S.-Japan Security Cooperation in the 1990s," pp.269–70 and pp. 278–85.

83. See Tadae Takubo, "Deadlock over Defense," *Bungei Shunju Digest,* January, 1990, pp.48–59.

84. Fisher, "How to Improve the U.S.-Japan Security Alliance," p.12.

85. "Joint-U.S. Defense Technology Groups to Form," Foreign Broadcast Information Service, *Daily Reports: East Asia*, 90–191, October 2, 1990, pp.5–6.

86. The 1984 Defense Science Board report noted above explicitly reviewed these trade-offs, as did the debate over the FSX.

87. These possibilities were raised but not elaborated on in Lieutenant Commander Paul G. Johnson, "Japan: A True Partner in Defense," *Proceedings*, March, 1990, p.37. Interviews revealed some broad interest for the possibilities both in the JDA and the DOD.

88. See Drifte, *Japan's Foreign Policy*, pp. 60–61, and Jones, "Post-INF Treaty Attitudes in East Asia," pp.483–85, for more detailed reviews of Japanese positions on various arms control issues.

89. This came through clearly in interviews with Foreign Ministry and Defense Agency representatives. Academic, business, and even some LDP political positions were less firm on this issue.

90. Peggy L. Falkenheim provides a detailed review of the motivations, history, and possible incentives of Soviet and Japanese interactions on arms control in "The Soviet Union, Japan and East Asia: The Security Dimensions," *Journal of Northeast Asian Studies*, Winter, 1984, pp.48–58.

91. This analysis is from an interview with the Kyodo News Service, reported in "Minister Kuriyama on Security Treaty Importance," Foreign Broadcast Information Service *Daily Report: East Asia,* 90–119, June 20, 1990, pp.1–2.

92. Interviews, June 1990 and November 1991.

93. The increasing security focus of aid remains politically controversial among opposition parties. The official government position is that aid is allocated based on a review of requests from individual countries.

94. Jones, "Post–INF Treaty Attitudes in East Asia," pp.483–85.

95. Some of these issues were discussed in a US–Japan Economic Agenda presentation by Susan Chira, "Currents of Change in Japan: Japan's Ability to be a Global Leader," June 28, 1989. See also Karen Elliott House, "Japan Lacks Global Leadership Qualities," *The Asian Wall Street Journal*, February 1, 1989, pp.1, 7.

96. The particular points made here are from a MITI advisory board report issued in May 1990. See Foreign Broadcast Information Service, *Daily Report: East Asia,* 90–095, May 16, 1990.

CHAPTER TWO

Japan's Strategic Options

Martin E. Weinstein

There is very little evidence suggesting that fundamental or dramatic shifts in Japan's basic strategy and foreign policy are imminent or likely during the next one or two years. Consequently, in looking at Japan's strategic and foreign policy options, I suggest that in addition to examining the recent and current foreign policy debate, we also attempt to peer into the next ten to twenty years, the 1990s and the first decade of the twenty-first century. Given the rate and extent of change occurring in the international system, especially in the Soviet Union and in Europe, and the Iraqi invasion of Kuwait, it is more likely than at any time since the late 1940s and early 1950s that fundamental changes in the international system will occur during the next decade or two, which could compel Japan to change its strategy and foreign policy.

Japan's strategy and foreign policy, including both its security policies and its foreign economic policies, have been highly successful and stable since the late 1940s and early 1950s, when they were formulated and defined. The success of these policies has generated an enormous inertia and an enormous reluctance to depart from them, until and unless it becomes clear to the Japanese government and the voters that it is necessary to do so. Although the Persian Gulf crisis generated an unprecedented level of international criticism of Japan, and the Japanese are now much more aware of the need to enlarge their international role, it is still not clear what the nature and scope of their response will be.

Japanese Policy Since World War II—The Yoshida Strategy

What are the defining characteristics of this highly successful policy? What is the baseline from which we begin our speculation about options and possible changes in the future?

Ever since the late 1940s, and indeed even back to the 1860s and 1870s when the Meiji oligarchs began Japan's industrialization, there has been a clear perception in the Japanese government that: (1) the building of a viable and then a competitive industrial economy and a stable, effective political system has been the primary objective of national policy; (2) the achievement of these goals is very heavily contingent on foreign policy; and (3) the security and economic dimensions of foreign policy are inextricably linked. It has been clear to Japanese officials since early in the modernization process that given its geographical position and resources, the success of Japan's industrialization would depend on access to overseas raw materials (and in the twentieth century, especially energy), and to overseas markets. The particular lesson of World War II, which was engraved very deeply on the national psyche, is that Japan cannot achieve this necessary access to the world economy by the use of military force. The Japanese concluded, therefore, that they must avoid as much as possible any military role in international politics, and that they must rely on peaceful, non-military means to build their economy and to make a decent life for themselves.

By the late 1940s and early 1950s, Japan's conservative foreign policy makers, especially Shigeru Yoshida, who served as prime minister from 1948 to 1954, had concluded that in the bipolar, U.S.–Soviet dominated international system, the best foreign policy for Japan was: (1) to become an ally of the United States (not a military dependent); and (2) to base Japan's economic future on the relatively free, open international economic system that the United States was constructing—most especially on cooperative economic relations with the United States itself, which would be a major source of raw materials and a major market for Japanese manufactured products. It is worth noting forty years later that while Japan's reliance on American raw materials has declined somewhat since the 1950s, it still relies heavily on American farm products, timber, and coking coal, and in the 1980s, Japan's exports to the United States reached record levels, approaching 40 percent of total exports.

Prime Minister Yoshida's strategy was rooted in the belief that the alliance with the United States would protect Japan against the Communist, Soviet threat to its military security and political stability. Within the secure, stable strategic-political framework provided by the security treaty, and by the United States nuclear deterrent and naval and air preponderance in the Pacific and over the world ocean and trade routes, the Japanese would be able to concentrate their energies and organizational skills in the 1950s on the task of economic reconstruction, and then on the goal of becoming a highly efficient, competitive industrial economy.

Recent Events Shake the Premises of Success

As we know, this foreign policy was highly successful—perhaps too successful. By the end of the 1980s, however, the basic premises of the Yoshida policy were being called into question by two related developments in Japan's external environment. First, the Communist, Soviet threat appeared to be diminishing to the point where it could cease being the negative force binding the United States and Japan into a security alliance. At the same time, Japan's successes in building a competitive, industrial economy were generating potentially dangerous levels of resentment, fear, and antagonism toward Japan in the United States. As a consequence, Japan-bashing became popular in the Congress and in the media, and the United States government began moving toward protectionist economic policies directed against Japan—such as the Super 301 provisions of the 1988 Trade Act. This mounting antagonism, and the creeping protectionism which accompanies it, threatened to undermine the General Agreement on Tariffs and Trade (GATT) and the relatively open international systems of trade and finance upon which Japan's prosperity and security depend.

Obviously, these two related, to some extent mutually reinforcing international developments call into question the basic premises and elements of the foreign policy that have served Japan so well since the Korean War (1950–53). Equally significant has been the call from abroad that Japan take on a larger role in the international community to a level commensurate with its economic power. At no other time was this more clearly stated, and Japan's actions as closely monitored, as during the 1990–91 crisis and hostilities in the Persian Gulf.

Japan's apparently lethargic response in the Gulf was in reality an abortive policy initiative encumbered by protracted legislative debate on issues of constitutionality, and exacerbated by the inability of a prime minister with a weak power base to win a timely consensus on either the allocation of funds or the dispatch of Self Defense Forces (SDF) personnel overseas. The result was predictable: criticism from the international community, led by the United States, that Japan was shirking its international responsibility and reaping the benefits of the "allied" military action, to which Japan contributed money, but not men.

The image of a Japan that reacts slowly and timidly only when forced to by an international crisis, or of an economic power that lacks geopolitical power, is indeed difficult to overcome, at home as well as abroad. "Tokyo would not have been criticized so harshly, if it had acted at the same time as Washington, or at least more promptly than it did," stated Professor Shin'-ichi Kitaoka in the April 1991 issue of *Chuo Koron*, "but because we were so slow, we always seem to be acting reluctantly in response to American pressure."[1] Following Japan's pledge on March 1, 1991 of an additional $9 billion to the Gulf effort (beyond the $4 billion previously promised), an editorial in the *Nihon Keizai Shinbun*, Japan's leading financial daily, accurately concluded that because the Japanese government had moved so slowly, its willingness to pay for as much as 20 percent of the cost of the war "was not really appreciated,"[2] even though an earlier report in the same paper cited official American appreciation of Japan's "generous and timely support," as expressed by Presidential Press Secretary Marlin Fitzwater.[3] Similarly, when a minesweeping group of six ships and approximately five hundred Marine Self Defense Forces personnel were dispatched to the Gulf in April, 1991, the editors of the *Yomiuri Shinbun* wondered in their headline: "Will U.S. Dissatisfaction be Mitigated?"[4] An article in the *Asahi Shinbun* noted the low priority given Japan by Secretary of State Baker in his meetings with individual leaders of the allied nations' foreign ministries.[5]

If nothing else, however, the events in the Persian Gulf may have heightened domestic awareness in Japan of the necessity of increasing its international role. In November 1990, before hostilities actually broke out in the Gulf and before criticism of Japan reached its peak, an *Asahi Shinbun* poll showed that public opinion ran very strongly against any Japanese involvement beyond economic support. As many as 78 percent of the respondents opposed the dispatch of SDF personnel to the Persian Gulf,[6] and 55 percent even rejected a plan for using SDF forces to transport Gulf War refugees.[7] By June of 1991, however, only 13 percent of those polled in a survey conducted by the *Mainichi Shinbun* were opposed to SDF participation in U.S. peacekeeping operations following the 1991 war,[8] and an *Asahi Shinbun* poll showed that 64 percent had come around to the view that, "It is now necessary for Japan to play a much more active role than before in settling international disputes."[9] Of course, one can argue that the Japanese public was more willing to consider SDF participation in a U.N. operation in June 1991, because the danger of imminent hostilities had passed. However, it is probably also true that the protracted barrage of intense foreign criticism of Japan's policy of limiting its involvement in the Gulf to funding while avoiding the fighting, also contributed to this shift in public opinion.[10]

The Current Foreign Policy Debate

The media in Japan is as open and free as any in the world, and the print media in particular is an extremely rich source in studying politics and foreign policy. Groups of journalists from each of the major national newspapers, organized into press clubs, have attached themselves to the prime minister, each of the powerful ministries, and to the powerful faction leaders in the political parties, who serve in the National Diet. Politics and foreign policy are covered in extraordinary, generally accurate detail and with extensive analysis. Moreover, there are in Japan monthly, intellectual journals, such as *Chuo Koron, Bungei Shunju,* and *Ushio,* in which foreign policy intellectuals of all political persuasions, from Marxists to right-wing nationalists, and everyone in between, criticize policy and tell the government what it should be doing. Based on a study of several hundred newspaper articles and several dozen journal articles and books on foreign policy published between 1988 and 1991, and interviews with senior Japanese foreign policy officials, there appears to be virtually no evidence that Japan is planning to fundamentally or even substantially change its foreign policy. These materials did indicate, however, that there is widespread awareness in Japan that the alliance with the United States is in danger, that its future is less certain than ever before, and that substantial, even fundamental changes in national and foreign policy may become unavoidable within the next decade or two.

One of the effects of the alliance's apparent vulnerability and uncertain future is that its Japanese critics have lowered their voices if not changed their minds. When, in the 1950s and 1960s, the United States had a position of unchallengeable economic and military strength, and when the reliability of its guarantee of Japan's security was hardly questioned, a slight majority of the Japanese voters consistently told pollsters that they did *not* support the Security Treaty. In those long ago days, there were many Japanese who believed that the Americans had too much military power, were excessively anti-communist and trigger-happy, and that to keep the United States from behaving recklessly, it was wise not to support the Security Treaty. Most of these critics were actually content to have Japan protected by the United States, and polls indicated that approximately 80 percent of the Japanese then believed that the United States would come to Japan's defense if it were attacked or threatened with attack.

Following the rapprochement with China in 1972, the defeat of the United States in Vietnam in 1975, the apparent weakening of United States naval and air strength in the Pacific relative to that of the Soviet Union, and the increase in trade frictions, Japanese belief in the reliability of the American security guarantee dropped to about 20 percent in the 1980s. It is not surprising that under these changed conditions, many former critics of the Security Treaty decided it was now necessary to strengthen the credibility of the treaty by supporting it.

As a result of these changing perceptions, during the last few years criticism against the United States–Japan Security

70

Treaty and the alliance has dropped to an all-time low. By the mid-1980s, a variety of opinion polls showed that between 70 and 80 percent of the Japanese voters had become supporters or had a favorable view of the alliance. During the general election in the fall of 1989, Ms. Takako Doi, at the time the new, more pragmatic leader of the Japan Socialist Party (JSP) (the English version of its name since changed to "Social Democratic Party of Japan"), bowed to public opinion by declaring that if the Socialists won the election and formed a government, they would *not* abrogate the U.S.–Japan Security Treaty. They would, instead, study the treaty and perhaps recommend some revisions. Because the JSP had been calling for abrogation of the treaty since the party was formed in 1954, Ms. Doi's change of line created dissension among her party cadres. A number of the more persistent, left-wing Socialists publicly disagreed with the Doi position. Nevertheless, the effect of Ms. Doi's change was to sharply reduce and divide the most harsh and consistent critics of the alliance.

At the same time, on the center and right of the political spectrum there has been a lively debate about the future of the U.S.–Japan alliance. The Toshiba Incident in the summer of 1987, the Trade Act of 1988 (which led to the Super 301 actions of 1988–89), and the FSX controversy have been given much more coverage and attention in Japan than in the United States. Moreover, critics of Japan in the Congress, such as Representative Richard Gephardt and Senators Lloyd Bentsen and John Danforth, and intellectuals, such as Clyde Prestowitz and James Fallows, probably have a larger, more attentive audience in Japan than they do at home. The natural and expected result is that many of the Japanese who have been publicly supporting and explaining the alliance for several decades have begun to wonder aloud about what has to be done to keep the alliance alive, or whether it can be saved at all. The following examination of several representative writings indicates the variety of analyses and views in this new genre.

Save the Alliance Even at the Cost of Wrenching Economic and Social Changes in Japan

Seizaburo Sato, who recently retired as a professor of international relations at Tokyo University, is one of the leading and most outspoken advocates of preserving the alliance with the United States. In March of 1990, Professor Sato published an article in *Chuo Koron*[11] in which he pulled together many of the ideas and arguments of those in and outside the Japanese government who believe that while the alliance has entered a period of instability and vulnerability, Japan has a vital stake in keeping it alive. To preserve the alliance, Sato argued, Japan should make dramatic and substantial changes in its own foreign economic policies as well as in its domestic social and political structures.

Sato believes that there is a tendency in both Japan and the United States to act as though the Soviet threat has disappeared. In his view, while the Soviets are clearly in a period of confusion and decline, they still have enormous nuclear and conventional military forces, and depending on how their current crisis is resolved, these forces could once again become a serious threat to both Japan and the United States. He concludes, therefore, that it is shortsighted and irresponsible to talk and act as though the U.S.–Japan Security Treaty were obsolete.

Professor Sato then goes on to argue that even if the Soviet threat does, in the future, virtually disappear, the United States and Japanese economies have become intertwined and interdependent, and that the economic dimension of the alliance is fundamentally beneficial to both partners, and to the entire world economy. He believes that the economic costs of abrogating or abandoning the present high levels of economic interaction and cooperation would be staggering. If Japan and the United States start fighting trade wars, and indulging in protectionism and techno-nationalism, Sato expects that not only the Pacific region but also the entire global political-economy would be dangerously destabilized.

Professor Sato's prescription for preserving the alliance is that Japan should take the lead in eliminating whatever restrictions remain on trade and investment. He advocates that Japan move quickly to reorganize its distribution system and business practices to make them more accessible and attractive to Americans. On the issue of technology, he urges the Japanese to make available to the United States whatever superior technology it may have developed, especially if this technology has military applications. Sato urges Japan to "offer its best technology to America . . . and help Americans to build the best possible FSX fighter."[12] (The FSX is an advanced, experimental jet fighter based on the F-16, and is being jointly developed by General Dynamics and Mitsubishi Heavy Industry. It is to be manufactured in Japan for the Air Self Defense Force in the late 1990s.)

Japanese (and Perhaps Americans) Underestimate the Danger of Their Economic Quarrels

Although this is essentially a variant of the Sato approach, it is worth examining because it indicates the seriousness and depth of concern among Japanese conservatives over the future of their relationship with the United States. Hisahiko Okazaki has thoughtfully expounded this theme. He is a senior diplomat who has served as ambassador in Saudi Arabia and Bangkok, and who is well known in Japan for his many books and articles on foreign policy and strategy. In the January 1990 issue of *Bungei Shunju*, Mr. Okazaki published an article entitled, "What Can Japan Learn From Holland?"[13] In this article Mr. Okazaki presented a scholarly analysis, drawing heavily on British sources, of the causes of the three Anglo–Dutch wars of the late seventeenth century (1652–54; 1665–67; 1672–78).

In these wars, Holland was defeated by Britain, and lost much of its overseas holdings and influence, as well as suffering severe economic damage and dislocation. The main point that Okazaki makes is that the Dutch did not expect war and persisted in believing that Britain and Holland were basically friendly, compatible countries beset by economic frictions and quarrels, which would be peacefully resolved by mutual, enlightened self-interest. After all, Holland and England had fought together against Spain and the Habsburgs in the Thirty Years' War. They were both Protestant states in a century when religion was as important as ideology was to be in the twentieth century. Both countries were proud of their commercial, trading, and manufacturing skills, and viewed themselves as rational and enlightened rather than passionate and military. The Dutch firmly believed that even after the defeat of the Catholics, and the decline of the Spanish threat, they and the English would continue as friendly trading partners, if not close allies.

Nevertheless, Okazaki draws on the writings of British historians to show that in the late seventeenth century, Holland's trade surpluses with England, together with its technological successes

73

and its banking skills, generated such resentment and jealousy across the Channel that enlightened English self-interest gave way to Holland-bashing and protectionism that did as much damage to England as to Holland, and which finally led to war, which did much more damage to Holland.

Okazaki cautions that there are many differences between the Anglo–Dutch relationship in the seventeenth century and the current U.S.–Japan relationship. But he concludes his article by asking:

> Was there some way that Holland, itself a model economic superpower, could have avoided conflict with England while maintaining its security interests and continuing its prosperity? If so, where did the Dutch take a wrong turn? Did they have a plan to avoid this wrong turn? Answers to these questions may provide Japan with vital information by which to chart its course for the years ahead.[14]

Save the Alliance, but Only as an Equal Partnership

Shintaro Ishihara, a novelist and a Liberal Democratic member of the National Diet, has gained a certain notoriety in the United States as a consequence of the unauthorized translation and distribution in the summer of 1989 of a book of essays he co-authored with Sony Chairman Akio Morita, entitled *A Japan That Can Say 'No' to America*. The controversy surrounding the initial appearance of this book seems to have led Mr. Morita to disassociate himself from it. However, an authorized translation of five of Mr. Ishihara's original essays, together with six additional pieces was published in early 1991 by Simon and Schuster, entitled *The Japan That Can Say No: Why Japan Will Be First among Equals*.[15]

For several decades, Ishihara has run for political office on two foreign policy planks. He has supported the U.S.–Japan alliance, but he has wanted Japan to stop being "subservient" to United States demands and "bullying." He has argued, long before the revisionists and Japan bashers appeared in the United States, that unless the growing economic and technological equality and interdependence of the two countries is matched by more equal influence and control over alliance policy, Japanese resentment and American arrogance are likely to destroy this highly successful and mutually beneficial relationship. Several of Ishihara's older essays in this vein appear in the new book, along with more recent pieces on the FSX controversy.

In the FSX essays, he expressed great irritation at those congresspersons and critics in Washington who attacked U.S.–Japan codevelopment of the FSX as a technological giveaway to Japan, which would endanger the United States aerospace industry. Ishihara wrote that Japan should have responded to those charges by developing the FSX itself. Probably the most controversial and inflammatory point he made was his contention that the Pentagon depends on Japanese chips to control its strategic missiles, and that if Americans continue to bash and bully Japan, Japanese should consider the possibility of selling their chip technology to the Soviets as well as to Americans. This, he argued, would awaken Americans to the reality of their technological dependence on Japan, and get them to talk about power sharing as well as burden sharing.

Ishihara's threat of selling chip technology to the Soviet Union faded quickly as the Soviet Union slipped into deeper economic and political weakness during 1990–91. Whatever one thinks of Ishihara's approach, it should be noted that while his arguments imply that the treaty is dispensable, he does not call for the abrogation of the Security Treaty, and repeatedly states his support for the alliance as a partnership of equals. It seems to me that the greatest difficulty in Ishihara's approach is that it is not clear what he wants to do about the military inequality between Japan and the United States. Sometimes he seems to be calling for Japan to become a military as well as an economic superpower—a message that raises as much fear within Japan as it does outside.

On economic questions, Ishihara's views overlap with those of Sato. He urges that Japan drastically reform its distribution system and transform itself into a model free market, free trading country. He believes that the Japanese consumer will benefit from such reforms, and he is confident that Japan is strong and competitive enough to thrive in this role. However, he contends that unless the United States undertakes whatever reforms are necessary to regain its financial solvency, to rebuild its industries and to educate its people, the American economy will continue to drift into ever greater difficulties, thus endangering the bilateral relationship with Japan and the entire world economy.

The Alliance Cannot Be Saved Because the United States Does Not Need It Anymore

In January 1990, Soichiro Tahara, a well-known writer on politics and foreign policy, published a brief article in *Ushio*,[16] in which he summed up the views of pessimistic conservatives who are supporters of the alliance but believe its days are now numbered. In this article, Tahara agreed with almost everything Professor Sato was to say in March, except that he was convinced that Americans had only put up with the U.S.–Japan alliance because of the Communist Soviet danger, and that Americans were prematurely concluding that the Russians were no longer a threat. Therefore, he wrote:

> . . . the United States needed Japan as an ally in the Cold War, and learned to tolerate us, even though our manufacturing success disrupted the American economy. But what will become of Japan if the Berlin Wall comes down, and if the Cold War disappears? The answer is obvious. Japan will become unnecessary. Unless Japan develops its own positive, acceptable strategy about what kind of a role it should play in the world . . . America and many other countries as well will turn more and more against us.[17]

Mr. Tahara's prescription for dealing with the post-alliance world is not a foreign policy as such, but rather a proposal for Japan to become the model of a successful, industrial, urban country, which he believes will elicit the respect and admiration of the world, including the United States. For Mr. Tahara, the essence of Japan's foreign policy problems is not the existence of powerful and potentially hostile military states, or economic disputes and frictions, but that there is something about Japan and the Japanese that makes them disliked and unpopular. He seems to believe that if Japan makes itself into a model industrialized, urban state, it will dispel suspicions and hostilities, will become universally respected and liked, and thus will have no need for alliances.

Japan as an Economic Hegemon

Although a number of non-Japanese writers have argued that Japan will overtake the United States as the world's leading economic power and will establish a *pax nipponica* early in the next century, it is not easy to find respected Japanese writers who take this position. It is, however, an option that bears examination. One of the more intriguing forecasts of Japanese economic hegemony has been written by Koji Taira, a Japanese economist, who is on the faculty of the University of Illinois. Professor Taira edited and contributed to the January 1991 volume of *The Annals of the American Academy of Political and Social Sciences*, entitled "Japan's External Economic Relations: Japanese Perspectives."[18] His article, "Japan, an Imminent Hegemon?," is the only one in the journal that focuses on the possibility of Japanese hegemony.

The first point to be noted is that Professor Taira expects that the post-Cold War world will be a relatively peaceful one, in which military politics will be almost entirely superseded by economic politics. In this world, he argues that Japan will achieve a hegemonic position based not on its capital surplus alone, which he believes will soon shrink, but based primarily on its unique organizational skills. He believes that it is organizational skills that have enabled Japan to attain the flexible, just-on-time manufacturing technology that has made it into the highest quality, most cost efficient manufacturer in the world. Professor Taira predicts that Japan will maintain its manufacturing lead well into the next century, and that Japanese manufacturing firms will continue to build plants worldwide. Japanese manufacturers, therefore, will assume leading positions in the American and European economies, as well as many other parts of the world. Since he also believes that there is and will continue to be a close, cooperative relationship between government and industry in Japan, he concludes that it is only natural that the Japanese government will use Japan's manufacturing and economic preponderance to serve Japan's political as well as economic interests. In Professor Taira's view (which he shares with writers such as Emanuel Wallerstein and Robert Gilpin), an economic hegemony is necessary to maintain a relatively open, orderly global economy, and Japan's economic hegemony will be benign and beneficial.

Professor Taira, in tune with Paul Kennedy's *The Rise and Fall of the Great Powers*, notes that Great Britain and the United States achieved their hegemonic positions partly as the result of lengthy, destructive wars that demonstrated their economic strength and staying power. He believes, however, that Japan will achieve hegemony in a peaceful environment without any dramatic confrontations. It will accomplish this feat by maintaining an unassuming, cooperative, nonthreatening posture in its foreign policy, while publicly continuing to treat the United States as the leading global superpower. According to Professor Taira, the *tatemae* (outward show) will be a U.S.–Japanese partnership with the United States as senior partner. The *honne* (hidden reality) will be quiet Japanese control and manipulation of this partnership behind the scenes. Taira believes the United States will be satisfied to appear to be in charge, while Japan will be satisfied to quietly run things.

My own view is that it is most unlikely, in view of the paranoia already demonstrated in the Congress and the media, that Americans will tolerate any form of Japanese hegemony, economic or otherwise. If the United States does not regain its economic vitality and self-confidence, I expect we will resort to protectionism and technonationalism, even though this will damage our own economy and the entire international economic system.

A Japan–United States–European Community Partnership Should Be Created to Shape and Maintain a New World Order

In Japan, Foreign Ministry bureaucrats are frequently criticized for being excessively conservative and unimaginative. Indeed, their harsher critics have characterized them as mere caretakers of the alliance with the United States. Although they are undoubtedly constrained by their official position in publicly expressing their views, the Foreign Ministry pitched into the public debate last May, with a rather bold article in its house journal, *Gaiko Forum*, written by its highest career official, Vice Minister Takakazu Kuriyama.[19]

Mr. Kuriyama's sober view of the post-Cold War world (published months before the Gulf crisis and the stalled negotiations in the Uruguay round of trade talks), was that unless new global security and economic systems are soon created to replace the rapidly disappearing bipolar, American–Soviet structure and the GATT-IMF structure, the world was in grave danger of drifting into instability and violence, and/or destructive trade wars. He made the point several times that in the 1990s the United States will not have the economic strength to either act as the world's policeman, or to take the lead in promoting a system of global free trade and investment. Since the United States (GNP $5 trillion), the European Community (GNP $5 trillion), and Japan (GNP $3 trillion) together produce about two thirds of the world's total goods and services ($20 trillion), he concluded that the best hope for the future lies in their forming a tripartite partnership that will make and implement the rules of a new international order.

Mr. Kuriyama was deeply aware of the antagonism developing against Japan in the United States, and his proposal for a global triumvirate was intended to help defuse the bilateral tension by transcending it. He also wrote that while Japan had reached a position of great wealth and influence in the 1980s, its economic achievements and prowess were frequently exaggerated in America and in Europe, as the 5–5–3 GNP ratio indicates. Nevertheless, he urged that Japan now take an active role in the triumvirate.

Since Japan is constrained by its constitution and by public opinion from assuming any military responsibilities, he proposed that Japan make its contribution by becoming the world's leading free trader and importer—playing an indispensable economic role which the United States no longer seems willing or able to perform, and which Europe is not yet prepared to assume. Mr. Kuriyama points out that since Japan failed so disastrously in its efforts to play the role of a great power before World War II, it is crucial that Japan now allay any suspicions about its intentions by continuing to be peaceful, unassuming and nonthreatening. Japan, he writes, should develop "the foreign policy of a great power without appearing to be a great power (*taikokutsura o shinai taikoku no gaiko*).[20]

Although Mr. Kuriyama indicates that "idiosyncratic nationalism" will become an increasingly serious threat to world political stability and peace in the 1990s, and that economic order and prosperity depend on political order and peace, it is not clear how the triumvirate would constitute a global security system, and what roles each of the partners would play, *except* that Japan could make no military contribution. The reader will have no doubt noticed that both Taira's "hegemon" and Kuriyama's "great power" bear a striking resemblance in their functions and disguises. The principal and crucial difference is that while Taira expects the post-Cold War world to be relatively peaceful and in no need of a military security system, Kuriyama sees a serious potential for political instability and violence, but makes no clear proposal for coping with it.

In the historical context of this essay, and set against the climate of recent opinion in Japan reflected in the articles we have examined, it is easy to understand why Prime Minister Toshiki Kaifu's government was unable to play any military role in the Gulf War, and limited itself to a monetary contribution of $13 billion, which was expected to cover about 20 percent of the cost of the war. As noted, critics within and outside Japan have argued that Prime Minister Kaifu's weak position in the ruling Liberal Democratic Party, combined with his unassertive personality, prevented him from using the Gulf War as an opportunity to give Japan a more prominent, clearly defined foreign policy. I believe that it was most unlikely that any of the prime ministerial candidates would have made a significantly different policy. Moreover, among foreign policy officials and within the foreign policy community, views were sharply divided and ambivalent. Writers such as Seizaburo Sato spoke out strongly for Japan to be more supportive of the United States in the Gulf, and for Japan to play some kind of a military role within the framework of the United Nations. Soichiro Tahara argued that President George Bush had decided upon a war in the Gulf without first consulting Japan, and that Japan's national interests in the flow of oil and political stability in the Middle East would have been better served by a policy of containing Saddam Hussein. Many Japanese officials publicly took a position close to Professor Sato's, while privately they leaned toward Tahara's views. There was a feeling among officials that Washington's idea of the "new world order" was a system in which the United States makes the decisions and Japan pays the bills—and gets criticized for not doing more.

Before moving on to look at the possibility that changes in the international environment will compel Japan to change its foreign policy, it should be noted that within the government and among most foreign policy officials, there is even more caution and uncertainty about future foreign policy than among the writers and publicists. Officials are working to preserve the alliance with the United States, and while they are aware of the strains and cracks in the relationship, they believe that for them to plan or speculate about alternative future foreign policies would undermine their work. Moreover, they believe that at this juncture in history the future is so murky and uncertain that contingency planning makes little sense. They are basically intent on shaping the future along the lines of Takakazu Kuriyama's U.S.–E.C.–Japan concert system. They believe that while the end of the Cold War is not going to quickly and automatically solve all the world's problems, it is an opportunity for the United States to channel more of its attention and resources to economic revitalization, and for the advanced, industrialized nations to coordinate their efforts to patiently and persistently help the poorer nations, including perhaps the Soviet Union and former satellites, to build better lives for their people. As long as these goals seem attainable, they see no need to devise alternative policies.

Three Scenarios for the Future

The foreign policy debate in Japan indicates that there is a keen awareness of the factors that are threatening to make the Yoshida strategy inappropriate in the coming decade. There is a sense that Japanese foreign policy has to be more responsible and more active, but that responsibility and activity seem to be limited almost entirely to economics. Although the Japanese themselves do not appear to be planning and preparing to make a new security or defense policy, if during the next ten to twenty years the bipolar international security system continues to unravel, and if the global economic system breaks into regional blocs, Japan will have to adjust to the new environment. For purposes of discussion, let me suggest three global futures and the impact they are likely to have on Japanese foreign policy, especially on the security component of foreign policy, which has been most resistant to change.

Scenario A

The Soviet threat continues to decline, the United States substantially reduces its conventional naval and air presence in East Asia and the Western Pacific, and U.S.–Japan relations continue to be basically cooperative within the framework of the security alliance, despite the trade imbalance and economic frictions. The decline of the Soviet threat could take place in the context of economic development and peace in the republics and Eastern Europe, or it could occur in an economically distressed and violent regional environment. As long as the U.S.–Japan–NATO system holds and the world economy remains intact, with high levels of trade and investment flowing between the United States, Japan, the European Community, and the rest of the world, the global outlook will be relatively good. Either the West will be able to assist in economic development in the former Soviet empire, or it will be able to contain whatever threats might emanate from this region. This scenario assumes that the U.S. economy becomes sounder and more competitive, and that Japan and the European Community continue to move in the direction of open, freer trade, services, and investment.

In this case, Japan would probably have to assume responsibility for its own conventional defense, while the U.S. nuclear deterrent would continue to offer protection against Soviet or other nuclear threats. Assuming that the Soviet conventional threat in Asia will continue to diminish, Japan could assume responsibility for its conventional defense with gradual, moderate augmentations to its present force levels, especially its air, naval, and short-range missile forces, that would not be seen as threatening by its neighbors. This is basically a scenario for moderate, incremental change within a relatively stable, less threatening international environment.

Vice Minister Kuriyama's proposal for Japan–U.S.–European cooperation would fit easily into this world. However, while the triumvirate would preclude wars among the great powers, it could not always prevent wars among the lesser states. The Gulf crisis suggests that the effective control of local wars will be difficult and could disrupt the tripartite system unless it becomes a military-security as well as an economic partnership. Although the Europeans and Japanese went along with American policy in the Gulf, they have probably sent the message to the United States that they expect to be consulted in the next crisis, and not simply called upon for support after the key decisions have been taken in Washington.

Scenario B

The Soviet threat continues to decline as postulated in Scenario A, but economic quarrels, protectionism, techno-nationalism, and trade wars lead to an end of effective U.S.–Japan security cooperation as the United States withdraws from military positions in East Asia and the Western Pacific, including the Philippine bases. In this scenario it is likely that U.S. relations with the European

Community will also deteriorate and that NATO will come apart. This would lead to the reemergence of a traditional, multilateral international system, with the United States, the Soviet Union or Russia, Japan, the European Community, and/or a unified Germany and China each operating on its own, outside the relatively cohesive alliances we have had since World War II. As long as none of these powers is perceived as militarily aggressive or threatening by the other major powers, this scenario could also lead to a relatively peaceful international security environment, albeit at lower levels of economic activity than in Scenario A.

Japan would probably respond to this environment by (1) attempting first to continue in its present non-nuclear, lightly armed posture; and (2) then, if necessary, building some kind of minimal, perhaps non-nuclear deterrent and augmenting its conventional air and naval forces, stopping short of an arms build-up that would cause military tensions with China, Russia, or the United States. Considering how difficult it would be to accomplish this build-up without generating tensions and instability, I believe Scenario B to be possible but unstable and extremely difficult to maintain.

In order for this kind of international system to survive, and in order for Japan to pursue this kind of independent but nonthreatening security policy, the five powers would probably have to operate along the lines of the concert system that prevented major wars in Europe from 1815 to 1914. They would all have to eschew ambitious foreign policies and be willing to negotiate and compromise whenever potentially disruptive disputes arose among themselves, and at the same time be prepared to cooperate on an *ad hoc* basis to intervene to keep conflicts among the lesser powers from disrupting the system. Again, the Gulf crisis suggests how crucial and difficult this kind of cooperation would be.

It is important to understand that while the breakup of the global economy does not necessarily lead to political conflict and war, the economic and ecological costs of a system of uncoordinated, competing spheres of national influence or regional blocs will be very high, and the potential for conflict in Scenario B is much greater than in Scenario A. The European concert system in the nineteenth century coincided with the early development of national manufacturing economies, and was supported by the relatively free movement of international trade, investment, currency, and people. In the far more interdependent global economy of the 1990s, the breakup of the global trading and investment system would be likely to leave the Soviet Union, Eastern Europe, and the lesser developed economies of the world in desperate straits, which will tend to push all of us into Scenario C.

Scenario C

The U.S.–Japan alliance ends as a result of economic quarrels as postulated in Scenario B, but after several years of economic decline and political disintegration, there is a nationalistic, militaristic, authoritarian backlash in Russia. Russia has thousands of advanced nuclear weapons and is using its conventional forces to reconquer and impose its authority on the various national groups within the Soviet Union—rebuilding the Russian empire. It has no intention of reviving the Cold War with the United States, but it is determined to prevent encroachments on its empire by a unified Germany, China, or Japan. It pursues détente with the United States, but takes advantage of the end of the U.S.–NATO–Japan coalition to assume a tough, truculent posture toward Japan, China, and/or Germany (perhaps allying with one of these against the others). In this anarchic, violent world, in which the global trading and financial systems have collapsed or badly deteriorated, it is likely that Korea would again find itself the cockpit for rivalry between Russia, China, and Japan.

In this kind of environment, Japan would probably see no alternative to protecting itself by becoming a major military power, both nuclear and conventional. This would be a dangerous, unstable world, and Japanese rearmament would aggravate the danger and instability.

Implications for the United States

It is difficult to conceive of a future international environment in which the United States would gain any substantial, lasting benefits by endings its alliance with Japan. If the Soviet threat does continue to diminish and we enter a relatively stable, less dangerous post-Cold War world, then the continuation of an effective U.S.–Japan alliance enhances that stability and promotes higher levels of economic activity and cooperation. This is the most beneficial scenario for the United States as well as for Japan.

Scenario B suggests that minimal American security interests could be met in a relatively peaceful post-Cold War world without an alliance or close cooperation with Japan, but the world of Scenario B is less stable than in A, less prosperous, and less likely to deal effectively with international economic-ecological and political issues. If Scenario B deteriorates into some variant of Scenario C, and I think it will be prone to do so, then we will have exchanged the nasty old days of the Cold War for a nasty, new world that will be at least as dangerous.

Notes

1. Masamichi Inoki and Shin'ichi Kitaoka, "Rekishiteki sokyo toshite no senso (The Gulf War and Pacifist Japan)", *Chuo Koron*, April 1991, p. 103.
2. *Nihon Keizai Shinbun*, March 2, 1991, p. 2.
3. *Nihon Keizai Shinbun*, January 27, 1991, p. 12.
4. "Beino fuman yawaraguka," *Yomiuri Shinbun*, April 25, 1991, p. 2.
5. *Asahi Shinbun*, March 15, 1991, p. 2.
6. *Asahi Shinbun*, November 6, 1990, p. 3.
7. *Asahi Shinbun*, February 5, 1991, p. 3.
8. *Mainichi Shinbun*, June 23, 1991, p. 6.
9. *Asahi Shinbun*, June 19, 1991, p. 15.
10. *Asahi Shinbun*, May 9, 1991, p. 2.
11. Seizaburo Sato, "Jidaino henka ga yori kyokona domeio motomeru (Changes in the Times Call for Still Stronger Alliance)," *Chuo Koron*, March 1990.
12. Ibid., p. 134.
13. Hisahiko Okazaki, "Oranda ni 'nihon' ga mieru (The Holland that Can Be Seen in Japan)", *Bungei Shunju,* January 1990.
14. Ibid., p. 305.
15. Shintaro Ishihara, *The Japan That Can Say No: Why Japan Will Be First among Equals* (New York: Simon and Schuster), 1991.
16. Soichiro Tahara, "Nichibeianpojoyaku wa ippotekini haki sareru (The US–Japan Security Treaty will be Abrogated Unilaterally)," *Ushio*, January 1990.
17. Ibid., pp. 67–68.
18. Koji Taira, "Japan, an Imminent Hegemon?" *The Annals of the*

American Academy of Political and Social Sciences, Vol. 513, January 1991.

19. Takakazu Kuriyama, "Gekidono 90 nendai to nihongaiko no shintenkai (The Great Upheaval of the Nineties and the Evolution of Japan's New Diplomacy)," *Gaiko Forum*, May 1990.

20. *Ibid.*, pp. 15–17.

Naval Power in the Pacific in the Post-Cold War Era

Robert S. Wood[1]

Naval power in the Pacific in the decade of the nineties and into the next century is being shaped by the dynamics associated with the end of the Cold War. Although the naval force postures of the former Cold War adversaries have not technically changed and regional naval powers are developing along established lines, these force postures may acquire different meanings or be seen from quite different perspectives from what they were at the height of the Cold War struggle.

Nothing in Asia and the Pacific has been quite as dramatic as the changes associated with the events in Europe in 1989. Recalibrations of powers are taking place, but the sharp breaks with the past are less evident in Asia than in Europe. The attempt to sort out the continuities from the discontinuities is therefore more challenging. As in Europe, however, one must begin with general perspective, determine what has in fact changed in the post-World War II order, and analyze how these systemic alterations affect the direction and meaning of seapower in Asia.

The New World Order and the U.S. National Security Strategy

Three forces have largely defined the turbulent and violent character of the twentieth century: *nationalist aspirations, totalitarian forms of political organization,* and *technology.* The attempt to unify national groups across state boundaries and to suppress the aspirations of other groups in deference to some conception of the nation held within it the seeds of hegemony and empire. The further attempt to organize the state along lines of state socialism or Marxist-Leninism removed many internal limitations on state power, and potentially state objectives, while destroying or eroding the connecting links of peoples across state boundaries. Technologies of communication, transportation, and combat both expanded the theater of competition to global dimensions and provided to ambition fearful instruments of power and conquest. The two world wars and the struggle of the Cold War were the natural consequences of these compulsions.

All three forces undermined the structural foundations of classical international law: state sovereignty, territorial integrity, domestic jurisdiction, and general international norms of peaceful and belligerent state intercourse. Without some sense of political understanding that both limits the range of power of rulers vis-à-vis their own citizens and encourages cooperative endeavors among states and peoples, it is difficult to escape the rule of brute force or to maintain the delimitations and moderation required for any system of law. The United States, along with a number of other states, has recognized the dangers of uninhibited political power within and between states and has, since the latter half of the nineteenth century, sought forms of state intercourse that would forestall these dangers.

The negotiation and codification of international norms before World War I gave way to the urgent search for forms of collective security after the devastations of World Wars I and II. Traditional U.S. policies of nonalignment and the contradictory interests of states, however, circumscribed these attempts. Perhaps more importantly, the great movements associated with the totalitarian revolutions of this century, the decay of traditional empires, the revival of ancient nationalities and the emergence of new ones, and the process of decolonization that jeopardized not only traditional imperial rule but territorial boundaries—all these constrained any scheme to establish universal norms and institutions. After World Wars I and II, however, there was hope that more adequate forms of international law and organization could be devised. The events of the late 1980s and early 1990s have again stimulated the search for policies and international understandings more sensitive to the challenges and the opportunities of a global society.

After a year-long examination of the changes taking place in the world and of the possible American response, President George Bush delivered on August 2, 1990 in Aspen, Colorado, what was intended to be a major policy statement on the *"new world order."* This was subsequently followed by a series of speeches by Secretary of Defense Richard Cheney, Chairman of the Joint Chiefs of Staff Colin Powell, Undersecretary of Defense Paul Wolfowitz, and other officials defining the political and military implications of the new order.[1] Most Americans failed to hear or respond to these elocutions, largely because their attention was riveted to the series of events that began to unfold in the Persian Gulf region on the same day as the Bush address. Many of those who heard the echoes of the "new world order" theme thought it was a new U.S. doctrine for the Middle East. But, in fact, the assumptions and policies of this concept preceded the Persian Gulf conflict and continue to transcend circumstances in that region. It is true that events in the Middle East and the Persian Gulf bear upon the new world order, but the issues of that region do not delimit the nature or the policy implications of that order.

The new world order can be seen both from a *descriptive* and a *prescriptive* perspective. Descriptively, it refers to the fundamental, sometimes dramatic, changes that we are observing in the patterns of global power and the understandings among heads of state and peoples about the appropriate ends and means of public policy. Prescriptively, it refers to interpretations being made of the national situation and recommendations proffered for national priorities, policy objectives, and strategic courses of action. Even if U.S. national interests and objectives remain relatively constant, the policies, instruments, strategies, and alignments associated with those interests and objectives may require rethinking and modification.

We may identify at least eight salient features of the current international landscape. Together they describe the patterns of power and the issue areas of the new world order:

1. The collapse of the Soviet East European empire and the social, economic, and political transformations and disruptions that are sweeping the former Soviet Union.
2. The political rise of Europe and Japan, no longer simply stages or stakes in a bipolar struggle but independent centers of global power.
3. The virtual completion of the process of decolonization.
4. The reunion of the states divided by World War II, save Korea.
5. The emergence of a truly planetary milieu: an international society defined and linked together by economic ties, demographic movements, communications, transportation, the physical environment, and the potential of being implicated in a common, planetary disaster.
6. The thorough, and, for many Americans, unrecognized, inclusion of the United States in a web of international and transnational interdependence.
7. The continuing and growing challenge of regional and intranational quarrels, ambitions, and competing principles of political organization, unconstrained by the post-World War II bipolar framework and subject to the manipulation of would-be regional hegemons.
8. The search for forms of political integration within states where communism or state socialism has been discredited but the conditions for the establishment of liberal democratic norms may still be unfavorable or not understood. The temptation in such situations to yield to racism, ethnicity, and religious exclusiveness is apparent, as are the dangers of such "tribalism" in an interdependent world.

Prescriptively, then, what should be the central tenets of policy? What would their implications be for the establishment of an international regime of security, economic growth, and peaceful change?[2] The objects of U.S. policy have been fairly constant throughout this century. It may be argued that changes in the current international environment provide a more favorable prospect for realizing those objectives on a universal scale than heretofore and at the same time pose challenges qualitatively different from those confronted at the height of the Cold War. The issue is thus less one of redefining fundamental interests and objectives than of designing policies and strategies appropriate to the contemporary international landscape that has emerged from the cumulative and revolutionary changes that have transpired since the development of earlier policies and strategies of containment.

The United States since World War II has sought a Eurasian political-military equilibrium; political and territorial integrity among states and peaceful change; restraints on the nature, size, and spread of weapons; economic growth; and a progressively universal framework of open societies and free markets. We have pursued these objectives through policies of containment, arms control, peacekeeping, trade liberalization, and human rights. Our instruments have been multiple: for example, the U.N., The Marshall Plan, economic development funds, The General Agreement on Tariffs and Trade (GATT), the Organization of Economic Cooperation and Development (OECD), the North Atlantic Treaty Organization (NATO), the Organization of American States (OAS), and a series of bilateral understandings. Our military strategies have been grounded in concepts of deterrence, forward presence, and power projection. But if the patterns of power and the issues have altered, what changes might be forthcoming in the balance of priorities among our chosen means?

In the first instance, the dissolution of the Warsaw Pact, the ongoing withdrawal of forces of the former Soviet Union from eastern and central Europe, the recent agreements on nuclear and conventional arms and the fitful process of perestroika and glasnost within the former USSR—all suggest the prospect of fundamental changes in U.S. relations with the successor states of the USSR and thus raise the possibility for the first time since the end of World War II of a true collective security system.

Technically, collective security is founded on an agreement to join together to establish or reinforce certain security conditions abstractly stated. It is not aimed at any state but rather is designed to favor a universally accepted and enforced international order. Hence, such an arrangement implies mutual obligations to respect common norms and to enforce, if necessary, such norms vis-à-vis any recalcitrant member of the collective security organization. Ultimately, a collective security system requires the assent and commitments of the "great powers," those who more than any other states can paralyze the enterprise. In the best of worlds, such a stance is difficult to maintain. In the bipolarization of the Cold War, it was virtually impossible to maintain and thus the basic aim of the United Nations was unmet. For all intents and purposes, the United States relied not on collective security but on collective defense for its security, a series of multilateral and bilateral alliances clearly aimed at a specific threat or threats.

Recent events suggest the possibility of transcending to some degree this pattern of relations. The cooperation in the recent Persian Gulf conflict of the permanent five members of the U.N. Security Council, especially the United States and Russia, signaled for many the prospect of a genuine collective security center in the United Nations.

Beyond the universal framework of the United Nations, there is as well the ongoing development of the political-economic transnational and interstate arrangements in Western Europe and of the pan-European structures of the Conference on Security and Cooperation in Europe (CSCE). The West European developments hold the prospect of genuinely independent postures and actions by the Europeans both throughout Europe and on the global stage. And the pan-European structures point to, if not a collective security organization for Europe and the North Atlantic, at least a political forum for the resolution of difficulties and for the development of cooperative measures. These and other institutions both in Europe and elsewhere indicate political, military, and diplomatic patterns different in their meaning and operations from those associated with the bipolar Cold War.

At the same time, the uncertainty of the evolution of the former Soviet states and Eastern Europe, as well as the fragility of cooperation in the U.N. and ambiguity about the range and character of the European institutions, point to the continuing relevance of such understandings as NATO and the U.S.–Japanese bilateral defense agreement. Moreover, regional problems provide no predetermined galvanizing threat and hence permanent defense arrangements are not in place. This means that many issues in the future may elicit *ad hoc* arrangements to meet emergent difficulties. In effect, policy must be based both on the possibilities of a permanent universal collective security framework and the prospect of more localized, *ad hoc,* and shifting arrangements. Neither the failure of the U.N. security system after World War II nor the certitude of bipolar conflict can any longer structure our policy.

In addition to the problem of reconciling the establishment or reinforcement of universal norms and institutional arrangements with regional and episodic security ventures, the United States confronts the comparable problem of relating international norms favoring free markets and open societies with the different levels of economic and political development and market competitiveness among states. This latter issue translates into policies that seek to gain the advantages of regional free trade areas or common markets, such as the North American Free Trade Area, while extending such arrangements to adjacent areas and at the same time upholding the more global trade liberalization orientation of the GATT. Moreover, there is the additional demand to extend the GATT order into Eastern Europe and into Third World areas earlier frozen by their statist and mercantilist systems.

Finally, there is a whole set of issues directly related to the interdependent, planetary milieu that has willy-nilly linked together the fates of disparate peoples: demographic movements, commerce in weapons and illicit drugs, energy markets, environmental impacts, financial flows, and technology spread. In a fundamental sense, none of these issues can be addressed or resolved within a purely national or unilateral frame of reference. Furthermore, the inability to successfully address these issues may inhibit economic growth, exacerbate international inequalities, and further stimulate arms competitions and military conflict.

In terms of international public order, U.S. policy in the new world order seeks to articulate universal norms of collective security and strengthen institutional mechanisms by which such norms might be enforced. At the same time, the United States is committed to the maintenance and development of forums within which rules of market liberalization, functional cooperation, and fundamental human rights might be favored. All of this is in keeping with aims adopted during the concluding days of World War II. Changes in the former Soviet Union may finally improve the prospects for realizing such aims, and heightened interdependence compels greater efforts toward their achievement.

The Bush administration believes, however, that it is also important to maintain intact the achievements successfully concluded among the advanced industrial states during the Cold War—that is, the political, cultural, economic, and security interlinkages among the states of North America, Western Europe, and Japan—as well as a multitude of other connections with Latin

America, Asia and the Pacific, the Middle East, and elsewhere. It was in fact to some degree the flourishing of these arrangements, as well as the purely defensive aspects of containment, that accounted for the end of the Cold War and the desire of other states to associate themselves with this liberal international order. The United States was a driving force behind this association of states and the free market and liberal democratic ethos that animated it. The maintenance of this order in the face of the diminishing, immediate threat of the former USSR and of protectionist temptations, will, in the view of the president, continue to depend on the policies and energies of the United States. The extension of this order to global dimensions of necessity will equally depend on the skills of the United States in articulating international norms and in organizing general and particular coalitions.

The defense posture being developed by the Bush administration seems in general terms to be well suited to this world order and this policy perspective.[3] The general peace requires the maintenance of a secure nuclear deterrent and the ability to reconstitute major forces in the event of a major deterioration in Eurasian stability and the rise of imperial ambitions. At the same time, the possibility of any collective security mechanism and of stability within different regions demands that the United States maintain forward presence and the ability to respond to a crisis with a smaller, restructured force. Such forward presence and crisis response compel a global legitimizing framework for the exercise of such force, international alignments and coalition understandings, arms regimes within regions, and rules by which military forces will deploy and employ.

President Bush has endorsed the concept developed by the chairman of the Joint Chiefs of Staff of a *"base force"* which could be augmented by reserves in the event of a major crisis. These forces would be further expanded through the "reconstitution" of general war capabilities should the general Eurasian balance of power be once again put in jeopardy. It is assumed that with the end of the Warsaw Pact, the withdrawal of forces of the former Soviet Union from eastern and central Europe, and the establishment of the Conventional Forces in Europe agreement (CFE), as well as the transformations taking place in the former USSR, that the United States would have at least two years' warning of a general military threat to the Eurasian balance of power.

94

As originally proposed, the base force was to consist of four types of capabilities: Strategic, Atlantic, Pacific, and Contingency. As explained by Pentagon spokespeople, the *Atlantic Force,* to include NATO Europe, would consist of approximately six carriers with one on the Mediterranean; major active/reserve army and air force units (with approximately 100,000 to 150,000 military personnel on the European continent); and two active and one reserve Marine Corps Expeditionary Brigades (MEBs). The *Pacific Force* would have a primarily maritime emphasis and would include six carriers with one based in Japan; smaller active and reserve Army and Air Force units; and four active and reserve MEBs. The *Strategic Force* would be in line with the Strategic Arms Reduction Treaty of 1991 (START) and would consist approximately of eighteen Trident ballistic missile submarines (SSBNs); a mix of B-1 and B-2 bombers; an MX/Mobile ICBM "hedge"; and some form of strategic defense. The *Contingency Response Force* would be primarily stationed in the continental United States and would consist of Army light and airborne divisions, MEBs, Special Operations Forces (SOFs), and selected units of the Air Force. These would be buttressed by carrier and amphibious forces.

As reported in the *New York Times* on August 2, 1990, the service force levels of the base force was to approximate the following:

- *Army*: twelve active, two reconstitutable reserve, six other reserve divisions (currently eighteen active and ten reserve).
- *Air Force*: twenty-five active and reserve tactical air wings (currently thirty-six).
- *Navy*: eleven to twelve aircraft carriers (currently fourteen).
- *Marine Corps*: 150,000 personnel (currently 196,000).

The collapse of the August 1991 coup in the former Soviet Union and the disarray in the military forces of the now defunct Union, as well as budgetary pressures in the United States, are likely to reduce the base force even further. For instance, there is now discussion of a carrier battleforce of 8 to 10 rather than 11 to 12.

Although these forces will be deployed and employed in combined and joint patterns, the mobility and flexibility of naval power may be the enabling factor in many enterprises and will be at the heart of the U.S. position in the Pacific. The criticality of naval power in the Pacific, the interdependent character of global politics, and the desire to identify U.S. interests with universal norms—all are stimulating in the United States renewed attention to international norms and institutions as well as the development of an oceans policy consistent with the U.S. interest in a stable, just, and peaceful global regime.

Naval Forces and Political Aspirations in the Pacific

Many of the principal states in the Pacific area have been engaged in naval construction and modernization throughout the eighties. There appears to be little or no slack in this development into the nineties. On the one hand, the Pacific naval balance can be seen as the result of broad systemic forces, i.e., the bipolar struggle between the United States and the Soviet Union or, alternatively, the emergence of multipolarity as the tensions between the United States and the former USSR abate. On the other hand, the naval policies of the regional powers may be viewed as responses to more regional external and internal demands, quite apart from the configuration of power and influence associated with bipolarity or multipolarity.

The proper assessment probably includes elements of both interpretations. Regional naval policies do seem most responsive to particular considerations. As long as the Untied States held maritime superiority and forward presence in the Pacific as essential conditions of its containment policy vis-à-vis the Soviet Union, however, the fears and aspirations of the regional states were to some degree bounded, as were their concerns about the naval developments of their neighbors. As the relative naval power and forward commitment of the United States lessens, then barely repressed anxieties and new or renewed hopes may become more salient. Regional military changes in general and naval developments in particular may take on a wholly different coloration.

If the Pacific naval balance in recent years has been largely defined by the relationship between the United States and the Soviet Union, the future evolution of regional navies and the external policies of their governments may generate forms of conflict and cooperation qualitatively different from the post-World War II order. Three states will probably be central to this evolution: China, India, and Japan. Lesser or more distant naval powers may also be more visible, i.e., Vietnam, the two Koreas, and Australia. Indeed, one of the crucial issues facing the United States is the impact of a significant reduction in U.S. naval forces and their presence on the calculations of the various regional powers. Hence, the first order of business in any analysis of naval power in the Pacific is a consideration of trends in the U.S.–Russian military balance in Asia and the Pacific.[4] As Russia is in many respects the successor state to the USSR and the exclusive heir to the Soviet Pacific Ocean Fleet, it is important to assess the character of U.S.–Russian military relations and the continuities and discontinuities in the Pacific naval balance.

Soviet and U.S. Naval Operations in the Pacific

The Russian Pacific Ocean Fleet, with headquarters at Vladivostok, is one of four Soviet fleets, the others being the Northern Fleet, the Baltic Fleet, and the Black Sea Fleet.[5] (Given the dispute between the Ukraine and Russia, the disposition of the Russian fleet is most problematic.) It is the largest and some even estimate it to be the strongest of the fleets. In any case, it underwent significant increases throughout the 1970s and early 1980s. At present the Russians have over six hundred major ships and submarines in the Pacific Fleet, including two aircraft carriers, about 160 large principal surface combatants, over one hundred principal general purpose submarines, and an estimated thirty ballistic missile submarines. From the mid-1980s onward, there has been some reduction in forces. Fleet Admiral V. N. Chernavin, named in November 1985 by Gorbachev to be commander-in-chief of the Soviet Navy, and now commander of the Russian navy and the combined fleets of the Commonwealth of Independent States (CIS), has asserted that the Pacific Fleet has been reduced by over fifty ships since 1984. All of these ships were old or obsolete vessels, and during the same period Kiev aircraft carriers, Akula nuclear-powered attack submarines (SSNs), Sovremennyy and Udaloy destroyers (DDGs), and Ivan Rogov amphibious landing ships (LPDs) were added. On balance, however, it appears that the Russian fleet of the nineties will have somewhat fewer submarines and principal combatants. Although qualitative improvements in Russian naval capabilities continue, fiscal constraints and the ongoing political turmoil in the former Soviet states have slowed such advances and reduced fleet operations.

Admiral Chernavin has implemented reforms that aim at greater combat potential through enhanced technological sophistication. Improvements in weapons systems, sensors, and command, control, and communications (C3) and the scrapping by 1996 throughout the fleets of around 450 pre-1970s combat ships, including forty-five general purpose submarines, may indeed yield a smaller but far more capable naval force. At the same time, there is a planned reduction of nearly 80,000 naval personnel afloat and ashore, a reduced overseas presence, and fewer deployments. Concentration on technological improvements coupled with reduction in forces and their deployment will, it is hoped, yield significant economic gains both in terms of immediate efficiencies and of longer-term structural changes.

The Russians have emphasized that future operations will support their declared "defensive doctrine." In practice, this may not represent a radical break with past naval missions. Both the Northern and the Pacific Ocean Fleets, including associated land-based air power, have been designed to protect those fleets' nuclear ballistic missile submarine (SSBN) forces. At the same time, the fleets have had the additional mission of protecting the seaward approaches of the former Soviet Union from sea, air, or amphibious attack and of securing the maritime flanks of the ground forces. These missions thus required maritime forces to hold at a distance or destroy dual-capable (i.e., nuclear and conventional weapons-carrying) vessels such as aircraft carriers, SSNs, and air- and sea-launched cruise missile platforms. At the same time, maritime forces would provide naval fire and logistical assistance, conduct amphibious assaults, and disrupt enemy sea lines of communications (SLOCs) in support of ground forces. Historically, these missions led the Soviet Navy to concentrate its SSBNs and most of its general purpose forces on so-called defensive barriers, waters adjacent to Soviet territory, and to employ a vast array of nuclear- and diesel-powered attack submarines, naval aircraft, and surface combatants to protect these barriers in layered defensive zones reaching thousands of miles outward. If anything, the doctrine of "defensive defense" reinforces this orientation and appears to be continuing under the policies of the Russian Federation.

It should be pointed out, however, that as the Russians improve the capabilities of their submarines in "quieting" (reducing the ability of the submarine to be detected by radar, acoustical devices, heat or motion sensors, etc.), endurance, and speed, it would be possible to "untie" their SSBNs from their general purpose forces and unleash a greater proportion of these latter forces to menace enemy sea lines of communication and hold distant targets at risk. Hence, whatever the current doctrinal orientation of Russia may be, their commitment to modernization may yield a force with far greater offensive capabilities than during the height of the Cold War. At the same time, however, the outcome of the current political and economic turmoil in Russia will probably be decisive in determining the solidity of these developments.

Asia and the Pacific reflect these general developments. Taking the Russian Far Eastern Theater of Operations (FETVD) as a whole, there has been a general reduction in air and ground forces in Mongolia and along the Soviet border with China. It is anticipated that by 1996 Russian ground forces in the FETVD will be reduced from the current forty-five divisions to thirty-eight and tactical air combat regiments will be drawn down from twenty-seven to sixteen. Bomber and strategic air interceptors will remain much the same and retain the capability of attacking targets in China, Japan, the continental United States, and throughout the Pacific.

As with sea power, the Russians hope that modernization and force restructuring, coupled with force reductions, will in fact yield a more capable military power. For example, an estimated 30 percent reduction in tanks has been accompanied by the introduction of modern T-80 and improved T-72 tanks; and the addition of advanced aircraft such as the modern Su-24 Fencer E., the MiG-29 Fulcrum, and the Su-27 Flanker has gone on apace with the elimination of older aircraft. At the same time, the Russians have substantially increased their air defense capabilities by 25 percent, with most of the augmentation in SA-10 Grumble surface-to-air missile battalions.

By the middle of the decade, the scrapping of obsolescent naval platforms should be completed and the size of the Russian

Pacific Fleet stabilized. However, the U.S. Department of Defense estimated in 1991 that current trends indicate an increase of 100 percent of surface-to-surface missile capacity, of 50 percent in surface-to-air missiles on surface platforms, and of 40 percent in the number of ships with long range antisubmarine weapons (ASW). Although attack submarines should decline in numbers from about seventy to sixty or sixty-five, their general performance and missile capabilities will substantially increase. All of these projections are likely to be significantly affected by the continuing economic crisis. Interestingly, given the defensive orientation of present Russian doctrine, it is anticipated that improvements in naval amphibious lift will by the end of the decade allow the fleet to move 80 percent of its tactical assault forces versus the current level of 50 percent.

The one area in Asia where there has been no appreciable reduction in Russian air and ground forces is in the military district opposite Japan. The four ground divisions in the Kuriles, on Sakhalin Island, and on the Kamchatka Peninsula have been largely unaffected even by the numerical cuts.[6] The visit to Japan by President Gorbachev in April 1991 resulted in fifteen agreements covering a range of economic and cultural issues, but accord over the disposition of the Kurile territories seized from Japan by the Soviets in the concluding days of World War II remained elusive. President Yeltsin, despite certain inconsistencies in his position, seems to be as intransigent over the Kuriles as his predecessors. In a real sense, stalemate over the Kuriles perpetuates a "cold war," however attenuated, in Japanese–Russian relations and hence may limit any fundamental alteration in the U.S.–Japanese security link. A fundamental shift in the Russian position could thus significantly unhinge this link, particularly given the growing tension in U.S.–Japanese economic relations.

Postwar Japan considered the entire thirty-two island chain composing the Kuriles, as well as South Sakhalin, as part of its Northern territories. However, since the sixties, the Japanese government has limited its definition of the Northern territories to only four areas: Kunashiri Island, Etorofu Island, Shikotan Island, and the Hobomai island group. Earlier it appeared that some compromise with the Soviets might be struck. In 1956 the Soviets offered to return Habomai and Shikotan, but this proposal was found unacceptable by the Japanese, constituting as it did of only

7 percent of the area in contention. As late as 1988, there was talk among Soviet spokespersons about the return of these two island areas upon the conclusion of a peace treaty with Japan. The disposition of the remaining two islands was to be postponed to a later generation. At best, what has been accomplished in recent years is the acknowledgment by the Russians that there is in fact a territorial dispute.

In many respects, it seems that in the new post-Cold War era, the Russians would have many compelling reasons to resolve this dispute in a manner calculated to induce Japanese gratitude. Given the Russian commitment to economic reform and their desperate need for capital and technical assistance, one might think that the good will of the Japanese might be worth the price of a territorial settlement. In fact, the most that Gorbachev offered in a joint declaration during the April 1991 talks was a "partial" reduction of the Soviet military presence on the four islands. In the subsequent meeting of the Western industrial powers, the Group of Seven, in July 1991, the Japanese were less than enthusiastic about offers of economic assistance to Gorbachev and to the former Soviet Union. In early 1992, there were greater formal commitments by the Japanese to assist the Russians, but these commitments still seemed tentative and restrained.

Beyond the improvement in political relations with Japan, with its promise of greater economic support, there would be, as mentioned earlier, the additional geostrategic benefit of removing one of the political reasons for the U.S.–Japanese security relation. There is already concern in Japan over the military budget and growing ill will between these erstwhile allies arising from the asymmetries in their economic relations. Should relations with Russia substantially improve, there could develop in Japan considerable pressure to reduce or remove the U.S. military presence. Even though the Russians might welcome some U.S. presence in the Pacific in order to "contain" Japanese revanchism (much as some have portrayed NATO and E.C. as "containment" of Germany in Europe), the consistent Russian desire to reduce the forward presence of the United States worldwide is probably more salient.

And yet, despite these various reasons, the Russians have not yet struck the grand deal such as they did with Germany. One might argue that growing hard-line discontent in the former

Soviet Union over these earlier moves in Europe preclude any major concession to Japan. As noted earlier, even reformers such as Boris Yeltsin, however, appear to oppose any major concession. It may still be, therefore, that the Russians continue to consider control of the Kuriles as vital to their conception of security.

The Kuriles have often been described as a gate, but a gate that can open in two directions. On the one hand, the Russians see the Kuriles, if under their control, as a defensive barrier for their Delta and Typhoon SSBNs in the Sea of Okhotsk. If the Kuriles remain under Russian control and the Sea of Okhotsk is maintained as a sanctuary, Russian submarines can deploy within this area from Petropavlovsk, and the passage to the fleet headquarters at Vladivostok is more easily secured as well. At the same time, control of the Kuriles provides a key element in the extension of the Russian defensive zone into the Pacific Ocean as well as a pivot on which to envelop Japan and disrupt that island state's sea lines of communication. The projected growth in naval amphibious lift also increases the potential for an assault on Hokkaido, which is already within range of Russian artillery. Under these circumstances, it is easy to understand why Japan maintains four of its thirteen divisions in Hokkaido and centers much of its military planning on this area.

On the other had, the Kurile gate can also be closed by the United States and the Japanese Self Defense Forces (SDF). If major elements of the Russian fleet can be confined to the Sea of Japan and the Sea of Okhotsk, they could then come under assault by U.S. and Japanese forces, removing pressure from the latter's sea lines of communication and threatening the Russian strategic missile force. If the "central front" has disappeared in Europe, there is still a lesser Asian equivalent.

On balance, therefore, there will probably continue to be in the Russian Far Eastern Theater of Operations a numerical reduction in air, land, and sea forces but an increase in technological sophistication, which will be most pronounced in maritime forces. In the areas adjacent to Japan, however, there is still no major decrease in numbers while force modernization goes on. Whatever the eventual character of the military balance in the military district opposite Japan, however, the inability to resolve the issue of the Northern territories will inhibit reduction in tensions and reinforce the defensive link between the United States and Japan.

What of the U.S. Pacific forces? As noted earlier, the region is largely defined as a maritime theater. U.S. forces have been centered in Japan, Korea, and the Philippines as well as on U.S. territories and operate within the terms of a number of bilateral and multilateral security arrangements. There are about 135,000 troops in the entire area. These forces are under the authority of the commander-in-chief of the Pacific Command and are characterized by their strong air and naval components. Japan is the home of the Seventh Fleet and Air Force tactical fighter wings. The United States maintains an Army division and two Air Force tactical fighter wings in Korea. As a result of the volcanic destruction in the Philippines, Clark Air Force Base will be permanently closed and its tactical fighter wing removed. With the failure of the Philippine Senate to accept the treaty for a new lease, U.S. naval forces will be effectively withdrawn from Subic by 1993 and facilities in Singapore, Japan, Guam, and Hawaii will become more central. There will be a major reduction of ground forces in Korea. U.S. Pacific forces in general face at least a 10 to 12 percent cut by the middle of the decade.

As with Russian forces, the United States is committed to fewer but more modern forces. This largely translates into stealth technology as applied to all military platforms; enhanced sensor and target acquisition capabilities; command, control, and communications advances; long-range precision-guided stealth missiles; and air defense systems. In a recent statement to the Senate Armed Services Committee, Admiral Charles Larson, commander-in-chief of the United States Pacific Command, spoke of the need "to project military power rapidly with ready and sustainable forces" and "to maintain maritime superiority and establish sea control during conflicts."[7] These requirements point to an emphasis on improvements in all-weather medium attack aircraft, modern smart weapons, anti-air and antisubmarine warfare capabilities, anti-mining forces, and strategic lift and amphibious ship assets, as well as a rather complex and robust logistical support system. Difficulties associated with the cost and complexity of a new naval advanced tactical aircraft and of a new attack submarine class are likely to stretch out the modernization process.

The sheer size of the Pacific basin will stretch U.S. forces. In no other area are U.S. forward operating bases so widely separated and putative areas of conflict so distant from the continental United States. Moreover, unlike Europe, there is no cohesive, multilateral security system. The political glue of the Pacific is in fact largely the bilateral arrangements into which the United States has entered, and the military glue is the U.S. Pacific Fleet, whose presence constitutes not only deterrence of potential adversaries but also reassurance of mutually-distrustful allies and nonaligned states.

Three factors will largely define the U.S. Pacific role in the next decade. First, reduction in U.S. forces, the continuing fiscally constrained modernization of Russian forces, and the emergence of regional military powers will erode, but not nullify, the predominance of the U.S. military position in the Pacific. Second, the commitment of the United States to maintain a forward presence in the Indian Ocean as a result of threats to U.S. interests in the Persian Gulf region will further stretch American forces. This will undoubtedly require even more flexible operations not only of the Pacific Fleet but of U.S. forces operating in the Mediterranean. For example, carrier battle forces will be less tied to particular deployment patterns. Third, heightened aspirations and increased military capabilities of a number of regional powers, and hence anxieties among their neighbors, may serve to reinforce the desire of the states in the region for a continuing, visible American presence as an element of stability and reassurance.

Force Expansion and Naval Policy of the Regional Powers

In a recent *Foreign Affairs* article, Admiral William J. Crowe, Jr., U.S. Navy (Ret.), a former commander-in-chief of the Pacific and chairman of the Joint Chiefs of Staff, and Alan D. Romberg noted the relatively small number of U.S. forces dedicated to the Pacific and cautioned against cutting those forces in the same proportion as elsewhere. The primary reason for their caution was the growth in military power of the regional states. As they argued,

> Only 6 percent of U.S. forces are forward deployed in the Asian–Pacific theater, and only 16 percent are "dedicated"

to the region. Given the space they are responsible for, they should not be proportionately reduced along with other cuts around the world. Indeed, with the political evolution in Europe, there is no need for such proportionality.

It is essential to retain enough of a presence in the region to assure mutually suspicious nations there that the United States is not withdrawing or contributing to the creation of a security vacuum. The concern is likely to grow as the military power of regional players grows, including their capacity to develop nuclear and other advanced weapons technologies. The sense of security that Asian nations have felt and the contribution this has made to their political, economic and social development has been of enormous benefit to American national interests. It is worth a great deal to the United States to preserve that sense of security and the development it fosters, including by maintaining both a force presence and a nuclear umbrella over those who feel the need to be protected by it. It is also important that regional nations bear their fair share of the burden.[8]

To understand the full dimensions of naval power in the Pacific in the years ahead, therefore, it is necessary to survey and assess the military build-up that is taking place among the regional states. In 1990 military expenditures in the region were over $86 billion, exceeded only in the NATO area. The most dramatic growth was in Korea, Taiwan, and the southeast Asian states of Brunei, Malaysia, the Philippines, and Thailand. Perhaps more important is the steady increase and modernization of forces in China, India, Japan, and Indonesia. Taking the Pacific as a whole, to include the Indian Ocean, both Australia and South Africa operate important, capable, and balanced navies.

The "Big Three": Japan, China, and India

Japan, one of the world's economic superpowers, has also developed an impressive military capability by devoting consistently over time approximately 1 percent of its GNP to defense.[9] In recent times, the rate of growth in the defense budget has been almost 6 percent, although it is likely to drop to 3 or 4 percent in the years ahead. It now contributes nearly $2 billion to offset the direct cost of U.S. forces in Japan and is scheduled to meet nearly 50 percent of those costs in the near future. It has more tactical aircraft than all U.S. forces in Asia and nearly twice as many destroyers as the Seventh Fleet. Although Japan has neither major offensive nor nuclear capabilities, it has developed an effective self-defense force. Depending on the geostrategic balance that emerges by the end of the decade, Japan may by the next century, however, develop a power projection capability.

More than 20 percent of the Japanese military budget is devoted to the navy, and it is currently replacing and modernizing many of its older vessels. Today the tonnage of the fleet exceeds 196,000 tons and the Japanese navy ranks as the fifth largest in the world. The primary missions of the Japanese navy are coastal defense and the protection of the sea lines of communications out to 1,000 miles. There is the continuing concern over the Soviet military posture in the Northern territories and hence special attention is paid to the protection of Hokkaido against any assault.

These missions translate into the acquisition of modern anti-aircraft destroyers equipped with Aegis air defense systems, attack submarines, anti-surface and antisubmarine warfare destroyers, and minehunters. Over all, the Japanese navy has twenty-nine modern and relatively new major ships with anti-surface or anti-submarine capabilities and sixteen highly capable attack submarines—a very credible if not overwhelming force. Among its three hundred aircraft, almost one hundred are high-performance maritime patrol aircraft, ranking it third after the United States and Russia in number of these planes. It has almost one hundred helicopters as well.

There are plans to include in future programs a 20,000 ton aircraft carrier capable of handling vertical short take off and landing system (V/STOL) fighter planes. Should the 1,000 miles patrol area dictated by internal politics and the external geostrategic balance be extended, it is likely that the navy will seek major construction of helicopter carriers or air support ships. To what degree these capabilities will be developed probably depends not only on the perception of any remaining threat from the successor states but also and more importantly on U.S.–Japanese relations and the extent to which the United States retains its military commitments in the area. Another factor will be the absence of competition with China—which again will be affected by the U.S.–Japanese link and the disposition of U.S. forces.

China

China's humiliating performance in the 1979 Sino–Vietnamese border conflict convinced the new leadership under Deng Xiaoping that the People's Liberation Army (PLA) stood in need of major restructuring and modernization. It was also clearly understood that such modernization depended very much on other modernizations in science and technology, industry, and agriculture. The relaxation of tensions and growing accord with Russia allowed the Chinese government to focus on internal modernization and reorient its defense posture toward issues along its southern and maritime frontiers. Since the early eighties, China has concentrated its military modernization on more mobile, quick-reaction ground, air, and naval forces with the ability to sustain limited operations across the national frontiers. Given this orientation, the highest budgetary priority has gone to the air force and the navy.[10]

China recently concluded an agreement with Russia to purchase, in part with barter, a regiment of twenty-four Su-27 combat aircraft, the largest arms purchase in its history. These craft could considerably erode Taiwan's air superiority and could provide air cover for the navy should Beijing undertake to assert its claim to the Spratly Islands in the South China Sea, an archipelago contested with Vietnam and, to a lesser degree, the Philippines and Malaysia. Moreover, the construction of an airbase in the Paracel Islands, six hundred kilometers from the Spratlys, and the purchase of air-refueling technology from Iran considerably enhance the projection power of its navy. The additional build-up of an air-transport fleet, an airborne early warning system, and improved missile technology should all give China much "longer legs" by the end of the decade.

Since the early eighties the Chinese leadership has diligently worked toward transforming its navy from a coastal defense to a blue water force with increasing power projection capabilities. In line with this, new or modernized destroyers and frigates are being introduced. It possesses about sixty destroyers and frigates and 350 to four hundred missile- or torpedo-firing patrol craft. It has developed a rather impressive amphibious capability, with 28,000 marines stationed with the South Seas Fleet. The cost and technological complexity of antiaircraft and antisubmarine systems still severely limit its surface force and make a robust blue water capability some years away. As to their submarine force, the nuclear submarine program has been virtually suspended, leaving them with only four operational but unreliable SSNs. They have resumed construction of conventional submarines and now possess an estimated 130 submarine force. As the Chinese are in the business of selling to Third World states sturdy and inexpensive ships and missiles, albeit outmoded by Western standards, they are beginning to acquire the financial and market base for a navy industry by the end of the decade.

Interestingly, despite a severe lacuna in capital and technological sophistication, the Chinese leadership is clearly looking toward the future development of an aircraft carrier. They are still unsure whether or not to develop a smaller helicopter carrier or a larger deck carrier to accommodate fixed wing aircraft. They also lack for any type carrier the requisite protection against submarines, surface ships, and missiles. Whichever direction they ultimately go, their aspirations are largely confined to research and training courses for carrier captains. Nonetheless, the Chinese leadership's decision to extend its strategic influence to the south and on its maritime frontiers seems to be confirmed by its attention to air and naval as contrasted with heavy land capabilities. Indeed, it is worth noting that the principal developments in land forces is in an army corps and helicopter regiment.

India

One perceptive commentator has recently argued that, whereas 1947 marked an ideological and administrative break between India and the United Kingdom, there has been a high degree of geostrategic continuity between the imperial British policy and the independent Indian policy.[11] In general terms, there were two tendencies in Britain's Indian policy: the first was to focus on external threats to India and hence concentrate on maintaining global naval supremacy and on constructing a ring of subordinate or neutralized states on the northwestern and northeastern frontiers; the second was to focus on internal threats to the integrity of India and hence concentrate on preventing the cultual heterogeneity of the subcontinent from fragmenting into separate political authorities. The Indian government has clearly been preoccupied with the second, internal issue, but it has also pursued with different emphases the first, external concern as well.

Since independence, the Indian government has been exquisitely obsessed with securing its internal integrity against what it perceives as external interference. This has led it in the direction of a policy of economic self-sufficiency and nonalignment. At the same time, although it sought to achieve accommodation with the USSR (rather than taking the United Kingdom view that Russia was the primary threat to its continental security) it was just as concerned about threats from the northwest and the northeast. In this case, however, these threats were seen as coming from China and Pakistan. In keeping with these concerns, India devoted its energies until the seventies to the achievement of political unity, autarky, and containment of its neighbors in the northwest and northeast. As a result, its primary military focus was on ground forces and it deemphasized naval modernization. This began to change by the mid-1970s, and in 1978 the Indian government announced a twenty-year development program, which is expected to yield by the year 2025 a balanced fleet of 250 to three hundred ships, including capital vessels and modern armaments.

The naval modernization program signaled the fact that India has now effectively adopted—and adapted—the naval component of British imperial policy. This naval program is linked to a reassessment of its geostrategic environment. The 1971 war with Pakistan and the deployment into the Indian Ocean of the U.S.S. *Enterprise* during that conflict was a turning point in Indian thinking. Subsequent events in the Persian Gulf and the growing links between Pakistan and the Arab states, as well as China, considerably added to Indian anxieties. The decision of the United States to expand the basing facility at Diego Garcia as well as to deploy a carrier in the Indian Ocean (perhaps now on an even more permanant basis because of the 1991 Persian Gulf War) raised Indian fears of encirclement and provided justification for naval modernization.

The Indian navy now possesses 165,000 tons of combat ships, making it the sixth largest in the world. It has acquired and modernized two ex-British aircraft carriers and has a contract with France to develop plans for a 30,000-ton aircraft carrier. Like China, although much further advanced, India is undecided as to whether to pursue the development of a conventional, large deck carrier or a V/STOL carrier. It appears in the short term to be oriented in the latter direction.[12]

The Indian navy currently has 150 vessels, including its two aircraft carriers, fifteen submarines (of which seven are of the Soviet Kilo class), five large missile-firing destroyers, twenty-eight frigates and corvettes, and assorted mine warfare, amphibious, and coastal forces. Its first-line aviation includes twenty-four Sea Harriers, three two-seaters, and over sixty helicopters. They have ordered eight Bear F maritime patrol planes from Russia and have received three thus far. They will in the future be able to conduct surveillance operations in the Indian Ocean. Although there are still problems in the endurance and sophistication of some of its systems, the Indian navy is the largest and most balanced fleet in the Indian Ocean and may by the end of the decade far outstrip in numbers and quality the Australian and South African navies.

In one way or another, both fears and aspirations are driving the Japanese, Chinese, and Indians toward fleet expansion. By the end of the decade or in the early part of the next century, the Pacific Ocean will see the coexistence of several very capable navies in addition to the forces of the United States and Russia as instruments of the new or revived geopolitical and economic visions of these regional states. If one includes the major military expansion taking place among the states in Southeast Asia and the continuing political-military stand-off between the two Koreas, the political and military tensions and balances in the Asia and Pacific Ocean area could prove to be both complex and, in some cases, intractable.

Southeast and Northeast Asia

What is striking about the states surrounding the East and South China Seas is the large build-up in their military capabilities without much evidence of heightened tension. There are, of course, a multitude of disputes in the area. The hostility between North and South Korea continues; Kampuchea is still shattered by civil strife; Vietnam and Laos are struggling with economic decay and civic cynicism; disputes over the Spratly Islands, offshore oil fields, economic zones, and maritime borders continue to arouse fears and ambitions among Vietnam, China, Malaysia, Brunei, and the Philippines; Thailand remains concerned about either the spillover of conflict from Vietnam into its own territory or the longer-range ambitions of Vietnam, as well as the security of its offshore economic zone. On the other hand, it cannot be said that any of these disputes has become particularly exacerbated in recent times. Moreover, there are still hopeful attempts toward a settlement in Kampuchea, fitful talks between the Koreas, internal economic and political issues within each of the states that may limit their ability to engage in external adventures, and the continuing engagement of the Association of Southeast Asia Nations (ASEAN) in the peaceful resolutions of disputes. It cannot be said that settlement of any one of the issues in the area is at hand; equally, it cannot be said that any of the problems has significantly worsened.[13]

In a real sense, the military build-up most likely results less from increased concerns for regional issues *per se* than a heightened sense of independence and the loosening of the geopolitical configuration that the end of the Cold War has generated. In any case, we see a whole variety of military purchases and developments that is altering the strategic complexity of the region. In Taiwan, recent programs have seen major modernization of attack aircraft, frigates, a variety of missiles, air defense systems, and main battle tanks. In Malaysia, there have been major improvements of military infrastructure and orders for diesel-electric submarines, helicopters, and corvettes. The Philippines, increasingly concerned over the control of the maritime territory of its archipelago and sea boundary with Malaysia, as well as the Spratly Islands, has plans for a major expansion of its patrol craft, medium landing ships, maritime patrol capabilities, and fighter aircraft. Thailand has increased purchases of fighter aircraft, helicopters, amphibious assault ships, frigates, tanks, armored personnel carriers, and air defense systems. South Korea is seeking not only to reinforce its ground and air position but also to develop doctrines and acquire an enhanced naval capability that would indicate a much greater attention to the issue of seapower. In 1985, North Korea began receiving delivery of MiG-23 fighter aircraft, the first major transfer of sophisticated Soviet aircraft in over ten years. Moreover, in 1988 and 1989 the USSR began delivery of MiG-29s and Su-25s. At the same time, however, the Soviets hinted that they might begin not only sales of MiG-29s but also of state-of-the-art MiG-31s to South Korea. Ideology is even less a barrier to arms sales. Even tiny Brunei has expanded its maritime patrol force with the addition of combat aircraft and offshore patrol vessels.

Further to the south, Australia maintains one of the best-equipped and professional forces in the region. Throughout the Southeast Asian area, it still has the most advanced aircraft and most potent submarine force, as well as a sophisticated over-the-horizon radar system. In general, however, there has been greater attention in recent years toward home rather than forward defense; and little serious attention is yet being given toward acquiring helicopter carriers like other states in the region, such as Japan, Thailand, and others. Internal economic considerations and a lessened sense of threat will likely limit Australian defense modernization and expansion in the immediate years ahead.

Independent calculations arising from local internal and external concerns thus appear to be the driving influence on the emerging strategic configuration throughout the region. The exigencies of the Cold War and the geostrategic bipolarization associated with the U.S.–Soviet conflict clearly weigh less heavily on the area. Enhanced "regionalization" of politics is giving rise to less predictable and more complex forms of cooperation and confrontation.

The New World Order and Naval Power in the Pacific

Although the two great armed conflicts in which the United States directly engaged during the Cold War, the Korean and Vietnam Wars, were in Asia, the central pivot of the American–Soviet confrontation was in the heart of Europe. The division of Germany and the organization of Europe into two alliance systems, reinforced by antagonistic ideological and economic regimes, were the crucial foci of the bipolar struggle. The "central front" was central not only in terms of the point at which the two alliances touched but also in terms of the geopolitical stakes at issue. It was the potential for direct warfare in this area that drove military planning and undergirded the concern for both nuclear holocaust and arms control.

In Asia, the crucial strategic relationship was that between Japan and the United States. The power potential of Japan and its increasing economic strength made it imperative that it not be subject to the intimidation of Soviet influence. Increasingly, moreover, it became difficult to conceive of a general deterrence system or general war capability vis-à-vis the Soviet Union without including Japan in the Western camp. The interdependence of the advanced industrial economies and the rise of Japan to a position of preeminence among those economies meant that the industrial base of Japan was crucial to defense planning for any general conflict. Hence, the defense of the Japanese Islands and the sea lines of communications connecting them with the United States and Europe became a matter of primary concern. "Trilateralism" was not only a political-economic connection between North America, Western Europe, and Japan but also a political-military link as well.

It was almost always assumed that should that link be activated in open and general hostilities with the Soviet Union, the trigger for the combat would be at the center of Europe. It was this distant trigger that led to the endless discussions among military planners about whether or not Japan would be "in" or "out" in the event of a European struggle, which few in Europe or the United States could see as being confined to a limited, regional engagement. By the late 60s and 70s, defense planners in both the United States and the USSR saw the possibility that a nuclear strike in the event of such a conflict could be postponed indefinitely. This meant that a global, conventional struggle might be more likely. In such a scenario, the importance of Japan increased. It was thus harder to accept the possibility of Japan being "out."

The decline, if not virtual collapse, of communism and the unification of Germany removed the "central front." The Conventional Force Reduction agreements in Europe (CFE) and the collapse of the Warsaw Pact, along with the continuing withdrawal of Soviet forces from Eastern Europe, made more distant the possibility of a general conflict arising from the center of Europe. Changes of regimes in Eastern Europe and attempts at reform in the former Soviet Union opened up avenues of positive cooperation among the states of NATO and the members of the erstwhile Warsaw Pact—endeavors centered on economic and technical assistance and the search for ways to incorporate the states in the east into the liberal international economic order constructed by the non-communist, industrial states after World War II. The Conference on Security and Cooperation in Europe (CSCE), which initially brought together the states of North America and of western and eastern Europe to reduce the perceptions of threat, has now begun to develop into an instrument of political, security, and economic integration of the heretofore separated parts of Europe. Given this evolution, can one expect that Asia and the Pacific will echo the harmony exhibited in Europe? Indeed, some in Japan, Australia, Canada, and the former Soviet Union have called for some form of regional association in that area, perhaps a kind of Conference on Security and Cooperation in Asia and the Pacific.

At the height of the Cold War, Asia and the Pacific were never integrated into well-articulated security systems confronting each other across a clear divide. And, as noted above, despite the great struggles over the divided states of Vietnam and Korea on the periphery of Asia, few believed that these conflicts ever had quite the same potential for exploding into general war as would an armed clash in Europe. These confrontations were generally seen as part of some "protracted struggle" fought out in the Third World and characterized by strategies of national liberation, counterinsurgency, and limited war. It is unlikely, therefore, that any general Asian and Pacific understanding will emerge out of the collapse of the Cold War. There will not only be schemes for regional security systems but also proposals for general naval arms control. However, the diverse goals and security concerns of the states in the regions will probably defeat—or defer throughout the decade—such approaches.

The key to stability and peaceful development in Asia and the Pacific is likely to be what it has been in the past—a generalized understanding between the United States, China, and Russia and also the U.S.–Japanese bilateral understanding. Close continuing relations between the United States and a number of other regional players, notably Australia, several of the ASEAN states, and South Korea will undergird this system. Crucial to these implicit and explicit accords will be the continuing role of the U.S. Pacific Command and the presence of the

U.S. Fleet. More important than actual deployment patterns will be the stability of expectations on the part of the states in the region that the United States will continue to play a preeminent role.

A major withdrawal of the U.S. naval presence from the eastern Pacific would open up in Japan a bitter debate over the appropriate external role of the state, generate fears over the prospect of a united Korea, and increase anxieties among the other regional states about the future course of Japanese power. The unpredictable behavior of North Korea would become more so and the strategic posture of South Korea more unsettled. The scramble for independent military forces among the various regional states would intensify, and fears about the meaning of this arms buildup would be heightened. The relationship between China and Taiwan, as well as between China and other states on its periphery, could become embittered. The uncertain evolution of the former Soviet Union would generate great concern, particularly on the part of Japan and perhaps China. The list of potential recalibrations of balances and recalculations of policies could go on. The great basin of the Pacific brings diverse states together. It is likely that the safety and relatively peaceful development of those states depend now as in the past on the stability of the U.S. position in the Pacific and its commitment to the general security of the area.

Notes

1. See remarks by the president to the Aspen Institute Symposium, August 2, 1990, Office of the Press Secretary, the White House; remarks by Secretary of Defense Dick Cheney to International Institute for Strategic Studies, the Homestead, Hot Springs, Virginia, September 6, 1990, Office of the Assistant Secretary of Defense (Public Affairs); address by Secretary of Defense Dick Cheney to the San Francisco Bay Area Council, San Francisco, California, September 14, 1990, Office of the Assistant Secretary of Defense (Public Affairs); remarks delivered by Undersecretary of Defense for Policy Paul D. Wolfowitz to the Hoover Institution, Stanford University, Stanford, California, December 8, 1989, *Defense Issues,* Vol. 5, No. 3 (American Forces Information Service).

2. See the 1991 *National Security Strategy of the United States,* President George Bush's statement to Congress.

3. See the statement of Secretary of Defense Dick Cheney in connection with the FY 1992–93 Department of Defense Budget, February 1991; remarks by General Colin L. Powell at the Royal United Services Institute, London, December 5, 1990, Office of the Assistant Secretary of Defense (Public Affairs); speech by Lieutenant General George L. Butler to the Center for Defense Journalism, the National Press Club, September 27, 1990, Washington, D.C.

4. General force structures, military balances, and orders of battle in the subsequent discussions of naval and military forces in the Pacific rely on *Jane's Fighting Ships 1990–91,* ninety-third edition, edited by Captain Richard Sharpe, RN, (Surrey, U.K.: 1990); *The Naval Institute Guide to Combat Fleets of the World 1990/1991,* edited by Bernard Preselin, (Annapolis: 1990); *Soviet Military Power 1990,* (Washington: The Department of Defense, September 1990); *The Military Balance 1990–1991,* (London: The International Institute for Strategic Studies, 1990); *Strategic Survey 1990–1991,* (London: The International Institute for Strategic Studies, May 1991).

5. For a more detailed analysis of trends in the Soviet position, see Robert S. Wood, "Soviet Naval Operations in the Pacific during a Global War," in *Korean Sea Power and the Pacific Era,* edited by Dalchoong Kim and Doug-woon Cho (Seoul: Institute of East and West Studies, 1990).

6. For background on the Kuriles issue, see David Rees, *The Soviet Seizure of the Kuriles* (New York: Institute of East and West Studies, 1985). For an analysis of some of the current dimensions of the issue, see Rex M. Takahashi, "The Kuriles: Passage or Impasse to Regional Peace?" *Naval War College Review* (Autumn 1991).

7. Statement of Admiral Charles Larson, commander-in-chief, United States Pacific Command, before the Senate Armed Services Committee, March 13, 1991.

8. William J. Crowe, Jr. and Alan D. Romberg, "Rethinking Security in the Pacific," *Foreign Affairs* (Spring 1991), pp. 131–32.

9. For a useful insight into Japanese political-military developments, see Fred Charles Ikle and Terumasa Nakanishi, "Japan's Grand Strategy," *Foreign Affairs* (Summer 1990), pp. 81–95.

10. Tai Ming Cheung, "China's Regional Military Posture," *International Defense Review,* Vol. 24, 6/1991, pp. 618–22.

11. Ashley J. Tellis, "Securing the Barrack: The Logic, Structure and Objectives of India's Naval Expansion," article in two parts, *Naval War College Review* (Summer 1990), pp. 77–97, and (Autumn 1990), pp. 31–57.

12. Captain Arun Prakash (Indian navy), "A Carrier Force for the Indian Navy," *Naval War College Review* (Autumn 1990), pp. 58–71.

13. For a useful survey of developments in Southeast Asia and Northeast Asia, see Robert Karniol, ''Asian Build-up—Regional Powers Strengthen Their Hand,'' and Dr. Young Koo Cha, ''The Changing Security Climate in Northeast Asia,'' both in *International Defense Review,* Vol. 24, 6/1991, pp. 611–16.

An American Perspective on Security and Tension Reduction in the North Pacific*

Sheldon W. Simon

Introduction

Radical restructuring of international security arrangements is a rare occurrence. It seldom takes place without a global war in which one or more major alliance is defeated. Fortunately, since the end of World War II, the world has not had to cope with such a traumatic change. Alliances have remained remarkably stable in both Europe and Asia; the superpowers have avoided war with each other; and the military actions which have been fought were located at a distance from great power heartlands (Korea, Vietnam, the Middle East, Afghanistan).

Nevertheless, even in the absence of great power conflicts, alliances will change over time as political suspicions abate and economic pressure for alternative, nonmilitary resource allocations grow. Unlike periods of war, however, the gradual erosion of great power tensions is a protracted process in which each alliance system tries to maintain its cohesion while simultaneously reducing the

---

*This chapter was completed prior to the dissolution of the USSR in late 1991. Much of the analysis of Soviet military capabilities in Asia can still apply to Russia, which has inherited the Pacific Fleet.

level of threat toward its antagonists. Even in a period of declining tensions, alliance maintenance is an important great power concern, for high status in the international system is still defined in large part by its number of dependent allies. Moreover, each great power and its allies fear that a precipitous change in arrangements could result in instability and unintended conflict. The continuation of alliance arrangements in a period of détente sustains deterrence until less threatening arrangements can be devised.

The purpose of this paper is to examine East Asian security arrangements in an early 1990s environment of growing superpower détente. It explores the prospects for and obstacles to tension reduction between the United States and the Soviet Union and their respective friends and allies, including Japan, China, and the two Koreas. The factors precipitating an interest in tension reduction are remarkably similar for both Moscow and Washington, though they are felt more intensely by the former. Domestic economic needs and social pressures in each society for the reallocation of resources away from the armed services can no longer be contained. For the USSR, *perestroika* is essential for its very survival as a great power in the coming decade. For the United States, successful economic revitalization will be the basis for the correction of domestic inequities—poverty and the lack of educational opportunities for a significant portion of the population. It is also necessary if the United States is to remain competitive in an information-intensive high technology global economy.

Indicative of the economic drain of military expenditure in the United States are the following figures:[1]

- For every one hundred dollars spent on civilian capital formation, forty dollars goes to the military. The comparable ratios for West Germany and Japan are thirteen dollars and three dollars respectively.
- From 1947 to 1987, the United States spent $7.6 trillion on the military, a sum roughly equal to the total value of the nation's infrastructure, plants, and equipment.
- Twenty-five percent of the U.S. scientists and engineers and 70 percent of all federal research and development money goes to the military ($41 billion in 1988).

At the very least, decades of postwar military leadership and its increasingly apparent economic and social costs to the United

States have led to an insistence that America's friends and allies bear an ever greater share of the alliance expenditures. In turn, these American demands have created new alliance strains, for they coincide with parallel pressures on these states to open their markets to U.S. products while revaluing their currencies to reduce exports to the American market.

Moreover, just as Washington is asking more from its allies to maintain decades-old security ties, the allies themselves are breaking out of the tight bipolar system on other dimensions. New trade and investment patterns have emerged between such traditional adversaries as South Korea and the Soviet Union, Taiwan and China, and South Korea and China—much to North Korea's consternation, the state least susceptible to the winds of political and economic change in the Asia–Pacific region.

U.S. interest payments on its foreign debt, $50 billion annually, are virtually the same amount needed to deploy over 330,000 members of the armed forces in Asia in pursuit of containment.[2] These forces include half the U.S. Navy, two-thirds of the Marine combat forces, two Army divisions, and several Air Force fighter wings. (At the same time, the growing democratization of governments throughout the Pacific rim has become associated with rising nationalism that objects to remaining part of the U.S. alliance system whose goals are determined more from Washington than their own countries.)

Seeing strains within U.S.–Pacific alliances and also hoping to acquire Asian resources for Siberian development, the Soviet Union has urged new security arrangements for the Pacific, including naval force reductions and the creation of buffer zones between Soviet and American naval deployments. The Soviets have also pledged unilaterally not to increase their deployment of nuclear weapons in the region.

China, too, is moving toward a more independent political position in Asia. Though agreeing with U.S. policy on Indochina and Afghanistan, the May 1989 normalization of Communist party relations between the CPSU and CCP signified the end of a lengthy era of entrenched Sino–Soviet hostility (1963–1989) and the inauguration of a new period in which Chinese diplomacy would work to avoid being drawn into Soviet–U.S. conflicts or shut out of their cooperation in the region.

Pessimistic analysts argue that if the United States continues its forward-deployed containment policy through the 1990s, then Japan would increasingly become America's mortgage banker, acquiring an ever greater amount of U.S. debt and real property as it recycles hundreds of billions of dollars back into the U.S. Treasury in support of American containment responsibilities. Political resentments on both sides of the Pacific would escalate, as Japan accused the United States of continuing to live beyond its means and Washington responded with allegations that Tokyo was a free rider on defense and unwilling to open its own domestic market to foreign goods and services.[3] Altering Japan's labor-intensive domestic distribution system to appease American demands, however, would entail considerable political risk for an already weakened Liberal Democratic Party leadership.

If the Soviet threat is seen to be waning, then U.S. allies may well find their side of the economic and security bargain with the United States a heavier burden than they are willing to bear. Redefining the bargain and the burden will be a major task for U.S. alliance diplomacy in the coming decade. Ideology has collapsed as the economic boundary between communist and capitalist states. Both China and the USSR are seeking trade and investment from the United States, Japan, South Korea, and ASEAN. These new economic relations could, over time, provide the rationale for a reduction of costly military commitments.

No precipitous change is anticipated, for an immediate dissolution of security arrangements could create disorder and instability, precipitating conflicts among other states in Asia. Rather, dependence upon the United States as the prime security guarantor and market must be gradually altered as new security arrangements are forged and markets diversified. These changes would not presage a U.S. exit from the region as a major player but rather a reduction and distribution of its role as prime mover to other regional actors. The development of new military doctrines and postures based on defensive rather than offensive intentions could contribute to reduced tensions and facilitate arms control negotiations in the Pacific. New resources freed by lower military expenditures could be invested in debt relief and economic development of the Philippines, Indonesia, and other Third World states. Increasing standards of living in the newly industrializing countries (NICs) and Third World generally along with greatly expanded markets in highly developed countries become major security tasks for the end of the twentieth century.

Asian Security Arrangements: The Problems of Builddown

Unlike the European situation where alliances are multilateral and opposing forces confront each other along clearly demarcated national boundaries, the Asia–Pacific region is characterized by bilateral alliances between the superpowers and their allies. With the exception of Korea, forces do not face each other along land boundaries. Rather, adversaries deploy along vast ocean and air spaces. The modification of defense arrangements and deployments, therefore, requires separate negotiations with a variety of allies located thousands of miles apart. Alterations in base arrangements in one country could offset the security of others even though the latter may not be involved in the diplomacy affecting their futures.

The United States has taken a cold and negative attitude toward Soviet President Mikail Gorbachev's Pacific disarmament proposals made at Vladivostok in 1986 and Krasnoyarsk in 1988. If American air and naval strength were significantly reduced, such U.S. allies as Japan and the ROK might well feel betrayed, with unpredictable consequences. Bilateral Soviet–U.S. disarmament talks for the Pacific would be insufficient, then. Allies would have to be included either directly at the bargaining table or indirectly through parallel negotiations between superpower allies. Even from the Soviet perspective, region-wide arms control talks are preferable. If not viewed in a regional context, an American deployment cap could be neutralized by strengthening allied forces. This is, after all, one of the goals of burden sharing.

Nor would arms control in the Pacific be successful without a modification of the U.S. maritime strategy. Its advocates argue that the forward deployment of U.S. nuclear carrier battlegroups near areas of potential conflict deter the Soviet Union from moving its forces away from the Sea of Okhotsk and northern Sea of Japan. The net effect is to keep most of the Pacific waterways free of Soviet ships and, therefore, open to international commerce.[4] Soviet naval strategy in the Pacific is driven by U.S. forward deployments. The Soviet Pacific Fleet is tasked with protecting its strategic ballistic missile submarines in the Sea of Okhotsk and defending the Soviet Far East by finding, and if necessary, attacking U.S. ballistic and attack submarines as well as its aircraft carriers and cruise missile-armed ships. Japan's additional anti-submarine warfare (ASW) capacity of about one hundred P3 aircraft makes the Soviet naval task formidable indeed.

Moreover, American officials are skeptical about Soviet arms control proposals for East Asia. They point out that Moscow has modernized the Pacific Fleet, adding forty new vessels in recent years. Thus, a regional naval freeze would find a modern Soviet force and prevent Japan from building its navy according to plans for the early 1990s.[5]

Despite the foregoing obstacles to Pacific arms control, the thawing of the Cold War has already affected Asia. U.S. Defense Secretary Richard Cheney has called upon American armed services to plan for substantial budget cuts in the early 1990s both because of the American deficit and in response to anticipated cuts in Soviet defense expenditures. At the same time, Washington is urging its allies to take up the slack. If the United States plans to withdraw some of its 46,000 forces from the ROK in the 1990s, then Seoul is pressed to compensate for this potential drawdown by buying additional U.S. fighter aircraft.[6]

A further complicating factor for the United States is found in the growing democratization of its Asian allies. While increased political openness in South Korea, Thailand, and the Philippines is welcomed, it has also rendered the alliances vulnerable to contentious domestic political debate. In the Philippines and South Korea, the presence of U.S. forces has exacerbated nationalist sentiments and fostered anti-American feelings in a younger generation that perceives little reason for their being there. Trade, investment, and security policy issues are subjects for heated parliamentary exchange, all of which focus domestic political-economic problems on relations with the United States.[7] Despite these new tensions, however, there is virtually no desire that U.S. forces leave the Asia–Pacific region. At a time of domestic political change, maintenance of a stable, secure international environment dominated by U.S. naval and air power seems to be preferred by both governments and opposition parties.

Like the United States, the Soviet Union is also faced with a transition in the Pacific. Without abandoning allies (North Korea and Vietnam), Moscow wants to demonstrate sensitivity to the security concerns of other Asian actors. It has normalized relations with China and seeks to diminish the anti-Soviet orientation of ASEAN, South Korea, and Japan. These policies are motivated partly by the traditional goal of weakening U.S. power in the region and partly by the need to attract Asian investment and technology for the development of the Soviet Far East. While most Asian states welcome the Soviet desire to reduce tensions, they also express new concerns. If, for example, Sino–Soviet rapprochement leads to a reduction of forces along their long mutual border, will China then turn its military attention toward Southeast Asia? This concern parallels another found among the ASEAN states: that economic limits will lead to U.S. insistence that Japan shoulder some of America's defense burdens south of Taiwan, that is, beyond Tokyo's current commitment to patrol within 1000 miles of Honshu.[8]

Soviet Security in the North Pacific

Soviet foreign policy under President Gorbachev is driven by the need to reduce defense costs and reallocate resources for the development of the civilian economy. Troop concentrations on the Chinese border are more expensive to maintain than strategic nuclear arsenals. An affordable defense requires an attenuation of the arms race with the United States. Détente with America and its allies is also seen by the Soviet leadership as the key to the trade, investment, and technology transfer required for perestroika's success.[9]

Soviet efforts in the late 1980s to settle such regional conflicts as Afghanistan and Cambodia and make unilateral arms cuts scheduled for both Europe and Asia are all demonstrations of good faith. They are designed to show how Gorbachev has distanced the USSR from his predecessors' policies of exploiting regional conflicts to improve Moscow's military position.[10] The defense reductions in particular will help lower the enormous Soviet budget deficit, estimated at 30 billion rubles in 1989, or 10 percent of Soviet gross national product. This is roughly triple that of the United States relative to GNP and a direct cause of the shortages crippling the Soviet economy.[11] It is essential that the Soviets create a new nonthreatening environment in which Moscow can be seen as an economic partner rather than a military and political threat.

To date, the most detailed Soviet proposal on Pacific security was made by President Gorbachev in the Siberian city of Krasnoyarsk in September 1988. Emphasizing interest in conflict resolution, he promised that the USSR would not increase the number of its nuclear weapons in Asia and called for consultations among Asian naval powers to reduce force concentraions where the sea boundaries of the USSR, PRC, Japan, and the two Koreas converge. He also called for the development of confidence-building measures to prevent air and sea incidents as well as a regional negotiating mechanism to examine all proposals dealing with Pacific security—in effect a preliminary blueprint of Gorbachev's view of a new central Soviet role in Pacific security concerns for the end of the century. To make these proposals especially uncomfortable for the United States, the Soviet President also offered to have the Soviet Union "abandon its naval material and technical supply point in Cam Ranh Bay" if the United States agreed to withdraw from the Philippines bases.[12]

Keen Soviet interest in becoming a part of the dynamic Pacific economy is apparent in its request to join the Canberra 1989 conference on Asia–Pacific economic cooperation in the incentives being devised for foreign investors in the Soviet Far East. Favorable tax arrangements are offered for joint ventures, not to exceed 10 percent of earnings. By late summer 1989, twenty-six such operations had begun: nine from Japan, six from the United States, three with North Korea, and two with China. The port of Nakhodka is to become a special economic zone of free enterprise based on foreign technology.[13]

The Soviet Union has rapidly followed the May 1989 normalization of interparty relations with China by withdrawing 23,000 troops from Mongolia and promising to reduce its total deployments in that country by 75 percent between April 1989 and December 1990.[14] Moscow is also negotiating a mutual drawdown of forces along the Sino–Soviet border, a procedure that should benefit both countries' economies. Some 200,000 troops are scheduled to be withdrawn from the eastern USSR by the end of 1990. These include twelve army divisions and eleven air force regiments.[15]

Soviet military officers declare that their armed forces configurations and maneuvers are now exclusively "defensive in nature." Reductions in tanks, artillery and combat aircraft presumably validate these changes. Moreover, Moscow has invited foreign observers and media to watch Far Eastern district exercises, including well-publicized Pacific Fleet maneuvers in July 1989. The Soviets claim that they will also be scrapping fifteen surface combatants of the Pacific Fleet by the end of 1990 in addition to the ground and air force reductions noted above.[16]

One major purpose behind this new highly visible Soviet openness is to put international pressure on the United States to reciprocate. Just as the USSR has inaugurated unilateral ground force reductions in Eastern Europe, the Soviets ask the Americans to respond accordingly with reductions in the environment where they hold the advantage—the navy. Soviet naval officers insist that the Pacific Fleet's role is not to obstruct sea-lanes (SLOCs), but rather to protect Soviet trade routes and coastal waters in the northern Sea of Japan. Pointing to the absence of full-size aircraft carriers in the Soviet navy, Admiral Genady Kvatov, Pacific Fleet commander-in-chief, contrasted Russian coastal defensive maneuvers with American power projection training activities in which land targets are the object of assault and occupation from the sea. The Soviets have particularly objected to the U.S. *Pacex 89* exercise, which involved maneuvers of four carrier battle groups along the Pacific rim from Alaska to the South China sea. A major portion of the exercise, according to Admiral Kvatov, focused on blockading the Kamchatka peninsula and the occupation of the Kurile islands, thus establishing full control over the Seas of Okhotsk and Japan. Moreover, Kvatov continued, "The U.S. and Japanese forces in the region are nearly four times larger in major surface ships armed with cruise missiles with the range of over 600 kilometers—we have no such missiles—and have an absolute superiority in aircraft carriers, of which there are none in the Soviet navy."[17]

The American response to Soviet claims of naval inferiority is skeptical. While granting that the Pacific Fleet has retired over fifty ships since 1984, U.S. officials states these were old, conventionally powered submarines and surface vessels due for retirement. New units joining the fleet, however, include nuclear-powered submarines (SSNs), guided-missile destroyers (DDGs), and amphibious transport vessels to enhance the USSR's ability to project forces from water to land. Although the fleet "may be somewhat fewer in numbers of submarines and principal combatants, . . . [it] is greatly improved in capability."[18] Moreover, if the Soviets deploy a large-deck carrier such as its new *Tiblisi* (undergoing sea trials) to Asia, the U.S. Seventh Fleet would potentially have to cover a genuine new threat to South China Sea control, one that could place Japan's long supply lines in jeopardy.

Despite these concerns, U.S. authorities acknowledge that, in fact, Soviet naval deployments away from Pacific coastal waters continue a decline begun in 1986. Naval aviation sorties have also diminished in this period. Moreover, force levels at Cam Ranh Bay have not increased since the early 1980s and consist of two or three submarines, three to four surface combatants, a squadron of TU-16 *Badger* bombers with anti-ship missiles, and a MiG-23 interceptor squadron, along with *Bear* D-F intelligence aircraft. No modern top-of-the-line aircraft have been deployed to Cam Ranh Bay. And, in late 1989, the MiGs and most of the *Badgers* returned to the Soviet Union. This relatively modest base fits with Moscow's 1988 offer to trade it for a U.S. withdrawal from the Philippines.[19]

Soviet naval arms control proposals since 1986 have concentrated on creating antisubmarine warfare-free zones, thus removing a combined Japanese–U.S. threat from the northern Sea of Japan. They have also asked for a ban on naval activity near international straits, freeing up choke points the Soviet Pacific Fleet must transit to move between their bases and open ocean.[20] In sum, the Soviets want to reduce the U.S.–Japan challenge to their strategic submarine deterrent (SSBNs) in the Sea of Okhotsk as well as their adversaries' ability to block the Pacific Fleet from reaching open ocean in a crisis situation.

Despite American naval reticence about Pacific arms reductions, there are some potential *mutual* advantages to their consideration. With a START agreement requiring a reduction of central systems by 30 percent, the number of Soviet SSBNs could be cut by more than half from sixty-two to fifteen to thirty, depending on the force structure chosen. In turn, the Pacific Fleet mission of defending these submarines would also be reduced, opening the way for a naval builddown discussion in the North Pacific.

The Soviet concern with sea-launched cruise missiles (SLCMs)—as the U.S. Navy continues to deploy them on most of its surface combatants—has led to radical proposals which include the inspection of launchers on each other's ships. U.S. National Security Advisor Brent Scowcroft has hinted that Washington will probably address naval arms control as one of the understandings arising from the 1989 Malta summit.[21] The advantage of a cap on SLCMs for the United States is found in the fact that much of America's population and urban centers are located near its coasts. SLCM controls would make the coasts less vulnerable to sea-based attack. Strong Soviet interest in reaching an agreement was evident in late 1989 when Russian negotiators suggested that ways of capping SLCM deployments other than direct inspection, to which the U.S. Navy vigorously objects, could be explored.[22] This point of contention was somewhat alleviated in 1991 when first President Bush and then President Gorbachev agreed to remove nuclear warheads from all surface vessels in their navies.

The Soviet–Japan Nexus

The most intransigent arms control problem in the Pacific rim for the Soviet Union is Japan. An increasingly formidable naval and air power adjacent to the Soviet Far East, Japan is, nevertheless, essentially uninterested in arms control talks by itself with the Soviet Union for several reasons. Bilateral negotiations would be seen by Washington as a break in the U.S.–Japan alliance. Moreover, Japan's forces are strategically meaningful only when combined with U.S. forces in an American-determined strategy. Japan also insists that reconciliation with the Soviet Union must be preceded by the return of the four southern Kurile islands adjacent to Hokkaido.

Although Boris Yeltsin's Russian republic is anxious to improve relations with Japan, the cession of territory acquired in the Great Patriotic War (1939–1945) is a politically risky prospect. The key question is: would the Russians be willing to offer the islands in exchange for massive Japanese aid and investment for Siberian development? Such an agreement would certainly signal a new more cordial stage in Russian–Japan relations, give Tokyo a significant stake in the Russian economy, and probably reduce military tensions as well.

Russian defense installations on Kunashiri, Etorofu, and Shikotan consist of about one division plus MI-24 *Hind* armed helicopters, long range artillery, and some forty MiG-23 interceptors.

These forces guard the entrance to the Sea of Okhotsk to protect Soviet SSBNs and are not included in force reduction plans for the Far East.[23]

Some Soviet scholars and deputies to the newly elected parliament have proposed to demilitarize the islands and even provide for a joint Russian–Japan administration. Although broadcast by Soviet media, there is no indication that President Yeltsin is contemplating such policy innovations.[24] Instead, the Russians insist that any reduction of their defensively deployed forces in the Southern Kuriles can only take place as part of a negotiated arrangement covering "the forces deployed in Hokkaido and other Japanese islands and South Korea as well as U.S. warships cruising in the sea off the Soviet coast. . . ."[25] In other words, the Russians will consider resolution of the northern islands dispute only as part of a broad North Pacific disarmament arrangement. Such a major change in the security structure of the region could greatly strain the U.S.–Japan alliance, especially if it covered the demilitarization of Hokkaido.

While the Russians insist on separating the issue of the Northern islands (Southern Kuriles) from Siberian development, Japan insists that the former's satisfactory resolution is a prerequisite for significant Japanese loans and investment. According to Soviet estimates, Siberian development would require an initial $320 billion in new capital by the year 2000.[26] Only Japan would be able to provide that kind of support. Yet, aside from political differences between the two countries, it is unlikely that Japanese investors are sufficiently interested in Siberia to warrant Soviet optimism. Japan's economy has changed since the 1970s, when interest in Siberian resources was strong. Now, Japan needs less energy and fewer raw materials. Its heavy industries are themselves being exported either to Third World countries where production costs are lower or to other industrial states so that goods will be produced within the markets in which they are sold. Thus, of the 165 joint ventures established in the Soviet Far East in 1988, only six were Japanese.[27] The question arises, therefore, of whether Japan's insistence on resolution on the Northern islands issue as a precondition for aid in Siberian development could be in fact a "red herring." That is, it could be a convenient excuse to cover a lack of interest in the project itself.

The Japan–U.S. Connection

The Japan–U.S. security treaty constitutes the premier defense pact in Asia. While no other Asian ally of the United States would be immediately involved in U.S. regional defense activities in the event of hostilities, Japan would almost surely be so. Either as a base for U.S. naval and air forces or by using its own services to monitor or possibly block the Japanese straits, Japanese armed forces are inextricably linked to America's North Pacific strategy.

Japan has more than fifty destroyers and almost one hundred P-3C ASW aircraft, more than twice and four times respectively as the U.S. Seventh Fleet. Its Air Self Defense Force flies two hundred F-15s, roughly the same number the United States deploys to defend the continental United States. Japan's forces are designed to counter the USSR's one hundred Pacific Fleet submarines and its two thousand fixed-wing landbased aircraft.[28] By the mid-1990s, Japan intends to deploy four escort flotillas with *Aegis*-equipped guided missile cruisers for air defense as submarine hunter groups. The *Aegis* system will provide instantaneous data links with U.S. ships.[29]

Moscow has urged Japan and the United States to meet with the USSR to discuss confidence-building measures (CBMs) and arms control for the North Pacific. The Soviets also invited Japan to observe their summer 1989 naval exercises in the Sea of Japan—to no avail. Washington and Tokyo have so far dismissed these initiatives as really geared to undermine U.S. naval strength and the Japan–U.S. alliance. Indeed, Japan's defense plan for the mid-1990s is designed to move forces closer to the Soviet Union to counter what the Defense Agency maintains is the USSR's continued military buildup in Asia.[30]

From the Soviet viewpoint, North Pacific arms control negotiations concentrating on forward deployed U.S. and Japanese naval forces is the linchpin for subsequent East Asian discussion. If the USSR demonstrates a willingness to cap its air and naval capabilities qualitatively as well as quantitatively in the Far East and/or if it agrees to return, say, the southern two Kurile islands to Japan, pressure on the United States and Japan to engage in arms control talks will be virtually irresistible. Japan has already declared its willingness to exchange inspection teams with the Soviet armed forces to observe military conditions if the USSR reveals the locations of its forces and bases. (Japan's are a matter of public record.) If genuine confidence-building is to occur, then each side must first know the capabilities of the other in the region.[31]

The prognosis for tripartite arms control talks in the North Pacific soon is not good. Japan is committed to a new five year defense plan which will witness the development of its next generation of combat aircraft (FSX) and does not want to jeopardize that commitment. The Maritime Self Defense Force (MSDF) is adding *Aegis* guided missile cruisers and also building an antisubmarine warfare (ASW) center which will be linked to a major U.S. facility in Hawaii. Japan will also be deploying Over the Horizon (OTH) radar, linked to U.S. systems in the Aleutians, which will provide the ability to monitor Soviet air activity well inside the USSR's Far Eastern region. Indicative of Tokyo's reticence to compromise these plans was Foreign Minister Taro Watanabi's insistence that arms control talks be preceded by progress toward the conclusion of a peace treaty, in other words, some change in Japan's favor with respect to the Northern islands.[32] If reversion of the Northern islands is, indeed, the prerequisite for tripartite arms control negotiations, the prospects are, indeed, bleak.

Korea and North Pacific Tension Reduction

Korea's importance for Northeast Asian security and tension reduction lies along several dimensions:

- The most heavily armed combat-ready ground forces in Asia have confronted each other along the middle of the peninsula for over three-and-a-half decades.
- These North and South Korean forces are backed respectively by the region's strongest powers (the USSR and China for the DPRK and the United States for the ROK). Although these great powers are involved in mutual détente, an outbreak of hostilities on the peninsula could rapidly lead to direct military action among them—an outcome no one desires.
- Korea's location between the Sea of Japan and the East China Sea suggests a potential *regional* security role. ROK naval forces could coordinate patrols of the Korea strait with Japan's monitoring of the Tsushima strait, possibly challeng-

ing Soviet Pacific Fleet movement into the open ocean. Moreover, both North and South Korean forces are sufficiently large and sophisticated that they could deploy beyond the peninsula, especially if provided air and sea lift capabilities by their Soviet and American allies. (Note, however, that these are hypothetical possibilities and do not form the basis of current policy by either of the Koreas, the Soviet Union, or the United States.)

The tensions and divisions listed above are deeply embedded in the international politics of Northeast Asia. Nevertheless, the 1990s may provide opportunities to reduce these dangerous legacies of World War II and the Cold War. Emerging from South Korea's dynamic economic performance of the past decade is a new foreign policy designed to separate the Roh Tae-wu government from its predecessors. Using its newfound economic strength to create international political legitimacy, South Korea is forging commercial ties with Eastern Europe, the Soviet Union, and China. Seoul's political goal is to give communist states a stake in the ROK's political survival, thereby undermining the communist states' reliability and support for any possible North Korean military effort to unify Korea. Indicative of South Korea's importance to communist states whose current primary concern is economic growth is the ROK's trade with China, estimated at $3 billion in 1988 or six times the value of the PRC's trade with North Korea.[33]

While prospects for the outbreak of hostilities on the peninsula seem remote—assuming rational decision makers—since a new war would devastate the economies and societies of both Koreas, war through miscalculation remains a possibility. One scenario that could lead to a North Korean attack would occur during a succession struggle in Pyongyang after Kim Il Sung's death. The contenders for power could choose war to rally the country behind them. Or, there could be a miscalculation in Pyongyang growing out of ROK–U.S. trade frictions and South Korean demonstrations against American pressures to open the Korean market. Popular anti-U.S. sentiment could be misinterpreted by the North as a retreat from the U.S. defense arrangement, especially if the United States withdrew ground forces from the 38th parallel during this period of political stress.

Ironically, the U.S.–ROK command structure for the South is probably North Korea's best guarantee against a South Korean decision to attack the North. Under current arrangements, the South may not initiate military operations against the North. Only the U.S.-led joint command may do so. Moreover, dependence on the United States for both deterrence and defense has delayed the development of a well-balanced ROK defense force. Both the air force and navy lag behind the army since air and naval protection have been essentially an American responsibility.[34] Without a new understanding between North and South, the reduction of U.S. forces on the peninsula and a change in the command structure producing greater autonomy for Seoul could actually be viewed as destabilizing by Pyongyang.

Korea presents an additional problem for East Asian arms control and tension reduction. While the prospect of some withdrawal of U.S. ground forces from the peninsula is increasingly probable in the 1990s as the ROK army grows, the American economic strains leading to worldwide military drawdowns have also generated a burden-sharing policy with allies. This policy requires an increase in allied forces to offset U.S. reductions. Burden sharing as a strategy reflects the belief that stability still depends on a strong air and sea based deterrent in the Pacific. If the Americans can no longer afford to bear the total cost of the deployments, then allies and friends should assist both through financial offsets for U.S. forces and by contributing more of their own.[35] Washington is undoubtedly encouraging ROK studies on the future development of a regional maritime role which could include coordinated straits control with Japan between the peninsula and the Japanese islands. This could, in turn, lead to the creation of joint patrols of U.S., Japanese, and South Korean vessels to help maintain the sea-lanes (SLOC) to the North Pacific, upon which the ROK's boom economy depends.[36]

The substantial South Korean shipbuilding industry could also provide repair and refitting services for U.S. ships as the navy leaves Subic Bay in the Philippines and if Sasebo in Japan becomes politically and financially problematic.

While South Korean strategic analysts express interest in three-way naval cooperation in Northeast Asia, particularly given the MSDF's enhanced ASW capability in the 1990s, traditional fears of a resurgent Japan persist. Should the United States choose to leave the major responsibility for North Pacific security to Japan, many South Koreans believe it will become an unacceptable hegemon once again.[37] American dominance in security relations with both Japan and the ROK appears essential for regional stability for the time being. The United States keeps Japan's growing forces within a regional balance for Asia in much the same way that NATO subordinates German military might in Europe.

Reinforcing trends in ROK internal politics and the liberalization of European communist states could also lead to tension reduction in Korea. Pyongyang may conclude that its political future will be best found in economic growth and greater participation in the global economy to avoid complete isolation in the North Pacific. If the ROK seizes this opportunity to negotiate commercial assistance to the North in exchange for arms reductions on both sides of the DMZ, disengagement may occur before the end of the century. Increased South Korean self-confidence, combined with a reduced American military profile and continually increasing political and economic relations between Seoul and Eastern Europe, the USSR, and China, could also open the ROK to compromise. North Korean demands such as the removal of nuclear weapons from the peninsula, an end to the ROK's anti-communist policy, single delegations to sports events and other international activities, mutual arms reductions, and the withdrawal of U.S. ground forces could all be topics for inter-Korean bargaining in a climate of global détente.[38]

A fundamental U.S. security problem will be reconciling these trends toward détente with burden sharing. The United States has called upon the ROK to provide financial support for naval operations in the Persian Gulf, to increase subsidization of U.S. forces in Korea to $45 million annually, and to participate in a multilateral aid program for the Philippines. Two of these three requests would link South Korea to extraregional security.[39] U.S. officials argue that the long-term viability of the alliance in an era of constrained American defense budgets can be sold to Congress only if mutual benefits are demonstrated. Thus, a regional defense role for the ROK may increasingly characterize bilateral planning. Some U.S. forces in Korea are already tasked with regional responsibilities. The Seventh Air Force, for example, counters Soviet threats in the entire Northeast Asian region.

Nevertheless, the extension of ROK defense responsibilities to the adjacent region is particularly controversial for the Roh government. It would seem to contradict its *nordpolitik* toward communist states. A defense role against the Soviet Pacific Fleet around South Korea could obstruct the economic and political ties that are being established with the Soviet Far East.

Even if the ROK agrees to a limited regional defense role in the 1990s, this policy change will probably not halt the withdrawal of U.S. ground forces by the middle of the decade. Bush administration officials argue that with the acquisition of 120 new fighter aircraft and the further modernization of the air force and navy, the ROK will have a sufficient deterrent by itself against the North. Secretary of Defense Richard Cheney has stated that troop withdrawals from Europe would ultimately be extended to Korea as well.[40] Interestingly, this development could become part of a broader North Pacific arms control arrangement that would encompass both Koreas, U.S. forces in the region, and the Soviet Pacific Fleet and Naval Air Force.

Disengagement on the Korean peninsula could be accelerated if Seoul and Pyongyang would agree to confidence-building measures such as the redeployment of North Korean forces in a less threatening mode, thus reducing the prospects of surprise attack. ROK opposition leader Kim Dae Jung has seized upon the prospect of U.S. force reductions later in the 1990s as an incentive for the North to engage in a dialogue on détente. Mr. Kim sees this policy as a way of appealing to younger voters who desire a country less dependent on the American security guarantee.[41]

ROK defense authorities seem less sanguine than their American counterparts concerning an independent South Korean defense against the North. Barring a change in North Korean policy, Defense Minister Yi Song-hun does not believe ROK forces alone will be ready to deter the North until the first decade of the next century.[42] In order to reduce the American financial burden of maintaining its forces in Korea, Seoul has promised to raise its cost sharing from $288 million annually to $340 million by 1992. (Other contributions, including real estate and tax exemptions, raise the total ROK contributions for U.S. forces to about $1.6 billion a year.)[43]

In effect, there appear to be two trends in U.S.–Korean defense affairs that could affect regional security: the first is a strong probability that U.S. ground forces will be reduced to around 10,000 or less by the mid-1990s, barring increased threat from the DPRK. U.S. naval and air power would remain the same. The second trend would involve reconfiguring the remaining U.S.

ground forces in the ROK for a regional role by changing the Second Division from a heavy mechanized force to a lighter mobile division with increased airlift.[44] From the Soviet perspective, however, this change would hardly be seen as desirable. It would mean that bilateral tension reduction between North and South Korea would increase local capabilities for regional defense against the Soviet Pacific Fleet.

The reduction of U.S. forces in the ROK had also provided an occasion for a peninsular agreement banning theater nuclear weapons. The utility of nuclear forces for either deterrence or defense in this densely populated area has been questionable for some time. Moreover, the political acceptability of U.S. nuclear forces in the South in the face of growing antinuclear sentiment in the ROK electorate meant the time was ripe for a withdrawal of these forces in hope that North Korea would reciprocate with a guarantee that its factories would be open for inspection. Pyongyang has proposed turning the peninsula into a nuclear weapons-free zone but refused to accept supervision of its own nuclear plants by the International Atomic Energy Agency through 1991. The USSR has urged the North to accept such supervision if the Americans remove their weapons and has offered to serve as a guarantor of DPRK compliance.[45]

Is the North ready to discuss confidence building measures (CBMs) for Korea in what still must be perceived as a hostile international environment? Pyongyang has made a number of proposals for arms reduction in recent years, though it is difficult to determine whether they are purely propaganda. In addition to the denuclearization of the peninsula, the DPRK has also called for force reductions on both sides. Yet the North also refused to engage in direct bilateral arms control talks with the South until 1991. To break this stalemate and demonstrate its good faith, the South Korean government could unilaterally reduce the scope and duration of the annual "Team Spirit" exercises with the United States as a prelude to its own appeal for arms control negotiations. Should these negotiations occur and make progress, Seoul could reward these developments by cancelling "Team Spirit" for one year. Finally, if the North agreed to redeploy its forces further away from the DMZ and in a more defensive arrangement, the "Team Spirit" exercise could be discontinued.[46]

Arms control on the peninsula, however, may be attenuated by movements toward the tripartite security cooperation among

Japan, the ROK, and the United States discussed above. Seoul's participation in bilateral simultaneous Korea–U.S. naval and landing exercises (*Pacex 1989* and *Rimpac 1990*) contrasts with the ROK's diplomatic and commercial efforts to improve relations with the Soviet Union, China, and North Korea.[47] Continuation of these two tracks seems probable for the next several years unless political changes in the DPRK open prospects for genuine arms reductions.

The China Conundrum

Security in the North Pacific must also consider China's growing capacity to project force beyond its borders and the political intentions of its leadership. Ironically, the PRC's reversion to a variant of Maoist paranoia toward the world after the June 1989 Tiananmen Square crushing of the pro-democracy movement has probably slowed the military's modernization. Both the reorientation of military units to domestic control and the centrally directed slowdown of economic development have undoubtedly constrained the People's Liberation Army's (PLA) professionalization and, therefore, its ability to operate in a regional setting.

Politically, the Deng Xiaoping/Li Peng regime is in a quandary. The industrial West, friends of the past decade, stands accused of indirectly fomenting the spring 1989 challenge to party leadership as Chinese youth agitated to adopt the free institutions they had observed in democratic-capitalist societies. But the disintegration of communist regimes in Eastern Europe and the Soviet Union itself are equally frightening, particularly as the Chinese Communist Party sees the execution of the Ceaucescus as an invitation to anarchy and a possible lesson for future Chinese (counter) revolutionaries. Only six months earlier Gorbachev had been praised for normalizing interparty relations after two-and-a-half decades of estrangement. Now he is excoriated as a traitor to Marxism-Leninism for espousing the anathema cause of social democracy.[48]

With China holding "a plague on both your houses" attitude toward the West and the USSR, there is little basis for the Bush administration's concern that Washington's condemnation of Beijing's repressive domestic actions will drive the PRC toward the Soviet Union. To the contrary, China's domestic problems have led to a kind of stasis in foreign policy. There is no indication of new radicalism. Indeed, China appears to be adhering to its previous statements on such issues as missile sales, nuclear non-proliferation, stability in Korea, patience on the Taiwan issue, and even a negotiated settlement for Cambodia.

Deng Xiaoping realizes, then, that despite the revival of domestic political conservatism, an extension of this policy to foreign affairs could have disastrous results. It would destroy China's standing in the international community so carefully developed over the past ten years and lead to neighbors in both Northeast and Southeast Asia once again regarding the PRC as a threat. With both the Soviet Union and the United States possibly reducing their military deployments in China's immediate vicinity in the 1990s, Beijing need only bide its time and continue gradually to build its navy to become a more significant regional actor by the early twenty-first century. According to Gary Klintworth of the Strategic and Defense Studies Center of the Australian National University, by the end of the century China will possess a "blue water deployment of multi-ship naval task forces supported by long-range bombers and air-refuelled maritime strike aircraft equipped with anti-ship missiles."[49] These would enhance the PRC's ability to control the Spratly Islands in the South China Sea.

On the other hand, if China adheres to its peace diplomacy of the past several years, then the reestablishment of diplomatic relations with Indonesia will be followed soon thereafter by Singapore. A subsequent settlement of the Cambodian problem would position the PRC very favorably in Southeast Asia and provide an opportunity for new ties with the burgeoning ASEAN economies.

Conclusion

Even with a hard-line regime in China, it is improbable that great power tensions in Asia will increase. Unlike the 1970s, the former Soviet Union is neither seen as dynamic nor expansive; therefore, a China–U.S. coalition against the Soviets is unnecessary. Moreover, Russia has little to offer the PRC since both seek to improve their relations with the industrial, capitalist world. Economic affairs take precedence over military concerns.

Détente among three of Asia's great powers (the United States, Russia, and China) means that other important regional actors will play more independent roles, particularly Japan and the ROK for the North Pacific. Their capabilities and intentions will become increasingly more determinative for regional security. For example, since both Seoul and Tokyo require open SLOCs for their prosperity, future negotiations with Russia could focus on free passage guarantees as an alternative to costly naval arms buildups.

A lower U.S. security profile in the North Pacific may also lead to new Japan–ROK cooperation with more direct military and political contacts. This will be especially important for both SLOC control and/or negotiations toward a free regional sea-lanes arrangement.

The knotty issue of Russian versus U.S.–Japan naval deployments in the Sea of Japan and North Pacific Ocean could begin to be unraveled through a series of CBM negotiations. On the Russian side, a cap could be placed on the introduction of new systems for the Pacific Fleet, precluding, for example, the deployment of a fixed-wing aircraft carrier such as the *Tiblisi*. The Soviets could also agree to continue to keep the bulk of their fleet within two hundred miles of Vladivostok in a defensive configuration. In exchange, Japan and the United States could honor a buffer zone around the Sea of Okhotsk, no longer sending task forces into the Soviet Union's SSBN bastion. This agreement could be facilitated if the START agreement leads to an SSBN reduction as one component of a strategic weapons builddown. All three countries could inaugurate reciprocal notification of major exercises while extending invitations to each other as observers. Finally, both the United States and Russia could place limits on the quantity and sophistication of weapons provided to such allies as North Korea, South Korea, Thailand, and Vietnam. Such policy changes would enhance regional stability, reduce the prospect of surprise attack, and lead to a degree of military disengagement.

These alterations in America's Asian security posture suggested for the 1990s logically grow from the Nixon Doctrine enunciated two decades ago. They presage a region increasingly independent of American military guarantees and responsible for its own security. These changes do not mean the end of U.S. alliance arrangements in the Pacific; but they do portend a reconfiguration as Japan and the ROK take positions on the world political stage commensurate with their economic strength.

Washington remains a friend but may no longer be able to serve as mentor. Nevertheless, a continued U.S. military presence in the Pacific remains essential to sustain the balance of power in the area—a balance that will be increasingly multipolar as the twenty-first century dawns.

Notes

1. Seymour Melman, "What to Do With the Cold War Money," *New York Times*, December 17, 1989.

2. Jerry W. Sanders, "America in the Pacific Century," *World Policy Journal*, Vol. 6, No. 1, Winter 1988–89, p. 54.

3. This point of view is effectively presented in Sanders' article (see note 2), especially pp. 66–68.

4. A recent defense of the maritime strategy is found in Alvin H. Bernstein, "Twin Dangers: Cost-Conscious Americans and Complacent Pacific Allies," *Pacific Defense Reporter*, Vol. 15, Nos. 6/7, December 1988–January 1989, pp. 82–85. Also see Sheldon W. Simon, *The Future of Asian-Pacific Security Collaboration* (Lexington, MA: Lexington Books, 1988), chapter 1; and Sheldon W. Simon, "Pacific Rim Reaction to U.S. Military Strategy," in Young Whan Kihl and Lawrence Grinter, editors, *Security, Strategy, and Policy Responses in the Pacific Rim* (Boulder, CO: Lynn Reinner Publishers, 1989).

5. Fred Greene, "The United States and Asia in 1988: A Changing Environment," *Asian Survey*, Vol. 29, No. 1, January 1989, p. 91.

6. Richard Halloran, "Cheney Opposes Licensing Accord for Jet Fighter Sale to South Korea," *New York Times*, July 20, 1989.

7. A good review of these difficulties in U.S. relations with its Pacific allies is found in Charles Morrison, "The Future of Democracy in the Asia–Pacific Region," presented to the National Defense University Symposium *Pacific Basin Strategies for the 1990s and Beyond*, Honolulu, HI, March 2–3, 1989.

8. Bilveer Singh, "The USSR's 'New Thinking' in the Asia–Pacific Region: Focus on the Sino–Soviet Détente," *The Indonesian Quarterly*, Vol. 17, No. 2, Spring 1989, pp. 177–83.

9. George W. Breslauer, "Linking Gorbachev's Domestic and Foreign Policies," *Journal of International Affairs*, Vol. 42, No. 2, Spring 1989, pp. 267–82.

10. Leszek Busznski, "The Concept of Political Revolution in Soviet Foreign Policy: The Case of the Kampuchean Issue," (Canberra, Australia: The Strategic and Defense Studies Center, the Australian National University, Working Paper No. 182, June, 1989).

11. Leonard Silk, "Aid for East Bloc Expected to be a Vital Summit Topic," *New York Times*, December 1, 1989.

12. *Pravda*, September 18, 1989, in *FBIS, Daily Report Soviet Union*, September 18, 1989.

13. These developments were discussed by Yuriy Akhrimenko, executive secretary of the Soviet National Asia–Pacific Economic Cooperation Committee, in *The Nation* (Bangkok) November 1, 1989, in *FBIS, Daily Report East Asia*, pp. 52–53.

14. Radio Moscow (in Mandarin) to Southeast Asia, November 29, 1989, in *FBIS, Daily Report Soviet Union*, November 30, 1989, p. 9.

15. Radio Moscow (in Japanese), October 16, 1989. Interview with Major General Yuriy Markelov, in *FBIS, Daily Report Soviet Union*, October 24, 1989, pp. 1–2.

16. Interview with General Viktor Novozhilov, commander of the Soviet Far East Military District, as carried by Radio Moscow (in Japanese) December 9, 1989, in *FBIS, Daily Report Soviet Union*, December 12, 1989, p. 16.

17. Interview with Pacific Fleet Commander Admiral Gennady A. Kvatov by Robert Horiguchi, "Eye Witness with the Pacific Fleet," *Pacific Defense Reporter*, August 1989, pp. 8–10.

18. Rear Admiral Thomas A. Brooks, Director of U.S. Naval Intelligence, "Soviet Naval Power—'Perestroika': Some Prognostications," *Asia–Pacific Defense Forum*, Fall 1989, p. 9.

19. Ibid., p. 14.

20. Ibid., p. 17.

21. Scowcroft interview on Cable News Network, December 3, 1989.

22. Michael Gordon, "Soviets Softening on Limits for Missiles at Sea, U.S. Says," *New York Times*, December 19, 1989.

23. Denis Warner, "Chinese Card Today—the Japan Card Tomorrow?" *Pacific Defense Reporter*, May 1989, p. 48; interview with Colonel General Moiseyev, chief of staff of the Soviet Armed Forces, Tokyo *NHK Television* (in Japanese), July 19, 1989, in *FBIS, Daily Report East Asia*, July 20, 1989, p. 2.

24. Radio Moscow (in Japanese), December 1, 1989, in *FBIS, Daily Report Soviet Union*, December 13, 1989, p. 24.

25. Interview with General Viktor Norozhilov, commander of the Soviet Far Eastern Military District, Radio Moscow (in Japanese) December 9, 1989, in *FBIS, Daily Report Soviet Union*, December 12, 1989, p. 17.

26. Robert Horiguchi, "Soviets Face Heavy Distrust," *Pacific Defense Reporter*, May 1989, pp. 49–50.

27. Ibid.

28. Statement by Assistant Secretary of State for East Asia and the Pacific Gaston Sigur, in *Sale of Aegis Weapons System to Japan: Hear-*

ings (U.S. General Printing Office, U.S. House of Representatives, Subcommittee on Asia–Pacific Affairs, June 16, 1988), p. 39.

29. Statement by Assistant Secretary of Defense Richard Armitage, in *Sale of Aegis Weapons System*, pp. 52–53.

30. *Kyodo*, September 28, 1989 and December 8, 1989, respectively, in *FBIS, Daily Report East Asia*, September 28, 1989, p. 4 and December 8, 1989, pp. 1–2.

31. *Kyodo*, November 28, 1989, in *FBIS, Daily Report East Asia*, November 28, 1989, p. 1.

32. *Kyodo*, December 5, 1989, in *FBIS, Daily Report East Asia*, December 5, 1989, p. 3.

33. These figures are cited in Edward A. Olsen, *Prospects for an Increased Naval Role for the Republic of Korea in Northeast Asian Security* (Monterey, CA: Naval Postgraduate School, NPS-56-89-007, March 1989), p. 26.

34. Cha Young-Koo, "The Trend of U.S.–ROK Security Relations," presented at the U.S. National Defense University Pacific Symposium, Honolulu, HI, March 2–3, 1989, especially pp. 10–12.

35. For a thorough assessment of the U.S. burden-sharing strategy in Asia, see Sheldon W. Simon, *The Future of Asian–Pacific Security Collaboration* (Lexington, MA: Lexington Books, 1988).

36. Edward Olsen cites a number of these studies in *Prospects for an Increased Naval Role for the Republic of Korea*, pp. 12–13.

37. Ibid., p. 19.

38. Larry Niksch explores these forces for change in "Political Change in South Korea and its Impact on U.S.–Korean Relations," *Asian–Pacific Review*, Vol. 1, No. 1, Spring 1989, pp. 23–25.

39. Ibid., p. 33.

40. Richard Halloran, "General Sees End to U.S. Troops in Korea in 90s," *New York Times*, August 15, 1989.

41. Mark Clifford and Shim Jae Hoon, "Welcome Wears Thin," *Far Eastern Economic Review*, July 13, 1989, pp. 28–29.

42. Seoul television interview (in Korean), July 20, 1989, in *FBIS, Daily Report East Asia*, July 28, 1989, pp. 25–26.

43. Steven Weisman, "Seoul Vows More for U.S. Troop Costs," *New York Times*, October 14, 1989.

44. This prospect is discussed in *The Christian Science Monitor*, October 12, 1989.

45. V. Ospov, "Nuclear-Free Zone for the Korean Peninsula," *Krasnaya Zvezda*, November 18, 1989, in *FBIS, Daily Report Soviet Union*, November 29, 1989, pp. 20–21.

46. These arms control prospects are discussed in a *Choson Ilbo* editorial, December 10, 1989, in *FBIS, Daily Report East Asia*, December 12, 1989, pp. 38–39.

47. *Yonhap* (Seoul), September 22, 1989, in *FBIS, Daily Report East Asia*, September 22, 1989, p. 21.

48. An internal Chinese Communist Party document was circulating among members in late 1989 condemning Gorbachev and political developments in Eastern Europe. See James L. Tyson, ''Sino–Soviet Tensions Rise,'' *The Christian Science Monitor*, December 27, 1989; and ''Worried Chinese Leadership says Gorbachev Subverts Communism,'' *New York Times*, December 28, 1989.

49. Quoted in Michael Richardson, ''New Fears of China's Military Power,'' *Pacific Defense Reporter*, August 1989, p. 15.

Japan's Role in Regional and Global Security

Robert H. Puckett

The decline in U.S.–Russian tensions has had a major impact on Europe, but its effects on the balance of power and interests in Northeast Asia are unclear. The prospects for a comprehensive arms control regime in Northeast Asia in the short term are negligible. The trend of the region is toward a multicentric balance, with the increase of medium-sized powers and with the United States as the presumptive balancer of power.[1]

In spite of cutbacks in operations and weapons systems, the former Soviet Union has continued to upgrade its weapons in the Far East. It has substituted more modern jet fighters, surface ships, submarines, tanks, surface-to-air missiles, and multiple rocket launchers.[2] Presumably, much of the Soviets' outdated military equipment will be sold to medium-sized powers in the region as well as elsewhere in the world.

Perhaps the most dangerous aspect of the emerging multicentric international political system is the structural weakness of the former Soviet Union, though. Its economic and ethnic problems dramatize the uncertainty and instability linked to the decline of a superpower.

However, Russia will remain a major military power in the region. With Japan as an economic superpower and the United States as both a military and economic superpower, the region is bound to be inherently unstable unless there is enhanced regional cooperation as well as a comprehensive arms control regime[3]

One author has postulated four possible scenarios for Japan's role in the emerging multicentric international political system:[4]

1. *Pax Americana* Phase II. In this scenario, the United States remains a comprehensive superpower (economic, political, and military), with Japan concentrating on its global economic role.
2. Bigemony. Japan and America would integrate their economies in the context of a Pacific economic community.
3. *Pax Consortis.* This scenario assumes that all major nations would become linked together through coalitions of consortia. No single actor could dominate the rest, especially in the context of détente, disarmament, strategic nuclear defense systems, and massive economic rehabilitation of poor nations. Japan's role in this scenario would be to increase its foreign aid, organize and represent the interests of Asian nations more effectively in multilateral organizations, and help to mediate conflicts.
4. *Pax Nipponica.* In this scenario, Japan's economic power would be preeminent, and Japan would in effect replace America as the global balancer of power.

It seems unlikely that Japan could replace the United States as a hegemonic power in the short or medium term.[5] It does not have the political will to support such a development, and it will become even more vulnerable and dependent upon other nations as it expands economically.

It is possible that Japan could drift away from the existing U.S.–Japan security alliance and toward nonalignment or "positive neutrality."[6] It could also organize an Asian–Pacific economic bloc which excluded the United States.

But another possibility that should be considered, in spite of the current trade tensions between the United States and Japan, is a "leadership coalition,"[7] with America providing strategic and political leadership and Japan playing an enhanced role in investment, foreign aid, and technology transfer. Such a relationship would be more likely than strategic integration of the two nations, which would entail coordinated military deployment and regional military alliance building.[8]

One of the principal factors affecting Japan's global role is the increasing degree of international economic interdependence. Some analysts have predicted the emergence of a "bigemony" in which the United States and Japan would continue to integrate their two economies and thereby "manage" the world economy.[9] (Together, the United States and Japan produce approximately 40 percent of the world's total output of goods and services.) Such a development does not seem likely in the short to medium term because of the variety of trade tensions between the two nations.

More likely is the continued development of regionalism in Northeast Asia—primarily economic but also including some political and security interests. To a certain extent, there is a "soft regionalism" emerging among Japan, China, and South Korea.[10] The United States is a player in this process but is not dominant. Throughout the Cold War, America exercised its influence in this region primarily through bilateral relationships.

In terms of enhancing a stable balance of power, the dilemma for the United States is whether to: (1) continue its bilateral relationships; (2) develop additional bilateral connections that cut across rivalries in the region; (3) assist in the development of regional attitudes and processes as an active member of the regional groups; or (4) remain as a military balancer of power.[11]

Imbalance and complexity often lead to international conflict.[12] International politics specialists traditionally have analyzed change in terms of balance of power assumptions. To what extent is this still valid? While some argue that the dynamics of interdependence have outdated balance of power theory, that conclusion is far from substantiated.[13] It does seem clear that "dominance" is no longer possible, but "leadership" is. Therefore the tensions between Japan and America are over degrees of leadership, rather than over preeminence. International politics, then, has become a process of varying degrees of conflict as well as cooperation among interdependent partners.[14]

In Northeast Asia, stability will be dependent upon continued economic growth and the inclusion of communist nations in the modernization process. In other words, interdependence is the prerequisite for a stable region. But there is still a major role for a military balancer of power (the United States); otherwise, arms races will escalate, thereby dampening economic growth.

America's role as a regional balancer of power is unusual, since there is no common enemy in Northeast Asia. The region's security concerns are quite complex and are linked as well to the general concept of interdependence. In particular, Japan faces several security concerns: (1) uncertainty about the impact of internal changes in the former Soviet Union and about the medium-term trends of its foreign policy; (2) substantial upgrading of Russian military power in Asia; (3) potential threats to regional stability from North Korea; (4) acts of terrorism in the region; and (5) uncertain transitions in China.[15]

Along with the security treaty with the United States, Japan has relied on advanced military technology to enhance its own national defense as well as to begin building a framework for regional defense. It has concentrated upon air defenses, antisubmarine war capabilities, surface naval forces to protect sea lines of communication, and advanced technology for sensor systems and for command, control, and communications.[16]

Until there is a comprehensive arms control regime in Northeast Asia, Japan faces approximately 390,000 Russian troops, 2,430 warplanes, and 840 naval vessels concentrated in various areas near Japan.[17] The Northern territories, islands claimed by both countries but controlled by the former Soviet Union, are heavily fortified with troops and fighter jets.

Japan and many other Asian nations are still concerned about the potential long-term hegemonic ambitions of both China and Russia as well as the uncertainty about North Korea's intentions. In this context, the United States is still expected to play at least a medium-term task as balancer of power or power broker. Such a role should enhance regional stability, prevent the development of a security vacuum, and preclude the creation of any regional hegemony.[18]

Over the past decade, Japan has steadily expanded its concept of defense. For example, in 1982 it decided to accept the urging of the United States to defend the sea-lanes 1000 miles from Japan. In 1985 it adopted a plan to increase its air and naval forces, and in 1989 it breached its self-imposed 1 percent of GNP limit for defense expenditures.

It seems clear that Japan's concept of security will continue to expand from a junior partnership with the United States into a regional "system." Beginning with its theory of "comprehensive security,"[19] Japan will likely insist on strategic reciprocity with America and will experiment with regional security organizations as well as economic ones.

Tokyo currently pays about 40 percent of the cost of keeping U.S. forces in Japan. The increasing capabilities of Japan's own defense forces have made it possible for America to stretch its own resources to other areas in the Pacific basin.[20] Of course, critics in America have insisted that Japan increase its share to 100 percent. But that type of pressure overlooks Japan's role in defending the region, its potential contributions in technology transfer, and most importantly the possible role of Japan as one of coresponsibility for a global security system.[21] For example, its technologies relating to optical scanning and instrumentation could enable Japan to make a substantial contribution to a space-based global defense system.[22]

In order to encourage Japan to increase its sense of responsibility for regional and even global defense, there must be a heightened degree of "strategic reciprocity," in which America would share power and decision-making authority with its key allies—and even with some of its erstwhile adversaries.[23] Such a relationship would emphasize "global partnership" and "sharing collective responsibility."[24] It would entail "joint leadership within a multilateral framework."[25]

"Comprehensive security" encompasses political and economic factors as well as military ones. The crucial core of this concept is that national security is linked to global security; and nonmilitary elements are as important as military ones.[26] The objectives of this approach are to minimize and defuse threats, reduce vulnerabilities, protect market access, and enhance the stability of the international environment.[27]

In order to create such an environment, Japan has been active in fostering the development of regionalization. For instance, the Asia–Pacific Economic Cooperation effort, begun in 1989, could help to coordinate trade, investment, and economic policy issues.[28] Further, in April 1991 the North Pacific Cooperative Security Dialogue was convened. It is intended to encourage the habit of dialogue and to prevent the current shifts in the balance of power from creating new conflicts. It could also lay the groundwork for confidence-building measures at first and then the development of a comprehensive arms control regime.[29]

Japan's position in the international arena is truly unique: it is the world's first "peace superpower."[30] It can exercise this role in the following ways: (1) promoting a regional arms control regime; (2) mediating conflicts; (3) taking a leading role in foreign aid and investment projects; (4) supporting United Nations activities; (5) sustaining non-exclusive Asian Rim regional economic organizations; and (6) assisting the development of a global space-based defense system.

Both Japan and Germany are economically dynamic and socially cohesive nations. They are examples of leading countries that can exercise "soft" (or persuasive) power in the changing international system, instead of "hard" power (the ability to dominate others).[31] Soft power implies the exercise of cooperative, partnership-type relations; concentration on economic means to achieve goals; and acceptance of supranational structures to deal with a variety of international issues, such as Third World development and environmental reconstruction.[32]

In 1989–90, Japan allocated over $10 billion for foreign aid, replacing America as the world's most generous donor. The purpose of Japanese assistance has been primarily commercial in nature, but as Japan expands its global political role, foreign aid will be a crucial device.[33] However, some experts caution that Japan is unlikely to pursue such a role since it has never transcended its own national interests in the past.[34] In the midst of a rapidly changing international system, though, it seems more persuasive to assume that Japan will *have* to set its own agenda for global relationships.

Japan has clearly asserted its presence in multilateral frameworks. In April 1991 it dispatched a flotilla of six vessels (four minesweepers and two support vessels) to the Persian Gulf to assist in mine clearing operations. This was Japan's first overseas commitment of military personnel on a non-training mission since World War II.[35] In addition, Japan sent a civilian delegation to help negotiate the Iran–Iraq cease fire and participated in U.N. civilian peacekeeping missions in Asia, Africa, Central America, and the Middle East.[36]

A potential future role for Japan would be as a major participant in an arms control regime. Such a system would use space-based communications, over-the-horizon radar, satellite intelligence, sensors, and theater missile defense systems.[37] Japan could help construct the technical means for this comprehensive arms control regime. It would be based on two principal pillars: surveillance and defense.

Such an approach would seem more beneficial to other nations in the Asia–Pacific region than for Japan to continue to expand its military forces in terms of power projection. That would alarm many of Japan's neighbors and probably cause a major arms race.[38] Instead, Japan could contribute to regional stability by supporting confidence-building measures as well as surveillance, interdiction, and defensive systems—especially as the United States continues to draw down its military forces in the Pacific.

Conclusion

Japan's role in the post-Cold War era is unique: it is the world's first "peace superpower." To fulfill that task, Japan will seek to develop joint leadership with the United States and other major powers, concentrate on economic means to achieve goals associated with stability, and assist in the development of supranational structures to deal with such international issues as Third World development and environmental reconstruction.

Instead of allowing tensions over trade issues and over degrees of leadership to intensify, it would be more beneficial for both Japan and America to accelerate a "leadership coalition" of the two nations. The United States will pursue its role as a balancer of power in Northeast Asia in the short to medium term. In the long term, however, the keys to stability in that region are: (1) enhanced regional cooperation to coordinate trade, investment, and economic policy issues; and (2) a comprehensive arms control regime.

The Commonwealth of Independent States, China, and North Korea should be encouraged to participate in regional economic organizations as well as in confidence-building measures. Such habits of dialogue and cooperation could eventually lead to a broader security framework—based on surveillance and defensive systems, rather than on bilateral and multilateral security treaties.[39]

Japan's contribution to an arms control system would be to construct some of the technical components for space-based communications, satellite surveillance, and theater missile defense. In addition, Japan and the United States could cooperate with the former Soviet Union in developing confidence-building measures to reduce "mutual uncertainty, miscalculation, or misinterpretation."[40]

Notes

1. Edwin O. Reischauer Center for East Asian Studies, *The United States and Japan in 1991: Discord or Dialogue?* (Washington, DC: Nitze School of Advanced International Studies, 1991), pp. 90–91.

2. Ibid., p. 90.

3. Gerald Segal, *Rethinking the Pacific* (New York: Oxford University Press, 1990), p. 385.

4. Takashi Inogachi, "Japan's Global Role in a Multipolar World," in Shafiqul Islam (ed.), *Yen for Development: Japanese Foreign Aid and the Politics of Burden-Sharing* (New York: Council on Foreign Relations Press, 1991), pp. 13–18.

5. See Reinhard Drifte, *Japan's Foreign Policy* (New York: Council on Foreign Relations Press, 1990), pp. 108–9.

6. See Raymond F. Wylie, "The US–Japanese Security Relationship: Retrospect and Prospect," in Paul Gordon Lauren and Raymond F. Wylie (eds.), *Destinies Shared: U.S.–Japanese Relations* (Boulder, CO: Westview Press, 1989), p. 70.

7. Ronald A. Morse, "Managing Cooperation Toward the Twenty-First Century," in Lauren and Wylie, *Destinies Shared,* p. 179.

8. See Raymond F. Wylie, *Destinies Shared,* pp. 68–69.

9. C. Fred Bergsten, quoted by Tashi Inoguchi, "Four Japanese Scenarios for the Future," in Kathleen Newland (ed.), *The International Relations of Japan* (New York: St. Martin's Press, 1990), pp. 213–14.

10. Robert A. Scalapino, quoted in R. Mark Bean, *Cooperative Security in Northeast Asia: A China-Japan-South Korea Coalition Approach* (Washington, DC: National Defense University, 1990), p. 28.

11. See Catherine McArdle Kelleher, "The Changing Currency of Power: Paper I: The Future Nature of U.S. Influence in Western Europe and Northeast Asia," *Adelphi Papers,* No. 256 (Winter 1990/91), pp. 23–36.

12. *The Economist,* Vol. 316, No. 7672 (September 15, 1990), p. 19.

13. See Hanns W. Maull, "Germany and Japan: The New Civilian Powers," *Foreign Affairs,* Vol. 69, No. 5 (Winter 1990/91), p. 101.

14. Ibid.

15. See Wendy Frieman and J. J. Martin, "Changing Military Technology and its Impact on Asian Pacific Security," in Robert A. Scalapino et al. (eds.), *Asian Security Issues: Regional and Global* (Berkeley, CA: Institute of East Asian Studies, 1988), p. 99.

16. Ibid., p. 97.

17. Stephen P. Gibert and William M. Carpenter, *East Asia in American Foreign Policy* (New York: Institute of Asian Studies, St. John's University, 1990), p. 51.

18. William J. Crowe, Jr. and Alan D. Romberg, "Rethinking Security in the Pacific," *Foreign Affairs,* Vol. 70, No. 2 (Spring 1991), p. 124.

19. See Robert H. Puckett, "Comprehensive Security in Northeast Asia," *Asian Profile,* Vol. 18, No. 6 (December 1990), pp. 509–14.

20. See Gerald Segal, *The Soviet Union and the Pacific* (Boston: Unwin Hyman, 1990), p. 9.

21. Islam, *Yen for Development,* p. 92.

22. Andrew Mack and Paul Keal, *Security and Arms Control in the North Pacific* (Winchester, MA: Allen & Unwin, Inc., 1988), p. A15.

23. Edward A. Olsen, quoted in Bean, *Cooperative Security in Northeast Asia,* pp. 168–69.

24. Shafiqul Islam, "Beyond Burden-Sharing: Economics and Politics of Japanese Foreign Aid," in Islam, *Yen for Development,* p. 216.

25. Ibid.

26. Puckett, "Comprehensive Security in Northeast Asia," p. 509.

27. Davis B. Bobrow and Stephen R. Hill, "Non-Military Determinants of Military Budgets: The Japanese Case," *International Studies Quarterly,* Vol. 35, No. 1 (March 1991), pp. 42–43.

28. Bernard K. Gordon, "The Asian–Pacific Rim: Success at a Price," *Foreign Affairs,* Vol. 70, No. 1, 1991, p. 157.

29. *The Economist,* April 13, 1991, p. 35.

30. Islam, "Beyond Burden-Sharing," p. 223.

31. Maull, "Germany and Japan," p. 92.

32. Ibid., pp. 92–93.

33. Donald C. Hellmann, "Contemporary U.S.–Japan Security Relations: Old Myths, New Realities," in June Teufel Dreyer (ed.), *Asian–Pacific Regional Security* (Washington, DC: The Washington Institute Press, 1990), p. 61.

34. Ibid., pp. 62–63.

35. *Japan Report,* Vol. 37, No. 2 (May 1991), pp. 1, 8.

36. Edwin O. Resichauer Center for East Asian Studies, *The United States and Japan in 1990: A New World Environment* (Washington, DC: Nitze School of Advanced International Studies, 1990), pp. 32–33.

37. Dreyer, *Asian–Pacific Regional Security,* p. 20; Crowe and

Romberg, "Rethinking Security in the Pacific," pp. 128–29; Islam, "Beyond Burden-Sharing", p. 93.

38. See Kelleher, "The Changing Currency of Paper," p. 31; Drifte, *Japan's Foreign Policy*, pp. 40–41.

39. For a substantially different view, see Segal, *The Soviet Union and the Pacific,* pp. 126–27.

40. Robert M. Orr, Jr., *The Emergence of Japan's Foreign Aid Power* (New York: Columbia University Press, 1990), p. 489.

Moscow, Seoul, and Soviet Strategy in the Asia–Pacific Region*

Stephen Blank

The Soviet rapprochement with South Korea was a major diplomatic event of 1990. By consummating this breakthrough, Moscow established itself as an inevitable "dialogue partner" in any future settlement of the Korean conflict. Resolution of this conflict or at least steps towards that end were Moscow's highest priority in Asia in 1990.[1] The opening of relations with the ROK has led Soviet commentators to claim that Moscow has decisively forsworn its former ideologically-based policies of socialist internationalism. Policies based on that formula effactually transferred class struggle onto the international stage. Now a policy of realism that is based on concrete interests will be applied.[2]

Arms control agreements for the Korean peninsula are one of those interests. Indeed, they appear to be a major interest in Soviet Asian policy. Inasmuch as the inter-Korean border remains the most dangerous one in terms of superpower proxies and hence superpower conflict, a Soviet policy based on new thinking

---

*The views expressed here do not represent those of the U.S. Army, Defense Department, or the U.S. Government. This article is an expanded version of "Soviet Perspectives on Arms Control in the Korean Peninsula," *Korean Journal of Defense Analysis,* Vol. 3, No. 1 (Summer 1991).

and conflict resolution by political means indicates Soviet goals for Korea and Asia. Therefore, careful examination of Soviet perspectives on Korean arms control shed light upon the depth of the change in the Soviet Asian policy.

Since Moscow does not directly participate in the balance of military forces on the peninsula, these perspectives are not couched in a formal negotiating paper or position. Rather, they emerge from the statements of Soviet politicians or spokesmen. And many of them antedate cross recognition with Seoul by several years. The oft proclaimed goals of denuclearization of Asia, creation of nuclear-free zones in Korea and across the Asia–Pacific region, a freeze in air and naval forces there, and restrictions on naval force movements and deployments all go back to Gorbachev's Vladivostok and Krasnoyarsk speeches in 1986 and 1988. So, too, do many of the suggestions for confidence-building measures concerning superpower naval forces and for withdrawal of U.S. forces from Korea as part of a settlement there. As a matter of fact, many of these calls for arms control and confidence-building measures, as well as for collective security in Asia, date back to the Brezhnev period. Thus, the continuity in Soviet arms control and security proposals is substantial notwithstanding the genuine innovations of new thinking.[3] These arms control proposals are tirelessly repeated by Soviet spokesmen, and clearly a Korean settlement process would involve a substantial Soviet effort to realize the proposals either in part or in whole.[4]

For example, Mikhail Nossov, writing in 1989 in *Asian Survey,* stated that Moscow supports the DPRK's proposals for converting all Korea into a nuclear-free zone, joint reductions of forces to 100,000 men by 1992 in harmony with a phased withdrawal of U.S. forces and nuclear weapons from the South, high-level talks on military affairs between the DPRK, ROK, and the United States, and negotiations on political affairs between the DPRK and ROK.[5] Soviet proposals for arms control and conflict resolution are also part of the process of bilateral and multilateral agreements among interested states, which would then provide the scaffolding for an overall collective security scheme in Asia that Moscow has insistently advocated since 1969.[6]

Finally, it must also be noted that both Soviet and PRC figures have privately and publicly told the United States that they would not support an attack by Pyongyang on South Korea. More recently it appears that both the PRC and the USSR, by virtue of their rapprochement, have successfully brought pressure to bear on North Korea to open up its nuclear program for international inspection, although this is not conclusive as of mid-1991. They also apparently agreed that both Koreas could enter the U.N. separately and that this would enable the U.N. to play a positive role in peaceful resolution of the Korean conflict.[7] However, this formulation leaves unresolved the issue of ambiguous situations that could lead to conflict, and does not fully assuage ROK security concerns.[8]

Nevertheless, in moving towards rapprochement with Seoul, Moscow has taken care to support North Korea's arms control initiatives concerning denuclearization, withdrawal of American troops, and so on, even as it publicly finds merit in South Korean positions.[9] Thus Moscow has publicly embraced the ongoing inter-Korean dialogue even as it supports the North Korean disarmament proposals of May 1990.[10] But it also churns out propaganda stating that unilateral American withdrawals from South Korea do not change the "essential nature" of U.S. force presence there in perpetuating the peninsula's devisions.[11]

In short, Moscow is attempting to perform a remarkable balancing act. On the one hand, it has supported the North Korean proposals for disarmament of 1988 (described below).[12] On the other hand, Soviet analysts were already developing ideas about confidence-building measures either between the superpowers or the two Korean states, which they published in 1989–90 in a conscious effort to prod Pyongyang further. In 1984 and 1988, Pyongyang advocated a tripartite conference with itself, Seoul, and Washington. First, American troops would have to withdraw as part of a bilateral North Korean–U.S. treaty. Then Pyongyang would be willing to issue a nonaggression pact with Seoul. Not only did this establish a precedent of bypassing Seoul, it also bypassed Moscow, Beijing, and Tokyo, a point that Moscow in particular must have forcefully brought home to North Korea.[13] During 1989–90, it also became clear that Seoul's success in achieving political stability at home as well as recognition from Soviet and East European states, plus Soviet pressure to climb aboard the train of new thinking, threatened Pyongyang with isolation and continuing economic stagnation if it did not alter its proposals.

Soviet suggestions, voiced in both domestic and foreign forums, included troop pullbacks from present lines, advance notification of maneuvers, regular meetings of military officials, reconfiguring units at the forward edge of the battlefield to reduce potential surprise offensives, creation of zones on both sides of the DMZ where offensive weapons would be banned, and hot line type mechanisms for communication between both sides' national command authorities to facilitate crisis management and prevent crisis escalation. The superpowers would duly begin a dialogue on Korea (which they did) to explore confidence-building measures, the reduction of threats to security, and/or stabilizing measures that could ultimately bring about a six-power dialogue including the two Koreas, the superpowers, China, and Japan.[14] A basic objective of the Soviet program was and remains the effort to secure, through this or an analogous process, a recognized status as guarantor of a peaceful status quo in all of Korea, thus giving it a veto over subsequent changes in the "regime" established on the peninsula.[15] That has been a constant and long-standing global aim of the USSR in all regional conflicts in Asia, Africa, and Latin America, and would secure by politics what has been denied to the USSR by its previous policy of intimidation and arms build-ups.

By May 1990 Pyongyang, probably under pressure from Moscow and Beijing, offered a program for both Korean states to issue a nonaggression pact, limit the size of exercises, give prior notification of maneuvers, establish a hot line between both sides' military commanders, halt qualitative improvement of military equipment including foreign arms, and develop means of verifying arms reductions including on-site inspections and removal of military equipment from the DMZ. Direct talks between the two Koreas, rather than with Washington first, would also take place.[16] By September 1990, after the Roh Tae Woo–Gorbachev meeting in San Francisco, the Far Eastern tour of then-Foreign Minister Shevarnadze, and the tremendous pressure of the impending Soviet recognition of Seoul, North Korea moved still further. It modified its insistence on immediate American troop withdrawals to a phased withdrawal of troops and nuclear weapons, and a three-stage inter-Korean troop reduction program to less than 100,000 men each by 1993–94. Once again the DPRK called for hot lines between military commanders and now added a call for a joint military group to resolve border disputes, on-site inspection, and the creation of a neutral force to monitor arms control in the DMZ.[17]

Moscow has clearly supported and encouraged North Korea's evolutionary policy and the DPRK's search for contacts with Tokyo and Washington that its own move towards Seoul has generated. Indeed, it appears that the Soviet move towards the South has led the DPRK to approach Japan in much faster and franker fashion, going directly to the major issues on their agenda, than Japan wishes to go.[18] Soviet spokesmen are also offering proposals for further arms control measures that appear to trade withdrawal of American nuclear weapons for North Korean adherence to a nonnuclear status under International Atomic Energy Agency verification, a moratorium on superpower arms transfers to both Korean states, and a reduction in both size and frequency of the ROK–U.S. "Team Spirit" maneuvers.[19] In this regard Moscow is trying to turn North Korea's obduracy on military and nuclear issues against the United States. Accordingly, one recent Soviet commentary states that,

> While trying to rule out even the possibility of the development of nuclear weapons in the DPRK, we should not forget that there is an excess of such weapons at U.S. military bases in the southern part of the peninsula. The demand of the DPRK to have them removed is quite legitimate. Given the current situation, the U.S. view of these weapons as containing the superior combat might of North Korea appears obsolete.[20]

In another article outlining these ideas, Ivanov also appears to hint at Soviet political goals in the region. He sees Moscow as outstripping every other foreign power in its ties with both sides and as the leading force pushing from without for a settlement of the Korean conflict. According to Ivanov, Moscow is already acting out the roles of a mediator suitable to both Korean sides as well as to the United States and of the force prodding Pyongyang into a DPRK "Sudpolitik" to the West.[21]

Moscow, Seoul, and Pyongyang: An Intricate Minuet

The Soviet initiative to South Korea is part of a broader political strategy to win for itself an unassailable position as an *interlocu-*

teur valable (reliable interlocutor or dialogue partner) in the solution of all security problems in Northeast Asia and beyond. That process serves as a prologue to the grand denouement of the collective security goal pushed since 1969 and in renovated form since 1985–86. Soviet recognition of South Korea is the USSR's entry fee to discussions of Korean and Asian security and also payment for access to South Korea's economic assistance, which is now vital to Moscow. And having paid those fees, Moscow is now reaping its benefits. Seoul has begun negotiations with Moscow on a friendship treaty whose terms are as yet unannounced and has agreed to sponsor Moscow's introduction as member in the Asian–Pacific Economic Council (APEC). The latter is a long-held ambition of Moscow and marks a decisive breach of the formerly closed world of Asian–Pacific economic organizations.[22] Thus, Soviet arms control programs are not disinterested even if they represent a considerable progress in tone and seriousness from past proposals.

But the fact that these proposals to avert conflict are in Moscow's broader interest hardly disqualifies them on those grounds. We may take it for granted that all such positions contain a large dose of self-interested motivation. A second observation is that historically Soviet arms control proposals have been advanced as part of an overall broader security strategy that is both political and military in its content and shape. Again, that consideration hardly disqualifies Soviet proposals as such or distinguishes them from other states' proposals. Rather, to assess the goals Moscow has in mind and what would occur should these proposals be realized, we need to look at them in the context of overall security policies in Northeast Asia.

First of all, despite Soviet proposals to freeze existing naval and air forces and to degrade both sides' strategic weapons, the fact is that the forthcoming strategic arms treaty's ramifications at sea directly contravene that injunction by allowing both sides a maximum limit of 880 sea launched cruise missiles. That figure is almost four times the then-Soviet capability and could never be achieved without a crippling naval arms race. Given South Korea's and Japan's proximity to Soviet naval platforms and the greater number of American strategic targets located near the Pacific coast, as well as the fact that SLCMs are the Soviet navy's major strike force, this augmentation of Soviet strategic capability for nuclear blackmail in the Pacific was not encouraging.[23]

A second disquieting factor is that Soviet commentators appear to have a double standard regarding Western, and specifically American, disarmament compared to their attitude towards the PRC's arms reductions. In this context it should be noted that the PRC between 1985–87 and the USSR between 1987 and 1990 unilaterally reduced the ground forces along their borders, a series of moves that received deserved acclaim. But insofar as Washington's unilateral arms reduction moves in the last few years are concerned, the tone changes. Chufrin observes that some Soviet observers remain suspicious of American disarmament moves because they are unilateral and can be reversed unilaterally as well. This factor is never mentioned regarding PRC moves. And because the American moves are unilateral, they do not answer to Soviet interests and concerns. Accordingly, the fact of unilateral American arms control actions proves that comprehensive and formal superpower arms control agreements are necessary, something that Chufrin never mentioned regarding the PRC.[24]

A third reason for skepticism concerns Soviet–North Korean relations. Chufrin again exaggerated when he said that Moscow had informed North Korea of its course in 1990 and, having not received a proper answer, decided to recognize South Korea so that its policy *would no longer be held hostage to Pyongyang* (my emphasis).[25] He exaggerated because more recently Deputy Foreign Minister Rogachev explicitly advised that Moscow support Kim Il Sung's May 1990 and New Year's Day 1991 proposals for reducing tension, confidence-building measures and a confederation in Korea.[26] Moscow's foreign propaganda now supports again Pyongyang's proposals for a nuclear-free Korea and hides the fact that Kim's 1991 New Year's Day speech represented an apparent step backward, strongly implying the need for immediate withdrawal of U.S. troops from Korea.[27] Soviet military media also strongly supported Pyongyang's breaking off talks with the ROK because of the 1991 "Team Spirit" maneuvers, even though the forces involved were reduced in numbers to lessen tensions.[28]

The Soviet Policy Debate

What appeared to be the problem was the ambivalent or divided Soviet power struggle over Korean policy and policy towards

Soviet allies in particular. While there is no love lost for Kim Il Sung in Moscow, it does appear that national security policymakers were deeply divided about Korean policy and about the "burden of empire," i.e., support of socialist states and socialist internationalism, in general. Chufrin's exclamations to the contrary, Soviet commentators admit that there was a deep division between old and new thinkers regarding Korean policy. The old thinkers supported Socialist allies and the structure of confrontation in Northeast Asia, saw the West as irrevocably hostile, and therefore recommended a continuing military policy of strength and force acquisition. Ideologically grounded, this approach saw Korea and other regional conflicts as zero-sum games where any concession detracts from Socialist strength and wins no plaudits from an always hostile imperialist bloc.[29]

The new thinkers claim to see things in terms of facts, (so Mikheyev claims), and view North Korea as an obstacle to Soviet policy, especially given the pressing economic need for ties to the ROK's dynamic economy. They exhibit a remarkable confidence that North Korea will fume and threaten but will eventually have nowhere to go other than to negotiate with the ROK and the world in a serious fashion. Indeed, one analyst baldly states that if and when Kim Chong Il, the son and designated successor of Kim Il Sung, comes to power, he will be overthrown within weeks by a combination of the army and the people.[30]

Naturally, the struggle between these factions holds back fresh Soviet approaches as Moscow gropes to find a military-political solution. Moreover, if the early 1991 rightward trend in Soviet politics had won, the military would have been strengthened; and we would have seen the kind of backsliding associated with Rogachev's support for the harder line proposals of January 1991 and for the cancellation of negotiations ostensibly because of Team Spirit. Soviet pressure on Pyongyang to open up its nuclear program, its support for Seoul's and Pyongyang's separate entry to the U.N., and the talks leading to a friendship treaty with Seoul did not invalidate the fact of continuing support for those proposals or for military assistance as mentioned below.

The gap between the two rival Soviet approaches can be summed up in Mikheyev's analyses of the problems each faces. The old thinkers cannot, he said, extricate the USSR from the contradiction of support for North Korean reunification programs on the basis of a confrontation with the South and the visible threat such policy contains to Soviet strategic interests. It also should be noted that their confrontational approach also applies to Japan and would thereby, according to the new thinkers, their critics, benefit only the United States and Japan. Sarkisov has argued that only conservatives will benefit from continuing tensions with Japan where each side perceives the other as "insidious samurais" or "wicked bears." Another reformer, Kunadze, argues that the only ones who win are those Japanese forces who are unwilling to open up to Moscow.[31]

The new thinkers even regard the prospect of a democratic, united, and neutral Korea, even if it subtracts from the world community, as a net plus because it balances the great powers in the East, especially Japan and China, promotes Moscow's security interests, and neutralizes the American deterrent. It also would promote a lucrative economic association for Moscow, which could be used to pressure Japan.[32] Other reformers believe that in order for the USSR to dissolve the Tokyo-Seoul-Washington military axis, a principled approach to resolving political and security questions in the region is called for. That approach would then make military partnership with America less profitable and commence the breakdown of this coalition, with military and economic benefit to Moscow due to its new access to Japan and South Korea. Though these states are American allies, they are by no means totally dependent upon Washington, and Moscow should lessen tensions to encourage that independence.[33] Or, as Vsevolod Ovchinnikov wrote in *Pravda,* due to the dialogues between Seoul and Beijing and among Seoul, Beijing, and Moscow,

> It is becoming increasingly hard to substantiate the need for the U.S. military presence on the Korean peninsula. Is it possible to speak seriously of a threat from the North, which has half the population of the South and whose economic potential is several times smaller? Whereas it used to be maintained that "two Communist giants" were standing behind Pyongyang's back, the improvement in Seoul's relations with Moscow and Beijing renders that conclusion groundless.[34]

South Korean analysts are well aware as well that even the new thinking is anti-American and anti-Japanese in its thrust and that its ultimate goals are to undermine the rationale for American military power in Asia with a consequent diplomatic *renversement des alliances* (reversal of alliances). Lee Haeng Goo, a member of the ROK's National Assembly, observed for a Soviet audience that Moscow believes that the purpose of keeping American troops in Korea (and for that matter anywhere in the Asia–Pacific region) is to prevent both Moscow and China from pursuing a more active role in the region.[35] Moscow does perceive the American forces in South Korea and Japan as direct threats to its security, and the belligerent period of the early eighties, where Moscow saw itself threatened by a warlike encirclement policy of the United States, is not forgotten.[36]

Thus, its attempts to solve the problem of American forward deployment in Asia by political means has taken the form of calling for and undertaking disarmament moves vis-à-vis China and the ROK. The apparent primacy of the military and right wing in then-Soviet policy raised the specter that these confident assertions of men like Mikheyev would not be tested. Rather, the high rate of military assistance will continue despite all the acrimony currently plaguing Soviet–North Korean relations. In contrast to the reformers, who allegedly place little stock in the American threat or in Chinese initiatives counter to Soviet interests, these groups supporting Kim Il Sung followed along a script written at least since 1984. Japanese security experts claim that in 1990 alone Moscow offered North Korea six top-of-the-line MiG-29 and ten Su-25 fighters similar to the ROK's A-10s. They also claim that not only are aircraft and support for ground forces being transmitted but also support for expansion of nuclear facilities.[37] Soviet Deputy Premier Maslyukov announced on January 22, 1991 in Seoul that while Moscow supports expansion of ties with the ROK, it "fully appreciates" Pyongyang's demand that the United States pledge not to use its locally-based nuclear weapons against Pyongyang in return for North Korean cessation of its nuclear program or opening up of the country to IAEA inspection (which Japan also wants). Moreover, Moscow will continue to support North Korea with unspecified "defensive weapons" under the terms of the 1961 treaty with Pyongyang.[38] Moscow announced in April, 1991 that it would not provide nuclear assistance to Pyongyang if it did not comply with IAEA inspection procedures, adding a new factor to this process, one apparently supported as well by the PRC. What this means for arms transfers of a conventional type will only be fully revealed with the passage of time.

Maslyukov also stressed that the weapons delivered by Moscow in the past are also strictly "defensive weapons."[39] These weapons transfers were part of a policy that has increasingly relied upon the transfer of state-of-the-art Soviet equipment as a means of enforcing Moscow's capability of deterring both attacks upon and apparently from North Korea. Those arms transfers have also been accompanied by expansion of the naval and air anchorages of the USSR to include North Korean ports, thus giving Moscow enhanced scope for aerial and naval maneuvers throughout the range of these weapons systems. Soviet policy, whether a form of deterrence through arms supply or something else, has also taken the shape of a substantial increase in Soviet–North Korean economic interchange. That economic relationship, like the military one, has the net effect of augmenting DPRK dependence upon the planned Soviet economy even as Moscow wrecks that economy at home and insists at the same time upon North Korean reforms. Thus Moscow's policy appears to Western observers as paradoxical and inconsistent if not dangerous.[40]

On the one hand, Moscow now insists upon payment in convertible currency for its goods and apparently its arms as well, and is loath to continue the annual naval maneuvers with Pyongyang that took place from 1986–90.[41] Polemics between the states occur with increasing openness, vitriol, and regularity and Soviet writers freely attack Pyongyang and Kim's super-Orwellian state. For its part North Korea, according to both Soviet and Japanese press reports, told Shevarnadze in September 1990 that if Moscow recognized Seoul it would reject inspection of its nuclear facilities, feel unbound by any pledges not to create nuclear weapons, support Japan's claims of the Kurile Islands against Moscow, and formally activate the provisions of its 1961 treaty with Moscow that stipulates that Moscow come to DPRK assistance (or vice versa) not only when one partner is attacked, but also when he finds himself "in a condition of war."[42] Yet despite this, Soviet spokesmen fully supported DPRK proposals for arms control, continued to export high grade weaponry to it, and maintained a burgeoning economic relationship with it.[43] Moreover, there has been no word from Moscow, despite foreign press speculation, concerning a renegotiation and amendment of the Pyongyang–Moscow treaty.[44]

The suggestions raised by the reformers and *Institutchiki* (members of foreign policy institutes) also are not as innocuous as they look. Suggestions calling upon the USSR and the United States to devise joint mediating postures for the two Koreas or to settle Asia–Pacific arms control issues without consideration of regional balances among Japan, China, and the two Koreas also have a mischievous impact. They are intended to divide the Western allies and introduce suspicions of sellouts or superpower condominiums. These proposals also point towards acceptance of the principle that the security of so-called "small states"—the two Koreas—may be negotiated in their absence and over their heads by the superpowers. Thus, Soviet suggestions like Vadim Medvedev's that Moscow mediate a denuclearization and disarmament of the Pacific in talks with Japan and the United States, and that it had already discussed denuclearizing the Korean peninsula with Washington, triggered a strong response by South Korea's foreign minister.

Choe Ho-Chung dismissed the idea that the surrounding powers could guarantee Korean security by themselves.[45] Therefore, it is hardly surprising that the author of the Soviet article spelling out Pyongyang's threats to Moscow in September 1990 rightly commented that Moscow's position approaches absurdity. It supports Pyongyang's conventional arms program and supported the nuclear weapons program while it avidly pursues maximum economic-political relations with Seoul and is subjected to harsh polemics from Pyongyang. Pyongyang, for its part, shows no sign of changing its violent longings for unification. Therefore the author calls for an "excessive dose of skepticism" about the initial hints of a thaw in the situation in the Korean peninsula and an end to the Cold War there.[46] Accordingly, actual Soviet policy casts great doubt upon the viability of Soviet arms control and CBM proposals and corroborates Donald Zagoria's observations:

> Moreover, many of Gorbachev's arms controls proposals are so patently one-sided that they inspire the belief that they must be largely intended for propaganda. The proposal to establish nuclear-free zones in Korea, Southeast Asia, and the South Pacific, where naval forces are stationed, while omitting any mention of the Sea of Okhotsk, the Kamchatka Peninsula, and the Soviet Union's own Maritime

Province, where nuclear forces are stationed, is one such example.[47]

Thus, despite claims to the contrary about the new thinking having a universal, expanding sum content, in Asia the fact remains that Soviet security proposals are one-sided in their effects. They aim to replace the U.S.-led security system, not with a multipolar one but with one of Soviet authorship stacked against both the United States and Japan. Soviet officials admit that their security proposals for Asia, outlined in the Vladivostok and Khabarovsk speeches of 1986 and 1988 and more recently in Gorbachev's April 17, 1991 speech to the Japanese Diet and ex-Foreign Minister Shevarnadze's speech to the Vladivostok conference in September, 1990, derive directly from the Helsinki process. These proposals are therefore irrelevant to Asian concerns, and cannot inspire confidence.[48]

Some Soviet analysts appear to understand that these proposals cannot really serve as a basis for genuine progress beyond opening the door to Seoul. Aleksandr' Bovin, a usually authoritative commentator, recently observed that Soviet Asian policy has been hurt by its addiction to a party propaganda approach over political and diplomatic ones. Great words and statements are not followed by actions but rather by "modest and bashful" commitments and a failure to take serious practical steps to realize declarations of intent. That is the main reason for suspicion about Soviet concepts of Asian collective security. And Bovin is not alone in his views. R. Sh. Aliev, something of a maverick Soviet Japanologist, made a similar observation in *Acta Slavica Iaponica* in 1989–90.[49] In the same issue of that journal, Jonathan Haslam also commented on this point. He noted that:

> In theory Gorbachev's consciousness of Russia's technological backwardness and his recognition of the urgent need for economic reform at home have led to a novel emphasis on the importance of economics in Moscow's assessment of international relations. Yet those domestic reforms above all require peace on all fronts abroad and it is this that has produced a foreign policy curiously at odds with the immediate needs of economic reconstruction. The priority abroad has hitherto been not that of winning over foreign investors—and Japanese investment could make all

the difference to the future of the Soviet Far East—but that of disarming Russia's adversaries. Where priorities have to be made, immediate requirements give way to the overriding primacy of the security imperative. In practice Moscow's foreign policy—despite the primacy of *Perestroika* at home—still assumes bombs are more important than bonds; that those with sufficient military capability to threaten the homeland merit greater concessions than those unable to do so.[50]

Hence the move to eject foreign troops from South Korea and defuse the war danger there—the greatest one in all Asia where superpower interests are concerned.

Bovin also observes, as have others before him, that the test of Soviet intentions in Asia is its own domestic behavior.[51] Failure to reform the economy, massive arrears to Asian businessmen, and persisting macroeconomic disequilibria, of which the most elemental is the nonconvertible currency, cannot be resolved by the neo-Stalinist policies of xenophobia and confiscatory policies followed by covert inflation currently in the ascendancy in Moscow.[52] Such policies only reinforce precisely those sectors most interested in pursuing a military-based policy in support of Kim Il Sung and the 1980s buildup in Asia. A clear domestic linkage between domestic and foreign policy emerged, and support for Third World allies was a major plank of the reactionaries, something discernible from Maslyukov's remarks above.

Bovin's argument here corresponds to Haslam's and explains why policy towards Japan has not yet broken free of the constraints of conservatives. While they see Japan as a threat in the future or more likely to the degree that it associates itself with American security and defense policies, they are counting on the explosion of American–Japanese rivalry to bring Tokyo to Moscow. Concessions to South Korea are part of that process that sets the ROK and a potentially united peninsula against Japan and forces it to approach Moscow.[53] Domestic reform is not so urgent, and certainly Moscow need not make concessions to Tokyo. But in Korea the danger of war and the irrationality of Pyongyang, coupled with uncertainty regarding its future policies, are good reasons for the current rapprochement with Seoul. In Korea, as opposed to Japan, there are grounds for convergence of reformers' and conservatives' policies, even if their ultimate vectors sharply diverge as they move away from the Korean peninsula.

Soviet Military Strategy and the Two Koreas

The Soviet arms control proposals remain one-sided and insufficient to the real task of disarmament and peace on the Korean peninsula. They ultimately attest to a policy that still elevates unilateral military-political considerations over economic interests and the international "balance of interests." It remains necessary to inquire as to the role arms control proposals play in overall Soviet security strategy when they are examined in the context of ongoing military programs. From a geostrategic standpoint, the Korean peninsula is vital to Soviet naval and air forces as a gateway either into Soviet air and naval bases in Asia or from them into the Pacific. The presence of strong ROK and U.S. forces, including perhaps tactical nuclear weapons and SSBNs, as well as similar situations in Japan, confront Moscow with grave threats should it try to threaten either Japan or the ROK.

By the same token the advent of naval missile technology and of air-delivered weapons has, in conjunction with Soviet naval doctrine, inescapably forced Moscow into a threatening posture versus those areas. Since naval and naval air platforms can deliver missiles from thousands of miles away with great accuracy and Soviet doctrine at present identifies the SLCM threat in particular as the gravest threat to it, Moscow perceives a necessity to construct counters or deterrents against such platforms. Secondly, Soviet doctrine and force-building programs increasingly stress that without air superiority, mobility at sea and control of the sea are inconceivable. For Moscow to defend its submarine and surface vessel bastions in the Pacific it must construct a far-flung air and air defense network combining both powerful shore and deck based aircraft and anti-ship missiles, either from the air, submarine, or surface vessels. Soviet naval construction programs have not slackened and stress this combination of submarines, carriers, and steadily upgraded land-based and sea-based aircraft along with carriers (what Moscow calls carriers for its fleet are more like heavy cruisers with carrier-based air forces). All these programs point to a strategic decision that in the Far

East, Moscow must consistently strive to expand its defense envelope, a policy which inescapably entails creating a naval, air, and air defense umbrella over both Korean states and Japan.[54]

Doctrinally, such a program evokes the idea of a limited theater of command or control of the sea that had emerged in Soviet thinking by 1946 and, according to some analysts, remains operative until now.[55] This notion entails both command or control of a portion of the naval or oceanic theater of strategic military operations (*Teatr' Voennykh Deistvii* in Russian) where the strategic operations will occur and also securing maximum freedom of movement to conduct the component parts of this operation. The greater the threat from sea-based platforms, including naval air, becomes, the more investment must be made against this threat and the more the strategic role of the naval, air defense, and air assets involved grows.

In this connection two other features must also be kept in mind. Many military leaders were Far Easterners, veterans of the Far Eastern TVD, even if they were army men as was traditionally the case. It is quite likely that they were not inclined to minimize the military dimensions of security policy throughout the region but had quite the opposite viewpoint. The second point is that despite the cutbacks in Soviet military spending, statements by high level officials such as Defense Minister Marshal Yazov and Chief of Staff Moiseyev indicated the navy's relative exemption from those cuts. In his speech to the Royal United Service Institute in 1989, Yazov stressed that priority was being given, for example, to antisubmarine and anti-air assets.[56] Traditionally these are submarines and both shore- and sea-based aircraft that the Soviets labelled offensive Western programs. That these platforms would now be Soviet ones does not change this fact.[57]

The political analogue of this effort to expand the reach of Soviet military power in naval and air forces is the effort to break up the threat, that is the so-called Tokyo-Seoul-Washington axis. One way is to stimulate a political process that leads to American demilitarization while Soviet assets at home remain relatively untouched. The new Soviet Asian policy is tailored precisely to this objective. It seeks to insert Moscow into Asian security processes in any conceivable way, either by multilateral or bilateral accords, while attempting to exploit Japanese–Korean tensions with each other and with the United States and to maintain influence over both Koreas or a united if neutral Korea.[58] At the same time, the prior and concurrent Sino–Soviet normalization, coupled with China's burgeoning trade with Seoul and disinclination to see conflict in Korea, constrains both Pyongyang and Beijing in their mutual relationship. The military benefit of the tie with China is also quite significant. Any potential Asian horizontal escalation or encirclement undertaken by the West needed the Chinese land forces and perhaps bases for air and naval assets to threaten Soviet Asian assets seriously. With China gone as a threat, the Soviets now have strategic depth for their naval and air bases on the Pacific coast. In addition, their military ties with Pyongyang offer opportunities for expanding their systems' range of activity and safety from a receding American forward deployment.

Should the united and neutral Korea envisioned by Mikheev come to pass, it would necessarily entail the departure of U.S. forces. And, by virtue of its burgeoning trade with Moscow, that state would be loath to offend the USSR. It would also be a counter to both Japan and China in economics, politics, and security policy. It would not be difficult for Moscow to always have at least one partner in Asia from among those three states and a judicious diplomacy could easily manage the level of rivalry among them. However, the continuation of the split on the Korean peninsula, a so-called German solution of mutual recognition, mutual membership in the U.N., and a diminution of tensions between the two Koreas, would also bring about reduction of the American presence. That situation would also give Moscow a *droit de regard* over the peninsula's affairs by virtue of its trade connections to both Koreas and its control over North Korean military development. In either case, Moscow hopes to stimulate a process that satisfies its traditional aims that the Korean peninsula not be a hostile base against Russia and in some sense be receptive to its influence.[59]

Thus, while reformers' and traditional military opinions divide in many ways, neither provides a sound basis for going beyond recognition of Seoul to satisfactory arms control and security processes in the Asia–Pacific region. For the moment, until Moscow decides its internal and external course more decisively, caution is warranted. The gains to date for the West from the new policy are impressive and real, but they do not mitigate the fact that behind the rhetoric of collective security and new thinking lies a sophisticated pursuit of self-interest and an unflagging military modernization. Whether Moscow adopts old or new thinking in its security policies generally and to the two Korean states in particular, its perceived self-interest ultimately is still antagonistic to the West (Japan, ROK, United States). That perception of interest is based on a desire to minimize American power from the region and on the simplistic view that American power in the area is directed solely against the USSR.

By the same token, the optimistic assumptions of the new thinkers concerning North Korea's supposed lack of alternatives remain unproven. First, at least some South Korean analysts can make a convincing argument that the ineptitude of Japan's approach to better relations with Pyongyang that was triggered by Moscow's moves toward Seoul could complicate the search for peace rather than abet it.[60] Secondly, many ROK analyses of the North Korean negotiating position see little or nothing that is new. These proposals still aim to unhinge the ROK government and disarm it and remove the U.S. troops while opening up South Korea to North Korean political influence.[61]

All of the foregoing therefore requires caution in assessing Soviet proposals and bona fides as a mediator for the Korean conflict. Indeed, all of Soviet security policy is in a state of complete rethinking, as a desperate political struggle rages in Moscow over the future direction of the USSR. Ultimately what will decide Soviet foreign policy is the course of domestic policy there. The current reversion to neo-Stalinist and xenophobic economic policy in the Soviet Union not only imperils the future of the economic ties to South Korea, Japan, and ASEAN in which so much has been invested, it also has ominous portents for Soviet foreign and military policy in the region.

The most alarming recent trend was one celebrating various authoritarian models of economic development from which Moscow may choose. These models range from Pinochet's Chile, the Generals' South Korea, or the PRC to the somewhat less alarming models of Singapore or postwar Japan. Though little noted, this is a dangerous trend because each model's advocates also then advocate a priority relationship with that country. In other words, advocates of the Sino–Soviet entente are mainly in the military, as are those supporting Pyongyang. One analyst writes that he has the impression that the North Korean–Soviet alliance is restricted to the sphere of the general staffs of each country.[62]

172

Another Soviet analyst is even more explicit about Sino–Soviet relations. He observes that:

> It must be observed that among a section of military and party figures in both countries there are those who support a sharp increase in collaboration. Certain Soviet officials openly approved the Chinese Army's actions to "suppress the counterrevolutionary rebellion" in 1989. To the commanders of the Chinese Armed Forces, which were set up according to Soviet principles and equipped with weapons copied from Soviet models, it may appear only natural to make a "great leap forward" in modernization on the basis of very up-to-date equipment and technology from the USSR, sold, moreover, at very accessible prices. In both capitals, people still survive who advocate a return to the Stalin or Mao Zedong model of orthodox socialism and hope for ideological, political, and other assistance from their great neighbor in realizing their dream. They find equally unacceptable the necessary reforms, which they see as the "intrigues of world imperialism," and are prepared once again to shut themselves off from the outside world with "curtains."[63]

That example indicates the linkages between such lobbies both internationally and with regard to their countries' full domestic and foreign policy or security policy agendas. The advent of such lobbies that link domestic and foreign policy stances in the Asia–Pacific region add to the volatility and uncertainty of future Soviet or Chinese policies and add substantial force to the possibility of a primarily military-driven and overtly anti-Western policy in contrast to the more subtle policies of the recent past. Such an outcome is by no means excluded. For instance, Bovin recently observed that Gorbachev could not resolve the issue of the Northern territories and unfreeze Soviet–Japanese relationships because his hands were "literally tied and bound. Whatever the president wanted to do, it was clear that he could not do it."[64] Undoubtedly domestic constraints will play a considerable role in future Soviet policies. And as long as the domestic situation there is uncertain, so too will foreign policies be liable to sudden shifts or abortive initiatives. Thus, while change is the law of life for Moscow and Pyongyang, caution and skepticism are still warranted because progressive change in both capitals that really meets Korea's and Asia's needs is not yet an ordained law. For now such change is only a hope, and an unproven one at that.

Notes

1. Aleksei Bogaturov and Mikhail Nosov, "The Asia–Pacific Region and Soviet–American Relations," *International Affairs,* January 1990, pp. 109–12.

2. Gennady Chufrin, "The USSR and Asia–Pacific in 1990," *Asian Survey,* Vol. 31, No. 1, January 1991, p. 15.

3. Hiroshi Kimura, "The Soviet Proposal on Confidence-Building Measures and the Japanese Response," in Joshua D. Katz and Tilly C. Friedman-Lichtschein, editors, *Japan's New World Role* (Boulder, CO: Westview Press, 1985), pp. 81–104.

4. Yu-Nam Kim "Perestroika and the Security of the Korean Peninsula," *Korean Journal of Defense Analysis,* Vol. 1, No. 1, Summer 1989, p. 160; "Shevarnadze Speaks at Reception," *Foreign Broadcast Information Service Soviet Union* (henceforth *FBIS SU*), December 27, 1988, p. 12.

5. Mikhail G. Nossov, "The USSR and the Security of the Asia–Pacific Region," *Asian Survey,* Vol. 29, No. 3, March 1989, p. 257.

6. Stephen Blank, "Violins with a Touch of Brass: The Soviet Design for Collective Security in Asia," *Conflict,* Vol. 11, No. 1, March 1991, pp. 281–305; and Stephen Blank "Soviet Perspectives on Asian Security," *Asian Survey,* Vol. 31, No. 7, July 1991, pp. 646–61.

7. Edward Neilan, "North Korea Hints at Nuclear Inspection," *Washington Times,* May 29, 1991, p. 7; for the opposite view, see George Leopold and Naoaki Usui, "North Korea Rejects Reactor Probes," *Defense News,* May 27, 1991; see also "Sino–Soviet Summit Views Nuclear Weapons in North," *FBIS East Asia* (henceforth *FBIS EAS*), May 21, 1991, pp. 28–29; "PRC–USSR Discussion on Reunification Reported," *FBIS EAS,* May 22, 1991, p. 26; David E. Sanger, "North Korea Reluctantly Seeks U.N. Seat," *New York Times,* May 29, 1991, p. A3.

8. Thomas W. Robinson, "The Soviet Union and East Asia," in Edward A. Kolodziej and Roger E. Kanet, editors, *The Limits of Soviet Power in the Developing World* (Baltimore, MD: Johns Hopkins University Press, 1989), p. 192; Alan D. Romberg, *The United States, the Soviet Union, and Korea: Beyond Confrontation,* Critical Issues series, No. 1 (New York: Council on Foreign Relations, 1989), p. 15; "Moscow–Seoul Ties Seen as 'A Matter of Time,' " *FBIS SU,* March 13, 1990, p. 14, annex.

9. See the entire section entitled, "Shevarnadze Concludes Visit

to DPRK," *FBIS SU,* December 27, 1988, pp. 10–18; and "Shevarnadze States Position on Korean Unification," *FBIS SU,* October 3, 1990, p. 20.

10. "Shevarnadze States Position on Korean Unification," p. 20 and "Shevarandze Concludes Visit to DPRK," pp. 10–15.

11. "Shevarnadze States Position," p. 20; "Pravda Publishes Joint Declaration," *FBIS SU,* December 18, 1990, p. 17; "Rogachev Visits ROK to Examine Regional Issues," *FBIS SU,* January 8, 1991, p. 4.

12. "Shevarnadze Concludes Visit to DPRK," pp. 10–18; "Shevarnadze States Position," pp. 19–21.

13. Peggy L. Falkenheim, "Soviet Security Perceptions in Northeast Asia," paper presented to the twenty-second national convention of the American Association for the Advancement of Slavic Studies, Washington, DC, October 18, 1990, pp. 14–15.

14. Bogaturov and Nosov, "The Asia–Pacific Region," p. 112; Rajan Menon, "New Thinking and Northeast Asian Security," *Problems of Communism,* Vol. 37, No. 2, March-June 1989, pp. 25–27; Aleksei Bogaturov and Mikhail Nosov, "Koreiskii Aspekt," *Novoe Vremia,* No. 23, 1989, pp. 26–27; Nossov, "The USSR and the Security," pp. 256–59.

15. Nossov, "The USSR and the Security," p. 257.

16. Kim Yong Nam, "A View From Pyongyang," *International Affairs,* January, 1990, pp. 142–45; Falkenheim, "Soviet Security Perceptions," pp. 16–18.

17. "Impact of Gorbachev–No Tae-U Talks Discussed," *FBIS SU,* July 12, 1990, pp. 12–13.

18. "Commentary Assesses DPRK–Japan Talks," *FBIS SU,* May 22, 1991, p. 6.

19. Falkenheim, "Soviet Security Perceptions," pp. 16–18.

20. "Significance, Effects of Cheju Talks Eyed," *FBIS SU,* May 3, 1991, p. 26.

21. "USSR's Role in East Asia Viewed," *Joint Publications Research Service* (henceforth *JPRS*) January 8, 1991, p. 34, translation of *Mirovaya Ekonomikai Mezhdunarodnye Otnosheniia,* No. 9, September 1990.

22. "Significance, Effects of Cheku Talks Eyed," p. 27.

23. "USSR's Role in East Asia Viewed," pp. 33–34.

24. Sheldon W. Simon, "Security and Uncertainty in the North Pacific," *Korean Journal of Defense Analysis,* Vol. 2, No. 2, Winter 1990, p. 95.

25. Chufrin, "The USSR and Asia–Pacific in 1990," p. 18.

26. Ibid., p. 17.

27. "Good Bilateral Ties with DPRK, ROK Sought," *FBIS SU,* February 21, 1991, pp. 4–6.

28. " 'Full Text' of Kim Il-Song's New Year Speech," *FBIS EAS,* January 2, 1991, pp. 6–12.

29. Civilian analysts, however, take a more balanced view, e.g., "Suspension of ROK–DPRK Premier Talks Regretted," *FBIS SU,* February 20, 1991, p. 3.

30. Vasilii Mikheev, "The Korean Problem in Future," *International Affairs,* September, 1989, pp. 143–44; Vasily V. Mikheev, "A Korean Settlement: New Political Thinking vs. Old Political Ambitions," *Korea and World Affairs,* Vol. 13, No. 4, Winter 1989, pp. 677–81; "USSR Not to Veto Separate ROK UN Admission," *FBIS SU,* October 25, 1990, p. 2 annex; "Soviet Official on Developing Seoul–Moscow Ties," *FBIS EAS,* December 21, 1990, pp. 16–18; Constantine V. Pleshakov, "Republic of Korea–USSR Relations: Psychological Choices and Political Challenges," *Korea and World Affairs,* Vol. 14, No. 4, Winter 1990, p. 696.

31. "Impact of Territorial Issue on Japanese–Soviet Ties Discussed," *JPRS, Soviet International Affairs,* July 6, 1990, p. 23.

32. Nossov, "The USSR and the Security," p. 258; Mikheev, "The Korean Problem in Future," p. 144; Mikheev, "A Korean Settlement," pp. 677–81; "No 'Early End' to Cold War in Korea Predicted," *FBIS SU,* November 30, 1990, p. 24.

33. "Problems of Soviet Far East, Listed Reviewed," *FBIS SU,* September 17, 1990, pp. 50–51.

34. "Seen as 'Catalyst,' " *FBIS SU,* November 26, 1990, p. 9.

35. "Plans for the Future," *New Times,* No. 6, 1990, p. 19.

36. "Rogachev, TV Panel Discuss Asia–Pacific Issues," *FBIS SU,* August 2, 1989, p. 8; Michael McGwire, *Perestroika and Soviet National Security* (Washington, DC: Brookings Institution Press, 1991), pp. 232, 236, 389.

37. Pleshakov, "Republic of Korea–USSR Relations," pp. 696–97; "USSR Reportedly Continues Aid to North Korea," *FBIS EAS,* December 6, 1990, p. 22.

38. "Maslyukov Reiterates Support for North's Goals," *FBIS EAS,* January 24, 1991, p. 17.

39. Ibid., p. 18.

40. Romberg, *The United States, the Soviet Union, and Korea,* pp. 16–17; Byung-Joon Ahn, "South Korean–Soviet Relations: Issues and Prospects," *Korea and World Affairs,* Vol. 14, No. 4, Winter 1990, pp. 672–77.

41. Shim Jae Hoon, "Détente's Orphan," *Far Eastern Economic Review,* January 10, 1991, pp. 18–19; "Soviet Policies Causing 'Difficulties' for DPRK," *FBIS EAS,* August 16, 1990, p. 20; "Verbal War Between North, USSR Heats Up," *FBIS EAS,* December 26, 1990, pp. 29–30.

42. Pleshakov, "Republic of Korea–USSR Relations," p. 697;

"DPRK Warns Moscow on Setting up Ties with ROK," *FBIS EAS,* January 2, 1991, pp. 2–3; "No 'Early End' to Cold War in Koreas Predicted," p. 24.

43. "Soviets Want to Turn Korean Peninsula into N-Free Zone," *Korea Times,* November 23, 1990, p. 1; "Soviet Sparks Nuclear-Free Korea Discussion," *FBIS EAS,* November 28, 1990, p. 16; "USSR's Role in East Asia Viewed," p. 35.

44. "Reporter on DPRK–USSR Friendship Treaty," *FBIS EAS,* July 10, 1990, pp. 32–33.

45. "USSR's Role in East Asia Viewed," p. 35; Mikheev, "The Korean Problem in Future," pp. 139–43; Bogaturov and Nosov, "The Asia–Pacific Region," pp. 109–12; Mikhail L. Titarenko, "Asian and Korean Security and Stability," *Korea and World Affairs,* Vol. 13, No. 3, Summer 1989, p. 293–94.

46. "No 'Early End' to Cold War in Korea Predicted," p. 24.

47. Donald Zagoria, "Soviet Policy in East Asia: The Quest for Constructive Engagement," *Korean Journal of Defense Analysis,* Vol. 2, No. 1, Summer 1990, p. 21.

48. Mikhail Gorbachev, "USSR Foreign Relations with Japan," *Vital Speeches of the Day,* vol. 57, No. 15, May 15, 1991, pp. 454–55; "Rogachev, TV Panel Discuss Asia–Pacific Issues," pp. 4–10; Blank, "Soviet Perspectives on Asian Security."

49. "Bovin Views Ties with Korea, China, Japan," *FBIS SU,* October 23, 1990, p. 7; "Soviet Policy in Asia–Pacific Viewed," *JPRS,* January 8, 1991, p. 23, translation of *Mirovaya Ekonomika i Mezhdunarodnve Otnosheniia,* No. 9, September 1990; R. Sh. Aliev, "Vneshnaia Politika Sovetskogo Soiuza v Vostochnoi Azil: Kriticheskii Analiz" *Acta Slavica Iaponica,* Vol. 8, 1990, pp. 67–84.

50. Jonathan Haslam, "Soviet Policy Toward Japan and Western Europe: What the Differences Reveal," *Acta Slavica Iaponica,* p. 113.

51. Aliev, "Vneshnaia Politika Sovetskoga," pp. 67–84; "Bovin Views Ties," p. 9.

52. Stephen Blank, "A Winter Storm in the Baltic: Operation Metel," in Susan L. Clark, editor, *The Soviet Military Factor in a Time of Change* (Boulder, CO: Westview Press, 1991), pp. 241–80.

53. Nossov, "The USSR and the Security," pp. 256–59; "Should the USSR Return Kuriles to Japan?," *Current Digest of the Soviet Press,* Vol. 58, No. 14, May 20, 1991, pp. 7–11; "Impact of Territorial Issue on Japanese–Soviet Ties Discussed," pp. 18–24; Mikheev, "A Korean Settlement," pp. 677–81.

54. Lt. General I. Perov, "The Aggressive Essence of New US and NATO Concepts," *Zarubezhnoe Voennoe Obozrenie,* February, 1988, pp. 7–17, Michael Rothenberg, trans.; Stephen Blank, "Carriers and Reasonable Sufficiency: The Soviet Debate," unpublished manuscript;

Derek da Cunha, *Soviet Naval Power in the Pacific* (Boulder, CO: Lynne Rienner Publishers, 1991); Aleksi G. Arbatov, "Arms Limitation and the Situation in the Asian–Pacific and Indian Ocean Regions," *Asian Survey,* Vol. 24, No. 11, November 1984, pp. 1109–16; Byung Kyu Kang, "Korea and Sea Lane Security," *Global Affairs,* Vol. 4, No. 3, Summer 1989, pp. 148–62; Joseph K. Woodard, "The Soviet Navy and Command of the Seas," *Global Affairs,* Vol. 4, No.2, Spring 1989, pp. 36–48; Hisatomo Matsukane, "Japan and Security of Sea Lanes," *Global Affairs,* Vol. 4, No. 2, pp. 49–64; Makoto Momoi, "The Emerging Strategic Environment and Prospects of Naval Arms Control in the Far East," *Korean Journal of Defense Analysis,* Vol. 1, No. 2, Winter 1989, pp. 61–66.

55. Robert W. Herrick, "Soviet Naval Strategy and Missions, 1946–1960," in Philip S. Gillette and Willard C. Frank, Jr., editors, *The Sources of Soviet Naval Conduct* (Lexington, MA: Lexington Books, 1990), pp. 165–91.

56. da Cunha, *Soviet Naval Power in the Pacific,* p. 247; "General Moiseyev on Cutting Defense Expenditures," *FBIS SU,* February 23, 1990, pp. 85–86; "General Moiseyev Discusses the Defense Budget," *FBIS SU,* February 26, 1990, p. 83; Stephen Blank, "The Heavenly Mission of Soviet Space Forces," *Defense Analysis,* Vol. 7, No. 1, March 1991, pp. 39–61; Blank, "Carriers and Reasonable Sufficiency."

57. Blank, "The Heavenly Mission."

58. Blank, "Violins with a Touch of Brass," Blank, "Soviet Perspectives on Asian Security."

59. Donald S. Zagoria, "The Superpowers and Korea," in Ilpyong J. Kim, editor, *The Strategic Triangle: China, the United States, and the Soviet Union* (New York: Paragon House Publishers, 1987), pp. 171–80.

60. Hong Nack Kim, "The Normalization of North Korean–Japanese Diplomatic Relations: Problems and Prospects," *Korea and World Affairs,* Vol. 14, No. 4, Winter 1990, pp. 664–70.

61. Dae-Sook Suh, "Changes in North Korea and Inter–Korean Relations," *Korea and World Affairs,* Vol. 14, No. 4, pp. 613–17, 621–23.

62. "Policy on Korean Unification Analyzed," *FBIS SU,* July 11, 1990, p. 12.

63. "Importance of Ties 'Not Exaggerated,' " *FBIS SU,* May 16, 1991, p. 13.

64. Aleksandr Bovin, "Japanese–Soviet Relations Must be Viewed in the Long Term Even Though President Gorbachev's Visit to Japan Bore No Immediate Results," *Mainichi Shimbun,* May 15, 1991, p. 6.

CHAPTER SEVEN

Japanese Policy Toward the Two Koreas in a Changing Security Environment

David Arase

I will argue that Japan has embarked on a cautious new policy toward the two Koreas characterized by a serious attempt to overcome bitter animosities between the Japanese and Korean peoples and, at the same time, gain a role in the settlement of the conflict on the Korean peninsula. The roots of this new policy are in the regional dynamic produced by the end of the Cold War and a new assertiveness by Japanese policymakers. The change has worked itself out through Japan's bilateral relations with the North and South. How these relations have been since the 1988 Seoul Olympics is described in order to draw more general conclusions about the motivations and future directions of Japanese policy.

Historical Background

Geography and history inextricably link the security of Japan and Korea. This linkage was illustrated as early as the thirteenth century when armies of the Mongol Empire launched from Korea two serious invasion attempts on Japan that failed only due to severe storms believed by the Japanese to have been *kamikaze*, or "divine winds." Early developments in Japan affected Korea as well. In 1592 the Japanese general Hideyoshi Toyotomi sent an invasion force of 150,000 to Korea where it slaughtered tens of thousands of Koreans. Hideyoshi's death in 1598 caused a Japanese withdrawal, but the brutality of this Japanese occupation is still remembered by Koreans today. Hideyoshi Toyotomi is widely regarded as being the second most-hated Japanese in Korea, surpassed only by Ito Hirobumi, the first Japanese governor of Korea after its incorporation into the Japanese Empire.

Japan's annexation of Korea in 1910 was the culmination of prewar Japan's security strategy up to that point. Meiji Japan's first major war was fought over the issue of influence in Korea, where Japan prevailed over China in the Sino–Japanese War (1895). To meet the subsequent Russian challenge to Japanese interests in Korea, Japan concluded the Anglo–Japanese alliance (1902) and achieved victory in the Russo–Japanese War (1905). After winning American recognition of Japanese predominance in Korea in the Taft–Katsura agreement (1907), Japan announced its formal annexation of Korea. This eventually led to the occupation of Manchuria in 1931, and subsequently to the Marco Polo Bridge Incident in 1937.

Postwar Japanese Policy Toward the Two Koreas

Defeat in World War II and incorporation of both Japan and the ROK into the U.S.-managed Cold War security system did not divorce Japan from Korean security issues but allowed Japan to be passive toward the Korean peninsula, since the U.S. presence there preserved Japan's security. Other factors such as Korean animosity toward the Japanese, Article Nine of the postwar Japanese Constitution, and popular Japanese resistance to remilitarization and exposure to the risk of another war also explain why Japan did not play an active role in peace and security issues on the Korean peninsula.[1] Thus, after regaining sovereignty in 1951 it took Japan fourteen years to normalize relations with South Korea, otherwise known as the Republic of Korea (ROK). Meanwhile, western alliance considerations did not allow Japan to recognize North Korea, otherwise known as the Democratic Peoples Republic of Korea (DPRK).

180

Japanese passivity toward affairs on the Korean peninsula did not signal the absence of a policy or lack of concern; rather, it reflected a policy choice dictated by domestic constraints and a desire to minimize its exposure to risk in a Cold War climate of great power military tension and ideological conflict.[2] The postwar legacy of Japanese militarism was important as well, for as Martin Weinstein observed, "Although the Cold War might have been expected to generate a degree of cohesion among Japan, South Korea, Nationalist China, and the Southeast Asian states, in fact the bitterness left behind from Japan's military aggression greatly retarded this process."[3]

Normalization with the ROK came finally in April 1965 because of leadership changes in both countries and new developments in the regional strategic environment. The accession to power of Park Chung-hee in 1961 brought in a less anti-Japanese leadership. In Japan, this development was welcomed. Park had served as a junior officer in the Japanese army and was viewed as someone with whom the Japanese could work. Park realized the ROK would need access to the Japanese economy to bolster the ROK's political and economic prospects, especially in view of the foreseen reduction of U.S. aid. Moreover, the economic crisis confronting the new regime gave Japan greater leverage in negotiating a more favorable war reparation settlement. This new willingness to move toward normalization surfaced at the June 1961 Kennedy–Ikeda summit, where Hayato Ikeda stated that "Japan and the United States must intensify economic aid to South Korea in order to bring about political stability there."[4]

A second factor motivating normalization was the fact that by the mid-1960s the ROK became a growing new market for Japanese exports. Finally, the regional security environment was affected by the intensification of the Vietnam War and the testing of a nuclear bomb by China in 1964. Both Korea and Japan came to acknowledge the merit behind U.S. pressure on both sides to normalize relations. For Byung-joon Ahn the strategic environment was the critical factor, for "what made Korea and Japan overcome [their] political and economic differences and psychological prejudices is the strategic relationship whereby each needs the other for its own security."[5]

The normalization agreement signed in 1965 called for $500 million in official development assistance (ODA) over a ten-year period, as well as an additional $300 million in commercial lending. Since then Japanese policy toward the two Koreas has been based on recognition of the ROK; nonrecognition of the DPRK; a willingness to participate heavily in the ROK economy (often portrayed as a contribution to ROK security); the maintenance of a modest trade relationship with the DPRK (dating from 1955); and an open-legged triangular security alignment whereby Japan and the ROK are indirectly linked by their respective bilateral treaties with the United States.

The strategic interdependence of the ROK and Japan was recognized implicitly by Japan in negotiations with the United States over the reversion of Okinawa when Japan agreed to the so-called "Korea clause" inserted in the Nixon–Sato joint communique of November 1969. It stated that the security of the ROK was "essential to Japan's own security."[6] This marked Japan's first official hint that the security of the ROK was linked to that of Japan.

Nonetheless, since then Japan has avoided any direct security commitments on the Korean peninsula and has relied on its economic resources to both support the ROK and create incentives for the DPRK to change its policies and intentions. This approach is, of course, premised on U.S. strategic predominance in Northeast Asia and a credible U.S. guarantee of Japan's security against unfavorable developments in the Korean peninsula.

The growth of bilateral economic ties after normalization has introduced certain imbalances in the Japan–ROK relationship. First, there is the imbalance between a broad and highly articulated economic dimension in contrast to the inchoate or implicit politico-strategic dimension. Second, within the economic dimension there are structural assymmetries in trade and investment which have become a chronic irritant in bilateral ties. The ROK's ranking as a supplier of Japan's imports rose from thirty-third in 1965 to tenth in 1975, while its ranking as a market for Japanese exports rose from thirteenth to fourth in the same period. By the 1980s the structure of the "interdependent" relationship was clear: Japan had the upper hand as the provider of needed aid, investment capital, and technology while South Korea suffered an unbroken and growing bilateral trade deficit with Japan since normalization.[7] In 1983 the ROK trade deficit with Japan actually exceeded (at 162 percent) the overall ROK trade deficit.[8]

The effect of the Nixon administration's rapprochement with China in 1972 on Japanese regional diplomacy was to prompt a move to a more "neutral" stance. Japan quickly normalized ties with China in 1972 and backed away from the commitment to the ROK implicit in the "Korea clause."[9] Japan interpreted the July 4, 1972 North–South communique on peaceful reunification as a sign of eased tension on the peninsula. Japanese Dietmen and journalists visited the DPRK starting in 1971, and a trade agreement was signed resulting in the rapid growth of two-way trade from only $59 million in 1971 to $361 million in 1974.

In this period, relations with the ROK deteriorated as a result of this and other factors. The imposition of the 1972 constitution and the assumption of autocratic power by Park hurt Japanese perceptions of the ROK, and this was followed by the kidnapping of Kim Dae Jung from a Tokyo hotel by the KCIA in August 1973, which caused an uproar in Japan. A year later South Korean sentiments were inflamed by an assassination attempt on President Park by a pro-DPRK Korean resident of Japan who managed to kill Park's wife using a gun stolen from an Osaka police station. Japanese officials put the blame on poor Korean security precautions, and then-Foreign Minister Kimura Toshio added fuel to the fire by saying that North Korea did not pose a threat to the South and that the ROK was not the only legitimate government on the peninsula.[10]

But the fall of Saigon in 1975 and Kim Il Sung's statement in Beijing in April of that year that the DPRK might resort to war to reunify the peninsula changed the strategic environment and caused Japan to reassess its Korea policy. Prime Minister Miki Takeo authorized a study of contingency plans for cooperation with the United States in the event of a military emergency. At his summit meeting with President Gerald Ford in August 1975, he confirmed the validity of the old Nixon–Sato "Korea clause" and took other actions such as cutting back economic and cultural relations with the DPRK and settling the Kim Dae Jung affair with the ROK. President Park welcomed this by stating that Japan should consolidate triangular strategic relations between the United States, Japan, and the ROK, and that it should give more economic aid to the ROK.

A kind of implicit ROK–Japan strategic partnership emerged as both sides shared concern over President Carter's proposal to withdraw U.S. troops from Korea. During his March 1977 talks with President Carter, Prime Minister Fukuda argued against a total U.S. ground troop pullout, and both Japan and the ROK were pleased by the eventual failure of this initiative. With the emergence of a new Soviet–Vietnamese partnership in 1978, the Vietnamese invasion of Cambodia, and an aggressive Soviet military buildup in Northeast Asia, Japan and the ROK formed a parliamentary group on security affairs and the director-general of the Japanese Self Defense Agency paid an unprecedented visit to the ROK in 1979. Increased perception of threat from the Soviet Union also facilitated the signing of the Sino–Japanese Friendship and Cooperation Treaty containing the "anti-hegemony clause" and the conclusion of a U.S.–Japan defense cooperation agreement.

What was conspicuously missing in Japan's diplomatic adjustments to a greater Soviet threat was a strengthening of security ties with the ROK. In 1981, new administrations in Washington and Seoul gave greater priority to security cooperation. In August 1981, Seoul requested Japan to recognize the ROK's contribution to Japan's security by giving South Korea $10 billion in economic assistance to be used in its fifth Five Year Plan (1982–87). The cabinet of Suzuki Zenko could not formulate a response despite U.S. pressure, and the negotiations ended when a controversy over Japanese textbooks intentionally altered by the government to downplay Japanese aggression in World War II dealt a blow to Korean–Japanese relations in the summer of 1982.

The start of a new phase in Japan–ROK relations began in January 1983 when the new Japanese prime minister, Nakasone, made an official visit to Seoul and pledged to extend some $4 billion in preferential loans as well as a promise to start a new political partnership with the ROK. Although the loans were not explicitly linked by Tokyo to security as the Koreans initially demanded, South Koreans justified the loans by referring to the ROK as Japan's first line of defense. Economic cooperation helped to improve the political relationship substantially.[11]

The 1983 Rangoon bombing may be seen in the context of the North's alarm over a perceived Seoul-Tokyo-Washington security axis, as can the May 1984 visit to the Soviet Union by Kim Il Sung, his first state visit there since 1961. Japanese–DPRK relations cooled after 1983 and in a rare 1984 Tass interview, Kim Il Sung put U.S. imperialism second to the threat of revived

Japanese militarism.[12] But if relations with the North deteriorated, the chance for consolidating a qualitatively new relationship with the ROK was lost when Emperor Hirohito expressed little more than vague regrets over the past when President Chun paid an official visit to Tokyo in September 1984.

Nonetheless, Nakasone and Chun stabilized the Japan–ROK relationship and set the parameters for Japanese policy toward the two Koreas to the end of the decade. Although Nakasone favored simultaneous seating of the two Koreas in the U.N. and some kind of cross-recognition formula in the belief that an isolated DPRK would be more dangerous, Japan nonetheless limited ties with the DPRK, moved closer to strategic alignment with the ROK and the United States, continued to apologize for the past, but would not go so far as to make an explicit commitment to ROK security.[13] Although some in Japan still wished better relations with the North, especially as the North was plainly eager to buy anything the Japanese would be willing to sell them, a tense strategic environment marked by incidents such as the 1987 KAL bombing by North Korean agents made it difficult for Japan to move in that direction.[14]

A New Turn in Japanese Policy

After the 1988 Seoul Olympics, a qualitatively different situation facilitated Japan's direct involvement in peace and security issues in the Korean peninsula. In 1990, the DPRK contacted the ruling Liberal Democratic Party (LDP) leadership through the intermediation of the JSP and renewed an earlier offer to return two Japanese sailors imprisoned by the DPRK on spying charges in exchange for the start of official talks with Japan. The offer was accepted and in September 1990 Kanemaru Shin, a senior leader in the LDP, flew to Pyongyang with Tanabe Makoto, vice-chair of the JSP (now renamed the Japan Social Democratic Party) and some thirteen government officials. Kanemaru gave Kim Il Sung a letter from Prime Minister Kaifu Toshiki containing expressions of regret over past unhappy relations, and on behalf of the LDP Kanemaru signed a declaration with Tanabe and Kim that promised normalization talks with the DPRK and monetary compensation for damage inflicted on Korea in both the prewar and postwar periods. In addition, an agreement to open direct flights and satellite communications was reached. In return Japan gained the release of two Japanese sailors imprisoned on spying charges by North Korea in 1983.

The Japanese opening to the DPRK appeared surprisingly narrow and awkward in that it seemed to offer the DPRK important concessions without gaining any promise of changed policies by the DPRK, and it was inconsistent with ROK and U.S. policies toward the North. The ROK objected to the communique signed by Kim Il Sung, Kanemaru, and Tanabe because of the promise of compensation for damages suffered by the DPRK in the postwar period, a consideration not given to the ROK at the time of normalization; and it denounced the idea of giving the DPRK compensation before normalization took place. In addition, no conditions regarding the inspection of nuclear facilities, the sponsorship of terrorism, progress in North–South talks, or tension reduction at the DMZ were attached to the compensation or normalization process, and this reportedly also raised concerns in the United States[15]

Fundamentally, the ROK was concerned lest Japan's initiative undercut its carefully planned strategy of forcing the DPRK into meaningful bilateral talks. The ROK feared that Japan would relieve the DPRK's isolation and give it enough money to allow it to resist external pressures for change. In addition, Japan's sudden initiative threatened the ROK's control over the peace process on the Korean peninsula, and some South Koreans even suspected that Japan's true objective was to keep the Koreans a weak and divided nation.

The Japanese response was that this initiative was not binding on the government of Japan since Kanemaru was merely a politician acting on his own initiative. When Kaifu paid an official visit to Seoul in early January 1991, he reassured the ROK by giving a pledge to accept all ROK demands regarding the Japan–DPRK normalization talks to start at the end of that month. Nonetheless, what concerned the South was the fact that the bureaucracy and all the political parties in Japan except for the Japanese Communist Party immediately welcomed the start of normalization talks as a step long past due.

The five main demands presented to Kaifu during his visit to Seoul were: full consultations with Seoul regarding Japan–DPRK normalization talks; Japanese support for progress in the North–South dialogue; a demand that Japan press the North to agree to nuclear inspections; no payment of compensation before normalization; and efforts to open up North Korean society to the outside world.[16] When official talks began in Pyongyang at the end of January 1991, the Japanese position reflected Kaifu's pledge. Yet a question remained: why did Japan ultimately honor Kanemaru's pledge to enter into normalization talks without preconditions?

Regardless of motive, the effect of the opening was clear: Japan now had a direct role in the ongoing effort to improve the peace and security situation in the Korean peninsula. Together with prime ministerial talks with the South, the Japan–DPRK talks began a process of opening up the North, which may promote pragmatic reform and ideological deradicalization. This has allowed both China and the Soviet Union to take a further step away from the DPRK without fear of leaving it in dangerous isolation. The talks not only gave Japan leverage over the North, but over other actors as well, for they must now involve Japan in the successful management of Korean affairs. Japan introduced conditions for normalization desired by the ROK and the United States, but to preserve its options Japan did not officially link its conditions to those of the ROK or the United States.

Changing Relations in Northeast Asia

One way to view the rapidly changing regional situation is to view the success of the ROK's "northern diplomacy." President Roh announced his initiative in July 1988 and it featured offers to reduce tensions and to start a high-level bilateral dialogue with the DPRK to improve trade and cultural relations. This was followed by Roh's October 1988 U.N. speech in which he also offered a North–South summit, a non-aggression declaration, and a six nation conference (the ROK, DPRK, United States, USSR, PRC, and Japan) on peace and arms control issues. To demonstrate good intentions and full coordination with the United States, during a visit to Washington ROK president Roh persuaded the United States to ease a few restrictions on relations with the North.[17] Toward the Soviet Union and China, the ROK used the offer of trade, investments, loans, and commercial technologies to improve the prospect for normalized relations.

The essence of northern diplomacy was to win normalized relations with China and the Soviet Union, and otherwise to isolate the DPRK in order to get it to accept an ROK offer of a high-level political dialogue and improved trade and cultural relations. A key premise was the ability of the ROK to coordinate policies with the United States and Japan while winning at least tacit support from the Soviet Union and China for this initiative. The hope was that an isolated DPRK with a deteriorating economy and no prospect for reunification through the use of force would have to settle differences with the ROK. By September 1990 there were signs of success: the ROK and DPRK were engaged in prime ministerial talks and the Soviets signed an agreement to normalize relations with the ROK, thus marking Soviet recognition of two separate states on the Korean peninsula. By agreeing in October 1990 to open a trade office in Seoul, China showed every indication of following the Soviet example and the ROK successfully gathered support for its admission to the U.N.

What gave the ROK hope for improved ties with the Soviet Union and China was the end of the Cold War, which implied a shared interest among the major powers to avoid war over a local conflict in the Korean peninsula. It also introduced a new element of fluidity since the old Moscow-Pyongyang versus the Seoul-Tokyo-Washington alignments (with some anti-Soviet participation by Beijing) became obsolete. The ROK's northern diplomacy enabled the ROK to seize the initiative in drawing a roadmap out of the Cold War period in a way that more or less served the major powers' interests while giving the ROK greater security, autonomy, and normalized diplomatic relations with the rest of the world outside the Korean peninsula.

That this opportunity existed was suggested by the successful holding of the Seoul Olympics in 1988 when only Nicaragua, the Seychelles, and Cuba honored the DPRK's request to boycott the event. The Seoul Olympics put on display the ROK's solid economic and national security achievements and strengthened its claim to legitimacy. By contrast the DPRK's absence—even as the Soviets and Chinese gladly participated—merely emphasized its own international isolation. The DPRK's eroding position was underlined by the fact that a day before the start of the Olympics, Gorbachev called for a six nation conference to discuss the situation on the Korean peninsula, and that afterwards the Soviets opened a trade office in Seoul.

In response to the ROK's northern diplomacy the DPRK sought to avert direct talks with the ROK, thwart Chinese and Soviet normalization with the ROK, and to open talks with the United States and Japan. With the exception of opening talks with Japan, the DPRK failed in all its objectives. Growing isolation and the need for hard currency to buy commodities previously given on concessional terms by the Soviets and China could explain why the DPRK agreed in July 1990 to North–South prime ministerial talks, as may a DPRK hope that these talks might bring diplomatic breakthroughs elsewhere.[18] The two rounds of talks actually held in 1990 implied that both parties accepted each other as legitimate and authoritative actors, even if they might not agree on an agenda for substantive negotiations.

The United States responded to DPRK overtures with small positive steps such as academic exchanges and diplomatic contacts with the DPRK, but the United States firmly resisted DPRK pleas for normalization talks unless and until it fulfilled the following conditions: inspection of nuclear facilities, disavowal of terrorism, progress in talks with the South, new confidence-building measures, and the return of MIA remains. These conditions were too steep, and so the DPRK turned to Japan after it was clear the United States would not deviate from the role assigned it in the ROK's northern diplomacy.

Meanwhile, in 1990 the United States announced its intention to reduce by 10 percent the amount of troops stationed in Asia within a three-year period, leaving open the possibility of further reductions if the regional climate was favorable. This meant an initial troop reduction of some five thousand men in Korea, and there was discussion about putting the top level of command of joint forces into Korean hands. This suggested that the United States would continue to play an important and responsible role, but would withdraw more forces if it helped reduce tension and improve stability, and would give over to the ROK the responsibility for actual management of security affairs on the Korean peninsula.

The flow of regional diplomacy, which in effect is redrawing the structure of relations in the region, has not put Japan in the mainstream of events or decision making. The fact that Japan has not been a central actor in the process is itself troubling to a Japan that wishes to be acknowledged as a great global actor and an arbiter of Asian affairs. Beyond this, however, the changed structure of relations must also raise concerns in Japan.

On the positive side, the new structure and dynamic in the region means Japan is less likely to become embroiled in a devastating war, and the general interest among nations in the region for enhanced economic cooperation gives Japan's economic power greater efficacy. On the negative side, after the threat of horizontal and vertical escalation is reduced, the United States may be less likely to intervene in or manage unresolved local conflicts. This must concern Japan because it has unresolved territorial disputes with all its neighbors and is heavily reliant upon a U.S. ability to protect Japan's broader security interests in Asia.

The end of the Cold War has affected the U.S.–Japan relationship by removing the anti-communist rationale for the U.S.–Japan Security Treaty. Both parties have had difficulty in finding a firm new basis for political partnership as demonstrated by the political frictions caused by the Persian Gulf crises of 1987 and 1990–91. At the same time, trade frictions now embrace a wider and more profound range of issues including high technology areas impinging on national security concerns. Looking into the future, different priorities in U.S. and Japanese regional agendas are bound to affect bilateral relations. Although the Security Treaty will likely last for the foreseeable future, Japan may seek to correct a perceived overreliance on the United States by developing a policy of more active and independent participation in regional peace and security issues.

This factor is compounded by the emergence of the ROK as a weighty regional actor. Its growing economic and military resources, effectively deployed through its northern diplomacy, have given it enough security and autonomy so that it can now turn its energies outward to define an active regional role for itself. According to the ROK's National Reunification Board, in 1989 the DPRK's GNP was one-tenth that of the ROK and the North's potential military manpower only half that of the South. A 1985 RAND Corp. report argued that by 1994 the military balance would shift "gradually and overwhelmingly" in favor of the South.[19] Aside from creating the prospect of a reunified Korean nation, it already has started playing an active economic partnership role with the Soviets and the Chinese, and because it has significant military capabilities it could engage in active security cooperation with others besides the United States. The emergence of the ROK as a new regional actor must concern Japan because the two countries still do not have relations that could be called close or friendly, and they have an unresolved territorial dispute over Takejima, or Tokto, an island in the Korean Straits.

Another aspect of the post-Cold War situation is that the Soviet military capability left intact in the Soviet Far East still overshadows that of Japan, and this may leave Japan in an exposed position in view of relaxed U.S. concern over a Soviet threat and an intractable Japanese–Soviet territorial dispute. The Soviet–Japanese relationship is the only regional major power relationship that has not markedly improved. Nonetheless, the visit by Gorbachev to Tokyo in April 1991 could only have occurred in the post-Cold War environment. The territorial dispute, however, is rooted in bilateral treaties and disputes going back over a century. It is a difficult bilateral issue that has grown in proportion as the Cold War has receded.

Here again Japan's post-Cold War prospects for close or friendly relations with a neighbor, in this case the Russian people, are clouded by the past. Moreover, the possible scenario of Soviet–ROK ties being stronger than Japan's ties with either one of them was suggested by the surprise Gorbachev–Roh meetings of June 1990 in San Francisco and of April 1991 immediately after Gorbachev's visit to Tokyo. The Japanese cannot afford to view this development with equanimity.

Japan may avoid being put at a disadvantage in the region by actively cultivating ties with China by means of economic cooperation. In return for Japan's willingness to supply China with official development assistance (ODA) and promote bilateral trade and investment despite events such as occurred at Tiananmen Square, it appears likely that the present regime is willing to forget the past and will rely more on Japan than the U.S. for help in achieving its post-Cold War strategic aims. Nonetheless, Japan cannot afford to be complacent, for it still has a territorial dispute with China over the Senkaku, or Tiaoyutai, Islands; and China reserves the right to use force to defend its sovereignty claims over these and other territories affecting Japan's vital sea-lanes such as Taiwan, the Paracel Islands and the Spratley Islands.

Thus, for Japan end of the Cold War has ushered in a new regional structure of relations that leaves it less threatened by general war but more exposed to local conflicts and in close proximity to neighbors with potent conventional military capabilities.

Factors Behind Japanese Normalization Talks with the DPRK

A changing balance of interrelated factors explains Japan's rather awkward and narrow opening to the DPRK. In contemplating Japan's long-term security interests in Korea the influential analyst Kamiya Fuji stated in 1980, "Whatever one may feel about the reunification of Korea, Japan's principal interest clearly lies in detente between North and South . . . The desirability of unification, as against maintenance of the present division, as a means of ensuring peace and stability does not lie within the scope of Japan's national interest."[20]

Today as the United States reduces its forces and the final fate of a divided Korean nation is being determined, Japan must be concerned about a more autonomous military actor next door whether or not reunification is actually achieved. A unified Korea could mean an advanced industrial nation with a population of 65 million and significant military capabilities unhindered by the constitutional limitations or the popular antiwar sentiments that constrain Japan. Yet even a secure and more autonomous ROK could greatly affect Japanese security. In sum, a new strategic actor in Northeast Asia may emerge in the post-Cold War period that has not had a very good historical relationship with Japan, and therefore how the Korean question is resolved is of vital interest to Japan.

There is also another way in which the security environment in Asia is changing, although this may be more to Japan's advantage by allowing it to influence peace and security issues more effectively. What helps define the post-Cold War period is the fact that all countries accept the need for outward-looking, market-oriented economic development. The desire for more international trade and investment has given all actors in East Asia, including the communist states, a shared motivation to settle regional conflicts and normalize relations with each other. It is this general desire for mutually beneficial economic relations that has been so successfully exploited by the ROK in its northern diplomacy.

This new environment gives Japan's wealth and technology more relevance to others' plans for reforming and upgrading their own economies. The degree of Japan's economic predominance over the rest of Asia may be seen in World Bank figures, which show Japan's GNP to be eight times greater than China's, and sixteen times greater than that of the ROK. Japan has three times the wealth of the combined GNP of the lower and middle-income countries of East Asia—even including China. The opening to the DPRK may indicate Japan's willingness to put this leverage to new use in areas of high-profile peace and security previously avoided by Japan.

Problems in Japan–ROK relations also may help explain Japan's normalization talks with the DPRK. The ROK's northern diplomacy relies on an ability to coordinate the policies of the United States and Japan toward the DPRK. Ironically, the May 1990 visit of Roh to Tokyo just before he headed on to Washington was intended to reinforce cooperation between Japan and the ROK, but it may have had the opposite effect at least temporarily.

The three major issues raised by the ROK during the Roh visit to Tokyo were the demand for an apology from the Japanese emperor for past mistreatment of the Korean people; the treatment of ethnic Koreans in Japan who were not allowed to be naturalized and were fingerprinted at the age of sixteen; and the problem of Korea's chronic trade deficit with Japan which in 1989 amounted to $3.5 billion. It is noteworthy that a request for Japanese cooperation with the ROK's northern diplomacy was not prominent, and this was perhaps an indication that this cooperation was taken for granted.

On all three main issues the Korean demands were only partially answered. The emperor expressed regret, but not a clear apology. The Japanese only promised to stop fingerprinting third generation Koreans, i.e., the children of Korean residents of Japan born after 1971, and this concession reportedly affected a total of only three ethnic Koreans in Japan. No concrete measures addressing the trade deficit issue emerged. The visit ended amicably, but the Japanese received no forewarning of Roh's impending meeting with Gorbachev just a few days after his departure from Tokyo.

Roh may have slighted the Japanese by keeping secret his upcoming meeting with Gorbachev in San Francisco. Beyond this, the Japanese were certainly annoyed when George Arbatov explained the Roh–Gorbachev meeting in terms of Soviet impatience with waiting for Japanese economic cooperation and the ability of ROK firms to fit the bill.[21] The lack of forewarning and consultation with Japan over events of vital Japanese concern must have been disturbing.

The Roh–Gorbachev meeting precipitated meetings between the Foreign Ministry, the LDP, and the SDP over Japanese relations with North Korea where they all agreed on the need to start talks.[22] Roh had stated before the Japanese Diet that he did not wish the isolation of North Korea, and this was taken to mean that talks with the DPRK would contribute to the easing of tensions on the peninsula. The message brought to Pyongyang by SDP leader Tanabe Makoto from Prime Minister Kaifu in July 1990 was that an LDP delegation would come to Pyongyang in September to have talks without any preconditions, although there was an understanding that the two imprisoned Japanese sailors would be released.

As mentioned above, the immediate ROK reaction to Japan's move was sharp and heated. Yet the Japanese opening to the DPRK meant that the South Koreans could no longer take Japan's cooperation for granted. The new message Japan wanted to drive home was that it wanted to bury the past and that it could be a valuable and trusted partner of the ROK in a broad range of Asian affairs. If this message was lost during the May visit to Tokyo by Roh, it was prominent at the November 1990 bilateral Japan–ROK ministerial meeting involving seven cabinet ministers from each side.

At the ministerial meeting Japan promised to end fingerprinting of all ethnic Koreans in Japan, and this issue was conclusively settled when Prime Minister Kaifu visited Seoul in January 1991. Japan also made promises to consult closely with the ROK over Japan's newly begun talks with the DPRK over normalization. In the area of economic cooperation Japan promised to include the ROK in the implementation of Japanese foreign aid projects, and both sides reached an agreement for Japan–ROK cooperation in giving development assistance in the Asia–Pacific region, especially among the Southeast Asian nations.

This emphasis on bilateral cooperation was broadened by the December 7 visit of Japanese Defense Agency head Ishikawa Yozo to the ROK where bilateral information and personnel exchanges were discussed,[23] and by Kaifu's January 1991 visit to Seoul where he and Roh agreed to seek an economic cooperation system in Asia in the face of growing trade protectionism and regionalism.[24]

This initiative in Japanese policy toward the ROK is part of Japan's response to the emerging post-Cold War order in Asia. It appears to be a genuine effort to overcome the burden of the past and to start a new meaningful bilateral relationship with the ROK over issues of shared interest and concern such as inter-Korean relations, regional security, regional economic cooperation, and the future of Japanese and ROK security policies. Japan's ability to push this new agenda of Japan–ROK cooperation was greatly enhanced by Japan's limited opening to the North.

Japan–DPRK Relations

Changes in bilateral relations with the DPRK also enter into the picture. In talks between Prime Minister Takeshita and President Roh at the start of the Olympics, the Japanese got the impression that they could play a significant role in opening up the North by gradually expanding bilateral relations. However, because of DPRK resistance to the idea of cross-recognition and vigorous anti-Japanese domestic propaganda line, they did not anticipate going as far as normalization talks. During the Seoul Olympics Japan lifted travel restrictions placed on the DPRK after the KAL bombing, and after Roh's October 1988 speech to the U.N. General Assembly the Japanese government expressed an interest to the DPRK in improving Japan–DPRK relations if the imprisoned Japanese sailors were freed. This message was delivered to Pyongyang by Soviet Foreign Minister Shevardnadze, who visited Tokyo in late 1988.[25]

In January 1989 North Korean Workers' Party representatives were allowed to attend the annual JSP convention, where they were assured Japan was interested in improving relations. Business delegations began travelling to the DPRK after a three-year break and in March 1989 then-Prime Minister Takeshita di-

195

rected an unprecedented apology for Japan's past behavior in Korea to the DPRK in a Diet statement. This was followed by an April 1989 JSP delegation visit to Pyongyang headed by Vice-Chair Tanabe Makoto, who had maintained personal contact with the DPRK leadership since 1985. Tanabe delivered a letter from Kanemaru Shin to Kim Il Sung expressing contrition over the past. Tanabe assured Kim that the Takeshita and Kanemaru expressions were sincere, and thus signalled the LDP's desire for improved relations. Kim Il Sung agreed to consider freeing the sailors on ''humanitarian grounds'' and invited an LDP delegation headed by Kanemaru to visit Pyongyang.

A variety of events in 1989 intervened to put off the trip, including the Tiananmen incident and the fall of Erich Honecker and Nicolae Ceaucescu in Eastern Europe, as well as the Recruit Scandal and an Upper House election in Japan. But according to the respected Japanese expert on Korea, Okonogi Masao, the meeting between Gorbachev and South Korean politician Kim Young-sam in March 1990, followed by the Gorbachev–Roh meeting of June, revived the idea of Japan–DPRK talks. At the request of the DPRK, Tanabe sent a JSP member to Pyongyang in early May to receive an invitation to Kanemaru to bring an LDP delegation to Pyongyang and perhaps gain the release of the imprisoned sailors.

This was followed up by a JSP member's visit to Pyongyang in July when it was decided that the Kanemaru visit would be a joint LDP–DSP mission to hold a meeting with the Korean Workers' Party leadership where agreement to hold official talks would be possible. A DPRK request that Kanemaru bring some kind of preliminary reparations package as a token of Japan's intentions to improve relations was represented by the North Korean front organization in Japan, the General Federation of Koreans in Japan, but they were met with the objection that official aid could not be made before official relations were established.[26]

Final preparations were made during a joint LDP–JSP delegation visit to Pyongyang in early September and the Japanese agreed that reparation issues would be discussed but warned that without official recognition nothing could be decided. To ensure the Kanemaru visit the North gave assurances that the imprisoned sailors would be freed if Kanemaru came to Pyongyang.[27]

The evidence suggests that the move by the North to seek normalization talks with Japan was not expected by the Japanese.

Yet during the Kanemaru visit on September 27 the DPRK suddenly reversed itself and proposed normalization talks with no preconditions even though normalization with Japan, a country recognizing the ROK, implied acceptance of the legitimacy of the ROK government and the division of the Korean people. The explanation given by the North to the Japanese was: (1) that international circumstances surrounding the North had changed; and (2) that the Japanese government would not grant official development assistance before normalization.[28]

Aside from its mounting economic difficulties and the need for new infusions of cash and technologies, made evident by the DPRK's inability to pay its foreign debts amounting to some $5 billion,[29] major setbacks suffered by the DPRK just before the Kanemaru visit may have forced it to rethink its position. It was clear that Chinese and Soviet recognition of the ROK was an impending *fait accompli*. This left DPRK policy in a shambles with no matching prospect that it would have new relations with the United States or Japan, a situation that could only please the ROK.

Viewed in this light normalization talks with Japan may have become desirable because they contained the prospect of Japanese aid and possibly a way to derail the ROK's northern diplomacy.[30] The two Japanese Foreign Ministry officials accompanying Kanemaru received the initial North Korean proposal for normalization talks without preconditions and they were reportedly greatly excited by the "historic moment." The LDP politicians accepted and took credit for being able to make a quick positive response to an unexpected proposal.[31]

Japanese Domestic Factors

Within Japanese society those actors perennially favoring normalization with the DPRK include the General Federation of Koreans in Japan *(Chōsōren)* accounting for one-third to one-half of Koreans in Japan, and the Socialist Democratic Party of Japan (SDP). These actors certainly played a crucial mediating role in events leading up to the Kanemaru visit, but they have neither direct access to policymaking nor the clout to move Japanese public opinion.

What is of greater significance in explaining Japan's change of policy toward the DPRK is the broad consensus among the government and the LDP over the desirability of eventual normalization with the DPRK. Normally the need to maintain a broad consensus among the bureaucracy, big business, the LDP, and popular opinion slows change—but in the case of Japan's opening of talks with the DPRK there was surprisingly little domestic controversy prior to the Kim-Kanemaru-Tanabe communique.

Mainstream analysts in Japan have long advocated adopting a special role in reducing tensions between the Koreas. The outlines of Japan's present policy were suggested as early as 1980 by Kamiya:

> Japan should take the lead with North Korea. I think of the process as one in which the U.S. initially assumes the major responsibility for dealing with Peking and Moscow on the Korea issue, while Japan is primarily responsible for Pyongyang. Talks . . . should focus on economic matters, as well as some political topics—such as the need for productive North–South talks . . . Japan should make a serious effort to expand its economic relations with North Korea, while continuing to place the highest priority on its relations with South Korea . . . Of course, a major purpose of this initiative would be to use Japanese economic power as a means of inducing Pyongyang to soften its confrontational foreign policy line.[32]

The broad agreement among the major domestic actors favoring an initiative toward the North does not mean, however, that there was a harmony of viewpoints among them. As explained by LDP Dietmember Ishii, who played the leading role in organizing the trip for the LDP, the substantive DPRK–LDP contacts were mediated by the JSP. In other words, they bypassed the Foreign Ministry. This understandably raised certain objections and reservations from the Foreign Ministry as it tried to protect its control over foreign policy, and it warned of the effect on relations with the United States and the ROK. The problem for the Foreign Ministry, however, was that besides Kanemaru other senior leaders in the LDP such as Noboru Takeshita and Abe Shintaro supported the existing initiative.

In contrast to the Foreign Ministry's caution, the JSP strongly advocated the interests of the DPRK and urged the conservatives to take advantage of a rare window of opportunity. The general position of the LDP was that it wished to take positive initiatives in foreign policy and it agreed with the JSP over the desirability of opening relations with the DPRK, but it also agreed with the Foreign Ministry over the need for caution. These different viewpoints were adjusted or put into an uneasy consensus in joint LDP–JSP–Foreign Ministry deliberations starting in May 1990 and in parallel LDP–Foreign Ministry deliberations starting in August.[33]

This process of opening to the DPRK needs to be put in the broader context of domestic opinion and Japan's foreign policy. A domestic debate over Japan's new role has been growing since the mid-1980s, when Japan emerged as the world's largest capital exporter and an important technological leader. Trade frictions— particularly with the United States—as well as the end of the Cold War and the Persian Gulf War have spurred Japan's search for a role beyond that of a merchant nation. Along with this, a blend of nationalistic pride and assertiveness has emerged, epitomized by the bestseller, *The Japan That Can Say 'No,'* authored by LDP Dietman Ishihara Shintaro and Morita Akio. The foreign policy emerging out of this ongoing debate emphasizes Japan's global economic importance, and this new Japanese nationalism expresses itself in aspirations for Asian political and economic leadership.

The search for a higher political profile has led to a desire for a direct role in the resolution of conflicts in Asia. Japan hosted a meeting of the warring Cambodian factions in June 1990 and followed this up with its own proposal for Cambodian reconciliation in early 1991. At the Tokyo meeting a senior Foreign Ministry official met skepticism over Japan's initiative by saying, "foreigners demand that Japan should contribute money to Indochina after the Cambodian issue is settled, but they tend to hinder Japan in taking an initiative or in playing a political role. This situation is absurd."[34] One cause of frustration for Japan's ambitions is that it is not a permanent member of the U.N. Security Council, which is managing the Cambodian peace process and will be important in brokering affairs in the Korean peninsula starting with the issue of U.N. membership for both North and South Korea.

One implication of Japan's desire for initiative and a higher political profile is that it may open differences between Japan and the United States in certain areas. In the Korean peninsula, the Japanese may share the U.S. and ROK desire to deny nuclear weapons to the DPRK, but may view with more concern the course of events on the Korean peninsula after the external powers have extricated themselves from the risk of conflict there.

Put in this context, Japan's initiatives toward the two Koreas fit into a broader general pattern. Japan's uncharacteristic eagerness to get involved in Korean peace and security affairs helps raise its profile as a leader in Asia contributing to peace. It also creates stronger ties with both Koreas, a task made more urgent by the end of the Cold War and the rapid transition to a new regional order in economics, politics, and security. Finally, it gives Japan more involvement in shaping its post-Cold War environment while marginally lessening reliance on the United States to protect Japanese interests.

Conclusion

From a certain viewpoint Japan's recent moves are consistent with a pattern in Japanese policy toward the two Koreas. When Japan perceives a lower risk of instability in the peninsula, Japan assumes a more equidistant position between the North and South. This can be observed in the 1951–65 period when Japan felt no great need to supplement U.S. efforts to stabilize the ROK, in the 1971–75 détente period, and today after the end of the Cold War. By opening talks with the DPRK, Japan is moving toward an equidistant, mediating role in the Korean peace process, something Japan has long desired.[35]

Another element of continuity is that Japanese policy is still based on the effective deployment of its economic power without the extension of any security guarantees or promises of military cooperation. Although there is a vigorous debate in Japan over the role of its Self Defense forces in international security and the peacekeeping efforts that may change the situation in the next few years, Japan is still unable to engage in overseas military cooperation due to restrictions imposed by Article Nine of the postwar constitution as well as the fears and suspicions of its Asian neighbors. The imbalance between Japan's economic and military capabilities shapes Japanese foreign policy in general, and constrains Japan's policy toward the two Koreas.

Japan's recent Korean initiatives, nevertheless, also mark a departure from past policies. Japan wants to be involved in the Korean peace process, even if it cannot make a military contribution. The opening to the DPRK demonstrates how in the post-Cold War environment Japan can and will use its economic resources to gain access to the diplomacy of regional conflict resolution. Making restitution to the North and starting broader ranging cooperation with the South also reflect Japan's need to settle differences with the Korean people and gain a partner in building a new regional order.

Yet Japan is entering unfamiliar areas of diplomacy where timing and coordination will be important. Japanese economic power and its application may not itself threaten the security environment, but as the awkward opening to the DPRK shows, its tactical application needs to be carefully watched. Many LDP politicians and intellectuals have taken to heart foreign criticisms of Japan's incrementalism and lack of political leadership. The initiative of politicians in the opening to the DPRK may indicate a general trend of greater unpredictability in the making of foreign policy in Japan due to the desire of LDP leaders to exercise "leadership." There is already a broad consensus in Japan favoring normalization with the DPRK, symbolized by the delegation of 350 Japanese politicians that visited Pyongyang in July 1991. If the nuclear issue is resolved, then agreement over reparations and normalization may follow quickly.

Finally, there is the longer term issue of how peaceful Northeast Asia will be in the post-Cold War period. If the ROK and Japan are successfully integrated into a stable set of security relations in the region, then attention could easily turn to Northeast Asian economic cooperation. The United States may still have the most important role in this process, but Japan and the ROK both show signs of greater independence and assertiveness. If not managed well, then the result could be persistent friction and a buildup of conventional arms, but if successfully managed, the prospect for peaceful cooperation should not be underestimated. China, the Soviet Union, and perhaps even the DPRK badly want economic cooperation with Japan and the ROK, while the latter two are willing to build the infrastructure and invest if certain political and economic conditions are met. To the extent that this vision of regional economic cooperation gains prominence Japan's ability to influence regional political and security affairs will naturally be increased.

In conclusion, events in Northeast Asia have developed in such a way as to present Japan with an opportunity to enter into the ongoing process of ending the Cold War in Northeast Asia while strengthening ties with both Koreas. Greater fluidity in regional relations gave Japan the opportunity for greater independence and political influence. Meanwhile, Japan's wealth gave it the ability to achieve this goal. Pressure to strike a higher political profile came from influential intellectuals and LDP members, and important developments in the Korean peninsula, practically on Japan's doorstep, constituted an important venue for exercising this new potential for influence. Whether Japan ultimately uses its influence to put historically troubled relations with the Korean people on an enduring basis will determine the success of Japan's broader efforts to gain political leadership in Asia and ensure a peaceful environment.

Notes

1. Lee Chong-Sik, *Japan and Korea: The Political Dimension* (Stanford, CA: Hoover Institution Press, 1985).

2. Ibid., pp. 25–34.

3. Martin E. Weinstein, "Japan and Asian Security," in *Changing Patterns of Security and Stability in Asia* (New York: Praeger, 1980), p. 99.

4. Okonogi Masao, "A Japanese Perspective on Korea–Japanese Relations" in Chin-wee Chung et al., eds., *Korea and Japan in World Politics* (Seoul: Korean Association of International Relations, 1985), p. 24.

5. Byung-joon Ahn, "Political and Economic Development in Korea and Korea–Japan Relations," in Chung et al., *Korea and Japan in World Politics*, pp. 62–63.

6. Chae-Jin Lee and Hideo Sato, *U.S. Policy toward Japan and Korea* (New York: Praeger, 1982), p. 44.

7. Bruce Cumings, "The Origins and Development of the Northeast Asian Political Economy: Industrial Sectors, Product Cycles, and Political Consequences," *International Organization*, 38, Winter 1984, pp. 1–40.

8. Chong-Sik, *Japan and Korea*, Tables 4 and 5.

9. Hahn Bae-ho, "Korea–Japan relations in the 1970s," *Asian Survey*, vol. XX, No. 11, November 1980, pp. 1187–97.

10. Chong-Sik, *Japan and Korea*, p. 85.

11. Evelyn Colbert, "Japan and the Republic of Korea," *Asian Survey*, Vol. XXVI, No. 3, March 1986, pp. 273–91.

12. Bruce Cumings, "The Conflict on the Korean Peninsula," in

Yoshikazu Sakamoto, ed., *Asia: Militarization and Regional Conflict* (London: Zed Books, Ltd., 1988).

13. Hong N. Kim, "Japanese–Korean Relations in the 1980s," *Asian Survey*, Vol. XXVII, No. 5, May 1987, pp. 497–514.

14. *New York Times*, September 9, 1984, p. 9.

15. Toshimitsu Shigemura, "Nittchō-Chōso o Mimamoru Washington no Embo" (The Long-Range Plan of Washington for Japan–DPRK and Soviet–DPRK Relations), *Chūō Kōron*, December 1990, p. 95.

16. *FBIS, East Asia*, January 9, 1991, p. 19.

17. See text of statement read on October 31, 1988 in *Department of State Bulletin*, January 1989, p. 17.

18. Young Whan Kihl, "The 1990 Prime Ministers' Meetings Between North and South Korea: An Analysis," *Asian Update* (New York: The Asia Society, October 1990).

19. *FBIS, East Asia,* Daily Report Supplement: North Korea Military Structure Viewed, April 16, 1991, p. 12.

20. Fuji Kamiya, quoted in Franklin B. Weinstein and Fuji Kamiya, eds., *The Security of Korea: U.S. and Japanese Perspectives on the 1980s* (Boulder, CO: Westview Press, 1980), p. 196.

21. Shin'ichi Hen, "Kaifu vs. Roh Tae Woo no 'Kokusai Seijiryoku' o tou (Kaifu vs. Roh Tae Woo: Who Has More Clout in International Politics?)," *Hoseki*, September 1990.

22. Masao Okonogi, *Nihon to Kita Chōsen: kore kara no 5 nen* (Japan and North Korea: the Next 5 Years) (Tokyo: PHP Kenkyujo, 1991), p. 125.

23. JDA Director-General Ganri Yamashita visited the ROK in 1981, but on an unofficial basis.

24. *FBIS, East Asia*, January 9, 1991, p. 18.

25. Masao, *Nihon to Kita Chōsen*, pp. 119–120.

26. Hajime Ishii, *Chikazuite kita tōoi kuni* (A Distant Country Getting Closer) (Tokyo: Seisansei honbu, 1991), p. 60.

27. Ibid., p. 44.

28. Okonogi, *Nihon to Kita Chōsen*, p. 125.

29. *FBIS, Northeast Asia*, April 30, 1991, p. 6.

30. Denny Roy, "North Korea's Relations with Japan," *Asian Survey*, Vol. XXVIII, No. 12, December 1988.

31. Ishii, *Chikazuite kita tōoi kuni*, pp. 138–139.

32. Kamiya, *The Security of Korea*, pp. 236–237.

33. Ishii, *Chikazuite kita tōoi kuni*, pp. 14–16.

34. *The Japan Economic Journal*, June 16, 1990, p. 3.

35. Jung Hyun Shin, "Japan's Two-Korea Policy and Korea–Japan Relations," in Chung et al., *Korea and Japan in World Politics*, pp. 269–90.

U.S. Forces in Korea and Inter-Korean Arms Control Talks

Tae-Hwan Kwak

Introduction

The end of the Cold War system, revolutionary changes in Eastern Europe and the Soviet Union, the shift of emphasis from security to economic issues by the major powers, U.S. economic difficulties and deficit problems, North Korean economic stagnation, three summit meetings between Presidents Gorbachev and Roh Tae Woo, and a growing détente in the Asia–Pacific region in the beginning of the 1990s are some of the major factors leading to inter-Korean prime ministers' talks in Seoul and Pyongyang and reassessment of the role of U.S. forces in Korea in the peacemaking process on the Korean peninsula.

In the spring of 1990, both the U.S. and ROK governments agreed to a three phase plan for U.S. troop reduction and partial, gradual withdrawal from Korea. It appears that North and South Korea are now willing to discuss arms control and disarmament issues to establish a durable peace on the Korean peninsula. The Democratic People's Republic of Korea (DPRK or North Korea) seems to respond slowly to the rapidly changing international security environment, while the Republic of Korea (ROK or South Korea) is quickly adapting itself to changing security relations

205

between itself and the United States, thereby showing a more flexible approach to a policy of status quo regarding the U.S. troop withdrawal issue.

The purposes of this paper are: (1) to reevaluate the roles of U.S. forces in South Korea in a newly changing international environment in the 1990s; and (2) to provide the author's timetable for U.S. troop reduction and/or withdrawal and to search for possible ways of using gradual, partial reduction and withdrawal of U.S. forces in Korea as a bargaining chip in negotiations with North Korea, the Soviet Union, and China to firmly establish a durable peace system on the Korean peninsula. In this paper, the author's two major arguments in implementing a timetable for U.S. troop reduction are: (1) U.S. troops stationed in Korea can play a new role in arms control and peace negotiations with North Korea; and (2) the U.S. troop reduction and withdrawal issue should and could be used as a political bargaining chip in arms control negotiations with the North.

The Roles of U.S. Forces in Korea

The security policy of the ROK since 1950 has been based upon a firm U.S. commitment to South Korea's defense that has kept U.S. troops in Korea for over forty years. America's firm commitment to South Korea provides a stable, credible deterrence against North Korea.

The U.S. security interest in Korea evolved from an American "Japanocentric" strategy of maintaining an effective and stable balance of power and deterrent force to contain Soviet expansion in Northeast Asia in the Cold War era. As a link in this strategy, U.S. policy-makers have perceived the Korean peninsula as a buffer zone for the defense of U.S. interests in Japan and the Western Pacific region primarily because of Korea's geostrategic position vis-à-vis Japan and U.S. bases in the Pacific.

Military Capabilities of U.S. Forces in Korea

The 1954 Mutual Defense Treaty between the United States and the ROK has been a cornerstone of U.S.–South Korean security relations, whereby the United States is firmly committed to the defense of South Korea by still maintaining the presence of its

206

43,000 troops along with some few hundred nuclear weapons in South Korea.[1]

Let us take a brief look at military capabilities of U.S. forces in Korea. Currently about 43,000 U.S. troops are stationed in South Korea, of which 29,100 are in the army, 11,200 are in the air force and 2,300 belong to KATUSA (Korean Augmentation to the U.S. Army). The U.S. troops have stayed in Korea since the end of the Korean War in 1953 to deter another war. The troop level has been maintained at roughly 40,000 personnel since the Nixon administration pulled out one army division in 1971. South Korea is the only place in the world where U.S. forces are kept at DEFCON 4 (Defense Readiness Condition Four), one level above normal.[2]

The U.S. Army stationed in Korea is the Second Infantry Division, the Eighth U.S. Army. Other armed forces in Korea include a surface-to-surface missile command, an air defense brigade, a signal brigade, and surveillance, logistics, and intelligence units. The Second Infantry Division and thirteen ROK Army divisions comprise the Combined ROK/U.S. Field Army. It is mostly deployed between the DMZ and Seoul, and its mission is to defend Seoul.

The U.S. ground forces in Korea are equipped with the most advanced, top-of-the-line weaponry. Major ground equipment of the U.S. forces in Korea include 155 medium tanks (M-55s), 105mm and 155mm artillery, 107mm and 88mm mortars, Vulcan air defense systems, I-Hawk and Redeye surface-to-air missiles, and TOW and Dragon anti-tank weapons. Chunchon houses the Fourth U.S. Army Missile Command, with Lance surface-to-surface missiles; while Osan is home to the Thirty-Eighth Air Defense Artillery Brigade.[3]

The U.S. Air Force stationed in Korea is part of the Seventh U.S. Air Force and is capable of carrying out independent operations. There are fifty-seven F-4Es, OV-10s and OA-37Bs located at Osan air base. Normally, U-2R reconnaissance craft also take off from Osan. Kunsan houses two squadrons of F-16s. Taegu air base has fourteen F-4Es and eighteen RF-4C reconnaissance planes, which will be withdrawn by 1992, according to the U.S. restructuring plan; and Suwon air base stations twenty-four A-10s.

As of February 1990, the total assets of the U.S. Air Force in Korea include sixty F-16s, twenty-four F-4s, twenty-four A-10 ground attack craft, and sixteen OV-10 counterinsurgency/reconnaissance aircraft.[4] In addition, the U.S. Air Force in Korea possesses AH-1S Cobra TOW attack helicopters and UH-60 Blackhawk transport helicopters. The air bases in Osan and Kunsan are equipped with Stinger antiaircraft missile systems.[5]

It is reported that a few hundred tactical nuclear weapons are stationed in Korea. Since the U.S. and ROK governments neither confirm nor deny the existence of nuclear weapons in Korea, it is difficult to verify this information. However, Kunsan air base is allegedly the storage location of the U.S. nuclear weapons. It is likely that some of the new B-61 tactical nuclear weapons for aircraft are already on Korean soil. The B-61 has four options of yield from one hundred kilotons to five hundred kilotons. (The nuclear bomb dropped on Hiroshima was twelve kilotons.) The 8-inch artillery shell can carry warheads from less than one kiloton to twelve kilotons. The 155mm artillery can carry 0.1 kiloton warheads. There are reportedly two kinds of atomic demolition munitions (ADMs or land mines) in Korea: small ones ranging from 0.01 to one kiloton and large ones ranging from one to fifteen kilotons.[6]

It is argued that the presence of nuclear weapons in South Korea serves as deterrence against another North Korean attack. The Center for Defense Information, in its recent study, concluded that "U.S. nuclear weapons in Korea serve no military function today and could be returned to the U.S. for storage."[7]

War-fighting capabilities on the Korean peninsula could be adequately maintained with ROK armed forces supported by the U.S. Air Force stationed in Korea. If conventional deterrence failed, and tactical nuclear weapons were to be used on Korean soil, the fallout effect would be devastating both to the Korean people and its neighbors, including the USSR, China and Japan. The use of nuclear weapons in Korea could endanger the survival of the Korean nation. In my view, nuclear weapons have outlived their usefulness in the post-Cold War era, and the withdrawal of nuclear weapons from Korea is desirable to the long-term interests of the Korean nation.

Military Rationale for Keeping U.S. Forces in Korea

The original objectives of keeping U.S. forces in Korea were to deter a North Korean attack and to prevent Chinese and/or Soviet military intervention in the event of recurrence of war in Korea. By preventing a renewed war in the Korean peninsula, the continued presence of U.S. forces has provided peace and stability in

Northeast Asia, thereby protecting U.S. interests in Japan and the western Pacific.[8]

The military justification for the continued presence of U.S. ground forces in Korea has been questioned in view of the changing international security environment, the end of the Cold War system, and changing policies of China and the Soviet Union toward the United States, Japan and South Korea. Some argue that China and the Soviet Union will promote peace rather than a war on the Korean peninsula in view of the establishment of Soviet–ROK diplomatic relations and new economic relations between China and South Korea.

Moreover, it is argued that South Korean forces can defend themselves against a North Korean attack because Seoul and Pyongyang now appear to maintain a strategic equivalence, although the role of the U.S. Air Force is to redress the imbalance in air power between the two Koreas. Also, the ROK still heavily relies on U.S. intelligence units stationed in Korea for its sources of information and intelligence. Thus, the military justification for the presence of U.S. ground troops in Korea appears weak, although North Korea's ground forces are numerically superior. However, the official rationale for the presence of U.S. ground forces in Korea is primarily political and psychological in nature. The presence symbolizes firm American determination to keep its defense commitment to South Korea in the event of a renewed war in Korea.

In the 1990s, under the rapidly changing international security environment, a gradual, partial U.S. troop withdrawal could be carefully considered in the context of the following four important factors.

First, one may argue that South and North Korea have agreed to three basic principles of Korean reunification in the July 4, 1972 Joint Communique: (1) an independent solution to the Korean problem without being subjected to outside interference; (2) a peaceful approach to the problem; and (3) the pledge to seek a great national unity, transcending differences in ideology, ideas, and social systems. The United States should not interfere in Korean affairs since U.S. forces in Korea could be considered a form of external interference. Thus, the United States should leave the two Koreas to determine the future of their own affairs by themselves. This argument basically supports "Koreanization" of the Korean dilemma. The Korean unification problem should be solved by Koreans themselves without outside interference.

Second, a gradual, partial reduction and withdrawal of U.S. forces in South Korea would be unlikely to invite a new war in Korea. Even if war occurred in Korea, Soviet and/or Chinese military intervention in Korea would appear extremely unlikely, and the Soviet Union and China would have to assess the impact of the war on their relations with South Korea, the United States, and Japan. Their intervention in Korea would not best serve their interests in the post-Cold War era.

Third, a gradual, partial American withdrawal would not threaten the balance of power in Northeast Asia. The Chinese would welcome an American withdrawal from Korea. It is unlikely that U.S. withdrawal could stimulate the rearmament of Japan and bring about Seoul–Tokyo military ties if a gradual, partial reduction and withdrawal of U.S. forces took place with an inter-Korean peace process.

Fourth, since South and North Korea appear to maintain their strategic balance on the Korean peninsula, it is unlikely that North Korea would strike first to its advantage. Furthermore, the changing international security environment and North Korea's domestic problems and economic stagnation make it more difficult for North Korea to make a decision to strike first at South Korea even if it intends to do so, because the North does not have the military capabilities to win a war.

The author argued elsewhere that the Seoul government needs to seriously consider the long-term strategic planning about the U.S. troop withdrawal issue and have serious discussions on this issue with the U.S. government.[9] In short, the ROK needs to seek "Koreanization of security" by improving and normalizing relations with North Korea in the 1990s. This strategic planning obviously requires a new adjustment to the current Korea–U.S. security relationship. The crucial question is: what steps could be taken to deal with U.S. troops in Korea if the two Koreas were to improve and normalize their relations? A clear argument is: the ROK needs to be prepared for U.S. ground troop withdrawal in the near future in order to improve inter-Korean relations, and the U.S. ground troop withdrawal issue needs to be used as a bargaining chip in arms control and peace negotiations with North Korea.

The rationale for this argument is based on the following factors. First, in terms of national power and capabilities, South Korea's economy is much stronger than that of North Korea, and an essential strategic equivalence between the North and the South appears to exist at the present time.[10]

Second, a well-planned and gradual reduction and withdrawal of U.S. troops would serve South Korea's interests better in the long run, thereby preventing a power vacuum on the Korean peninsula. More importantly, North Korea has already proposed a phased withdrawal of U.S. troops from Korea and arms reduction for establishing a durable peace on the Korean peninsula.

Third, changing policies of the four powers concerned surrounding the Korean peninsula will put pressure on "North Korea's perestroika and glasnost" in the 1990s, and Seoul's Northern policy will continue to improve political-diplomatic relations between South Korea and China, the Soviet Union, and East European states.

Fourth, North Korea's policy is slowly changing by showing moderate and conciliatory attitudes toward South Korea in recent months, and it has clearly indicated its interests in a South-North summit meeting. South Korea is also pursuing its pragmatic policy in line with its July 7, 1988 policy statement and principles of a new unification formula for a Korean National Community.

Fifth, in view of the changing international security environment, South Korea's elevation of international status to that of a middle power in the 1990s, growing anti-American sentiment in South Korea, continuing trade surplus of South Korea vis-à-vis the United States, and American budget deficit problems, Washington made a decision to reduce the level of U.S. troops in Korea.

Recent Inter-Korean Arms Control Proposals

South Korea's "Northern policy" toward the Soviet Union, China, and East European socialist states has led to significantly improved new relationships with these states. Furthermore, a new détente between the Soviet Union and the United States, a newly developing détente between the Soviet Union and China under Gorbachev's perestroika and glasnost and China's economic reforms, and other changes in the Northeast Asian security system will eventually be conducive to the firm institutionalization of peaceful coexistence between the two Koreas.

Let us take a brief look at the two Koreas' policy proposals in the changing international political-security environment surrounding the Korean peninsula. ROK President Roh Tae Woo announced a special declaration on July 7, 1988, known as the July 7 Declaration, in which he put forward a six point policy on reunification: (1) exchange of visits by a broad spectrum of the people of South and North Korea and free visits to both parts of the Korean peninsula by overseas Koreans; (2) exchanges of correspondence and visits between members of divided families; (3) open trade between South and North Korea as a single community; (4) no opposition to nations friendly with the South trading with the North unless it involves military goods; (5) giving up the competitive and confrontational diplomatic war between the South and North while ensuring the North makes a positive contribution to the international community; and (6) cooperation with Pyongyang in its efforts to improve ties with the United States and Japan while seeking improved ties with the Soviet Union and China.[11]

President Roh has repeatedly proposed a summit meeting between himself and DPRK President Kim Il Sung without any conditions. In an address by President Roh at the Forty-third Session of the U.N. General Assembly on October 18, 1988, he proposed that South and North Korea "agree to a declaration of nonaggression or non-use of force in order to better construct a framework for mutual trust and security." He also stated that "the Republic of Korea will never use force first against the North." He proposed an agenda for discussion at a summit meeting by suggesting that "we discuss sincerely and resolve all the problems raised by either or both sides with regard to disarmament, arms control and other military matters."[12]

In response to his proposal, Kim also made a proposal for a summit meeting in Pyongyang to discuss several issues, including U.S. troop withdrawal, North Korea's confederation plan, and a joint declaration of nonaggression between the South and the North. North Korea launched a peaceful offensive by proposing multichannelled inter-Korean talks, exploiting politically unstable situations in South Korea. Among many proposals, the most significant was North Korea's November 7, 1988 proposal of a "comprehensive peace plan" for the reunification of the Korean peninsula in which North Korea presented four steps to guarantee peace: (1) phased withdrawal of U.S. armed forces from South Korea; (2) phased reduction of North and South Korean armed forces; (3) information about and inspection of the above steps; and (4) tripartite talks involving North Korea, South Korea, and the United States. North Korea also made a proposal for easing the present political and military confrontation between North and South Korea.[13]

In response to announcements by the United States and South Korean governments of the U.S. troop withdrawal plan for the 1990s and the changing international strategic environment, on May 31, 1990, North Korea made a new proposal for arms control and disarmament for peace on the Korean peninsula.[14] This proposal contains new features for a peace process in which North Korea has substantially accepted previous South Korean proposals for military confidence-building measures. This new proposal has the following measures: (1) South-North Korean military confidence-building measures; (2) reduction of South-North Korean armed forces; (3) withdrawal of foreign forces; and (4) peace guarantees after disarmament. It is evident in this regard that North Korea has substantially changed its previous positions. Both sides now agree to military confidence-building measures prior to reduction of armed forces and withdrawal of U.S. forces from Korea.

Both sides wish to have a summit meeting, but the North set its preconditions for a summit meeting. The North wants to have high-level political-military talks prior to a summit meeting. The South agreed to hold prime ministers' talks which deal with political-military issues. In the fall and winter of 1990, there were three inter-Korean prime ministers' meetings. There has been a little progress in these talks, but both sides failed to conclude a basic relations agreement, including a declaration of nonaggression between the South and the North, primarily due to both sides' conflicting approaches to peace and unification processes. In February, 1991, the North unilaterally suspended the scheduled fourth round of inter-Korean prime ministers' talks because of the annual joint ROK–U.S. military exercises, code-named Team Spirit.

Team Spirit is the annual defensive joint military exercises for the security of South Korea. The North argued that inter-

Korean talks could not continue if Team Spirit were under way. If Team Spirit were suspended, would ongoing multichannels of inter-Korean talks continue? The North says "yes." Why then couldn't South Korea suspend Team Spirit? According to South Korean authorities, Team Spirit is essential to South Korean military defensive training, and therefore could not be suspended. Nevertheless, the South does not have much choice but to participate in joint military exercises with the United States as long as the U.S. government wants Team Spirit.

The 1989 joint military exercises were held for only ten days—a short period of time compared to the usual two months—probably to improve inter-Korean relations. Team Spirit '90 was scaled down and short in duration. In February 1990, the North unilaterally suspended ongoing inter-Korean talks again because of Team Spirit '90. The same patterns of North Korean behavior were repeated in the spring of 1991. North Korea suspended the scheduled prime ministers' meeting in February 1991 in Pyongyang.

Since the ROK government agreed to discuss political-military issues with the North, it remains to be seen whether the South can accept some measures in the North's "comprehensive peace plan" and a new May 31, 1990 disarmament proposal, including phased withdrawal of U.S. forces and arms reduction of South and North armed forces. It is clear, however, that in view of changing international security environments surrounding the Korean peninsula, the ROK could favorably respond to the North's arms reduction and disarmament proposals.

Pyongyang has reiterated time and again in its news media the issue of U.S. troops stationed in South Korea. Pyongyang's demand for U.S. troop withdrawal from South Korea has not been changed. In North Korea's view, the presence of U.S. troops is the basic obstacle to inter-Korean dialogue and Korean reunification. However, Seoul has just as strongly insisted that U.S. troops stay in South Korea because their presence helps achieve a military balance between the two Korean states and provides a credible and stable deterrence against North Korea. The U.S. troop withdrawal issue will be discussed in detail in this paper.

North Korea insisted on inter-Korean political and military talks first to reduce tensions on the Korean peninsula, and/or at the same time, the existing channels of inter-Korean Red Cross, economic, and parliamentary talks would be resumed. On the other hand, South Korea equally insisted on the resumption of the existing channels of inter-Korean dialogue in order to build up mutual trust and cooperation, and then high-level political and military talks would begin to discuss all issues relating to peace and unification on the Korean peninsula. Both positions were mutually incompatible. In response to the changing international security environment, South Korea changed its earlier position on this issue and is now prepared for high-level talks with the North.

Does Kim Il Sung Really Want U.S. Troop Withdrawal?

Pyongyang's demand for U.S. troop withdrawal has not changed. North Korea has consistently maintained that the presence of U.S. troops is the basic obstacle to inter-Korean dialogue and Korean reunification.

It has become imperative for South Korea to take a new look into the role of U.S. troops in Korea and to pursue a new security policy toward North Korea in view of changing domestic and international environments. In other words, both a "status quo" policy favoring permanent presence of the U.S. troops in Korea and an "anti-status quo" policy calling for unconditional and immediate withdrawal of U.S. forces in Korea are not conducive to the peace process on the Korean peninsula.

As an alternative, the ROK government could adopt a "policy of pragmatism," seeking to use the U.S. troop withdrawal issue as a bargaining chip in negotiations with the North Korean government for improving inter-Korean relations. The Republic of Korea could be flexible toward the U.S. troop withdrawal issue.

It should be pointed out that North Korea also agreed on a phased withdrawal of U.S. forces from Korea. North Korea wants a step-by-step, but complete, withdrawal of U.S. forces for achieving national reunification.

Why did North Korea want the complete withdrawal of U.S. forces from Korea? It appears that North Korea's demand for U.S. troop withdrawal was linked to the following assumptions. First, the complete withdrawal of U.S. forces could contribute to the demise of the Seoul government, which would lead to a "South Korean revolution," thereby creating a sympathetic, friendly government in Seoul. Thus, the North argues that the presence of U.S. troops in Korea is the basic obstacle to Korean reunification. Secondly, North Korea believes that the Democratic Confederal Republic of Koryo unification formula could be achieved with the complete withdrawal of U.S. forces, and then Kim Il Sung's unification dream could be realized. If these assumptions are indeed accurate, one can understand why the North has consistently insisted on complete U.S. troop withdrawal. Nevertheless, in reality, even if U.S. forces were to be withdrawn, Kim Il Sung is keenly aware that Korean reunification would not be achieved on North Korean terms under the present international environment.

In the meantime, North Korea has been effectively using the U.S. troop withdrawal issue for domestic and international propaganda purposes. Domestically, the Kim regime has used it for political stability and legitimacy of his autocratic rule for the past forty-five years. Internationally, the U.S. troop withdrawal issue is also used as a tool of enhancing his status as "a leader of the anti-imperialist movement" in the Third World. In the South, Kim also appeals to some radical students and progressive forces as "an anti-American hero."

Kim may face serious problems of justifying his rule and legitimacy as a "great leader" in North Korea, if and when U.S. forces are completely withdrawn from Korea, because the presence of U.S. troops has been used as a rationale for his rule for the past forty-five years. Furthermore, Kim may be afraid of South Korea's possible use of force to unify the Korean peninsula if U.S. troops were no longer present in South Korea. If this analysis is accurate, then Kim's demand for U.S. troop withdrawal appears to be nothing but political propaganda.

Since the end of the Persian Gulf war, Kim Il Sung may have thought about the necessity of the continued presence of U.S. troops in Korea because he wants domestic stability in the North and a peaceful transition of power to his son, Jong Il, in the near future. He may have even concluded that the presence of U.S. troops in South Korea would continue to serve his regime's interests by contributing to the stability of the Kim Il Sung–Jong Il system in the 1990s.

In sum, since it is not unreasonable to conclude that Kim Il Sung's interests would be best served by the presence of U.S. troops stationed in South Korea, he and his son do not really want the complete withdrawal of U.S. forces from South Korea in the 1990s.

U.S. Strategic Planning For Three Phase Force Reduction/Withdrawal

The United States and South Korea worked out a gradual, partial reduction of U.S. troops and readjustment to the U.S.–Korea security relationship in the 1990s. The Bush Administration has made preparations for a gradual reduction and withdrawal of U.S. troops from Korea.

Defense Secretary Richard Cheney visited Seoul in February 1990 to have a conference with South Korean Defense Minister Lee Sang Hoon. They agreed, in principle, on a number of significant items.[15] First, South Korea accepted in principle the gradual withdrawal of about five thousand to six thousand noncombatants from U.S. forces in Korea. In January 1990, the United States announced that it would close three of its five air bases in South Korea and withdraw about two thousand Air Force support personnel from Korea by 1992.

Second, both sides agreed that the American role would gradually change from its leading role to a supporting one, while South Korea assumes more leadership, including the eventual command of key units of the Combined Forces Command. South Korea would consider taking over operational control of its own armed forces during peacetime, with the United States resuming command in times of war.

Third, both sides agreed to work out more cost sharing of South Korea's annual contributions to U.S. defense costs. The United States suggested that South Korea should double its $300 million in annual direct contributions to the $2.4 billion cost of maintaining its troops in Korea. Both the United States and South Korea agreed to work out the details and hard numbers of the proposed new arrangements later on.

The detailed agreements between the United States and South Korea were disclosed in a required report to Congress in April 1990.[16] What is significant in this report is that the U.S. government decided on a gradual, partial reduction and eventual withdrawal of U.S. forces in Korea in the 1990s in light of the changing international security environment and U.S. domestic conditions.

The U.S. Department of Defense announced a timetable for a planned U.S. troop reduction and withdrawal from Korea.[17] The Defense Department's three-phase plan for the restructuring of U.S. forces stationed in Korea during the 1990s is described below.

Phase I—One to Three Years: The United Nations command must be retained, essentially in its present form. During this phase, the United States will reduce administrative overhead and phase out units whose mission can be assumed by the South Korean forces. By 1992, the United States will reduce about seven thousand personnel, including two thousand Air Force personnel and about five thousand ground force personnel. These reductions are based on steady improvements in South Korean defense capabilities.

Phase II—Three to Five Years: During Phase I, the United States will reexamine the North Korean threat, evaluate effects of changes in Phase I, and establish new objectives for Phase II. The restructuring of the U.S. Second Infantry Division will be considered at this point. An additional withdrawal of the Second Infantry Division will be considered in terms of the state of South-North relations and further improvements in ROK military capabilities.

Phase III—Five to Ten Years: If the earlier phases were successfully completed, South Koreans should be ready to take the leading role in their own defense. During this phase, fewer U.S. forces would be required to maintain deterrence on the Korean peninsula.

The U.S. government spelled out the following specific bilateral security objectives in this report.[18] These are: (1) to deter North Korean aggression or defeat it if deterrence fails; (2) to reduce political-military tensions on the Korean peninsula by encouraging inter-Korean talks and the institution of a confidence-building measures regime; and (3) to change the role of U.S. forces in Korea from a leading to a supporting role, including some force reductions. These security objectives clearly indicate an American firm commitment to the security of the Republic of Korea in the 1990s. An additional U.S. troop withdrawal during Phase II and Phase III will depend on the peace process on the Korean peninsula and improvements in ROK military capabilities. It appears that U.S. forces in Korea will remain even after the year

2000 unless South and North Korea firmly establish a durable peace system on the Korean peninsula.

Agreements at the Twenty-Second ROK–U.S. Security Consultative Meeting in 1990

The Twenty-Second Security Consultative Meeting between the United States and the ROK was held in Washington on November 13–15, 1990. ROK Defense Minister Lee Jong-koo and Secretary of Defense Cheney led their respective delegations, which included senior defense and foreign policy officials of both countries. They discussed a variety of important topics, including Team Spirit, the proposed cost sharing of maintaining U.S. forces in Korea, moving the Eighth U.S. Army compound out of Seoul, the pricing of the Korean Fighter Program, future reduction of the American military presence in Korea, a shift in the operational control over the combined forces and the sending of medical military supplies to the multinational force in the Persian Gulf. Among mutually agreed items, three important ones will be discussed here.[19]

First, both sides reaffirmed their commitment to the maintenance of peace and stability on the Korean peninsula. The United States plans to reduce its military presence by five thousand ground and two thousand air force personnel do not indicate any change in the close and long-standing security relationship between the two allies. Both sides reaffirmed that any future reduction or readjustment of U.S. forces in Korea should be made gradually and in a phased manner after a careful evaluation of the changing Northeast Asia security environment in and around the Korean peninsula.

Second, both sides agreed that Korean generals will take over the two posts of commander of the U.N. Command's Ground Component Command and top representative of the U.N. Command's Military Armistice Commission by 1992. Since the Korean War, U.S. generals have taken the posts, and a four-star U.S. general still retains the post of commander-in-chief of the ROK–U.S. Combined Forces Command (CFC). The agreement heralded a reduced role of the U.S. ground forces stationed in Korea and also reflected the process of the ongoing inter-Korean talks.

Third, both sides agreed that South Korea would increase its direct contribution to the cost of maintaining the U.S. forces stationed in Korea. Seoul will pay $150 million for the 1991 share of the defense burden, compared to $70 million in 1990.

Both sides also assessed the impact of the ongoing inter-Korea talks and the Persian Gulf crisis on the ROK–U.S. security relations. The ROK is gradually preparing for upcoming inter-Korean arms control talks in the near future.

In accordance with U.S.–ROK bilateral agreements, the United Nations command appointed a South Korean army general as chief delegate at the Military Armistice Commission talks at Panmunjom in March 1991. The appointment of Major General Hwang Won Tak as senior delegate provided more authority and responsibility to South Korea in defense against North Korea. North Korea refused to accept General Hwang's credentials by arguing that a South Korea military delegate cannot represent the U.N. Command since the South refused to sign the 1953 Armistice Agreement.[20] The United States, however, maintains that anyone appointed by the U.N. Command can represent it. The North will eventually accept General Hwang. If the North does accept Hwang, the inter-Korean arms control and disarmament issue will be discussed between the two Koreas.

Author's Timetable for Reduction/Withdrawal of U.S. Forces

What should and could be done to establish a peace system on the Korean peninsula? The time has come to seriously consider the U.S. troop withdrawal issue as a political leverage in dealing with North Korea as the author has advocated since 1983.[21] How could the U.S. troop withdrawal issue be used as a bargaining chip in dealing with North Korea? Both U.S. and ROK authorities could use it as a policy instrument for achieving security and peace on the Korean peninsula in the 1990s. The instrument could be very effective with U.S.–Korea security cooperation. Herein a new role of U.S. troops in Korea can be defined as a bargaining chip in arms control negotiations with North Korea.

To be specific, I would like to suggest a timetable for U.S. troop reduction and withdrawal from South Korea during the 1990s. The following timetable is subject to changes in North Korea's attitudes toward South Korea and in the Northeast Asian security environment. The timetable consists of three step-by-step stages.

Stage I (1991–93): The U.S. and ROK governments should take unilateral initiatives to temporarily suspend Team Spirit for three years (1991–93), reduce about five thousand to six thousand noncombatants, close three U.S. air bases in South Korea, and withdraw two thousand Air Force support personnel from South Korea by 1992 as planned.

Judging from the North Korean Foreign Ministry's March 5, 1990 statement demanding that the United States take a practical step for troop withdrawal, North Korea will favorably respond to these initiatives. It states that, "If the United States practically takes at least a step for partial pullout which would mark the start of the complete withdrawal of the U.S. forces from South Korea, we will welcome it and we are ready to take more necessary measures corresponding to it for military confidence and disarmament between the north and the south."[22]

In response to the American–South Korean announcement of a planned reduction of U.S. forces in Korea, on May 31, 1990, just prior to a summit meeting between Soviet Union President Gorbachev and ROK President Roh, North Korea made a new "disarmament proposal for peace on the Korean peninsula," in order to ease tensions on the Korean peninsula and create a peaceful climate for national reunification.[23] The contents of the proposal are: (1) confidence building between the North and South; (2) arms reduction in the North and South; (3) withdrawal of foreign forces; and (4) disarmament and guarantee for peace after disarmament.

North Korea has changed its earlier position on its insistence on holding trilateral talks among the United States, the South, and the North. Now it proposes to hold inter-Korean bilateral talks about disarmament and arms reductions for peace on the Korean peninsula. It is expected that the ROK government will favorably respond to the North's new proposal.

As discussed above, these unilateral initiatives need to be done with U.S.–South Korean military cooperation. Prior to the final decision on the temporary suspension and the reduction of U.S. troops, the U.S. and ROK governments should inform North Korea, China, and the Soviet Union of these initiatives, inviting North Korea to make a similar move to reduce tensions on the Korean peninsula. For instance, the North could be encouraged to substantially reduce its offensive forces deployed along the

DMZ. South Korea could seriously discuss military confidence-building measures with North Korea as the latter recently proposed to induce Pyongyang to take positive actions toward the South in many channels of inter-Korean dialogue.

During the first stage, the ROK government needs to take over its military operational rights in times of peace, and needs to assume more cost sharing of keeping U.S. forces in Korea. During this stage, a summit meeting between President Roh Tae Woo and President Kim Il Sung or Kim Jong Il needs to be arranged to discuss all issues of mutual concerns, including an adoption of the basic relations charter and a declaration of mutual non-aggression.

Stage II (1994–96): The second stage would involve substantial cuts of U.S. troops in Korea. The Second Infantry Division would be withdrawn along with the total withdrawal of U.S. tactical nuclear weapons from South Korea, leaving a brigade with supporting personnel. This stage cannot be completed without concessions from North Korea, China, and the Soviet Union, such as a South–North Korean basic relations agreement based on the institutionalization of peaceful coexistence between the South and the North, a peace charter replacing the Korean Armistice Agreement of 1953, and two sets of a four party conference (the United States, Soviet Union, South and North Korea; and the United States, China, and two Koreas) to discuss arms control issues.

Stage III (1997–2000 and beyond): At this stage, U.S. ground forces should be withdrawn, along with a 50 percent cut of U.S. air and naval forces in Korea. If and when South and North Korea agree to the establishment of the Korean Commonwealth, the South–North Korean confederation stage (fourth stage) in my "block-building model of Korean political integration,"[24] there will be no need for keeping the remaining U.S. air and naval forces in Korea.

The timetable for U.S. troop withdrawal in the 1990s could be subject to changes in inter-Korean relations and international and Korean domestic environments. I would like to make it very clear that this timetable should be used as a bargaining chip in arms control and peace negotiations with the North Korean government, and that a phased withdrawal of U.S. forces from Korea in the 1990s should not endanger a strategic balance on the Korean peninsula.

It is necessary and essential for South Korea and the United States to agree in principle on a phased withdrawal of U.S. troops from Korea in the following order: (1) the removal of nuclear weapons from the South; (2) U.S. ground troop reductions in exchange for a peace treaty between the United States and North Korea, and a nonaggression declaration between the South and the North; and (3) withdrawal of U.S. air forces after the firm establishment of a peace regime on the Korean peninsula. Even after the U.S. ground troops are withdrawn, the U.S. air forces should remain for some time to provide strategic stability on the Korean peninsula. In addition, the U.S. early warning system should remain even longer until the ROK has an independent warning system.

Conclusion

As discussed in this paper, the author argues that the U.S. troop reduction and withdrawal issue be used as a political bargaining chip in arms control and peace negotiations with North Korea.

Pyongyang will eventually accept the principle of peaceful coexistence with South Korea. The North Korean government accepted a phased withdrawal of U.S. forces in Korea, although the time frame for such a withdrawal could be readjusted. The South Korean government has also accepted a gradual, partial reduction and withdrawal of U.S. forces in Korea with the clear understanding that a gradual reduction should not in any way endanger the security of South Korea.

Since both Koreas and the United States have accepted a phased withdrawal plan of U.S. forces stationed in Korea, there is a high probability of an inter-Korean summit meeting in the near future for further discussions on confidence-building measures, and on the U.S. troop reduction/withdrawal plan in particular.

On June 1, 1985, in his interview by the editor of *Sekai* (The World), a Japanese monthly magazine, Kim Il Sung said that, "North Korea has neither the intention nor the capability to invade the South." North Korea recently reiterated that statement by stressing that it "unilaterally reduced the Korean People's Army by 100,000 men by the end of 1987 in order to make a substantial breakthrough in arms reduction on the Korean peninsula and, earlier, took a positive step of relocating 150,000 troops in peaceful construction."[25] Nevertheless, the U.S. and South Korean authorities neither trust the reduction of the North Korean army nor Kim's words. Herein the credibility gap is a serious problem for North Korea. Thus, Pyongyang needs to build its credibility and image as a civilized nation so that its words can be trusted by the international community.

Now is the time for Kim to sincerely and seriously show his deeds, not just words, to the world. For instance, North Korea signed the Nuclear Non-Proliferation Treaty in December, 1985, but it refused to sign a safeguards accord with the International Atomic Energy Agency (IAEA) for inspection of the North's nuclear facilities. It is reported that North Korea is now capable of building nuclear bombs.[26] A North Korea nuclear weapons program would certainly contradict its nuclear-free zone proposal for the Korean peninsula and Kim Il Sung's 1986 statement that North Korea would not build a nuclear bomb. North Korea demanded the withdrawal of U.S. nuclear weapons in exchange for IAEA's inspection of nuclear facilities in North Korea. However, North Korea is expected to eventually sign a safeguards agreement with the IAEA because of international pressure, just as it finally decided to apply for U.N. membership separately.[27]

Kim could unilaterally take his own version of common security-building measures on the Korean peninsula by signing a safeguards agreement with the IAEA. If Kim demonstrates a sincere attitude and good behavior, there will be meaningful and productive inter-Korean arms control talks, and also improved relations between the United States and North Korea.

Notes

1. The number of U.S. nuclear weapons stored in South Korea is uncertain. In the mid-1970s, the presence of over six hundred nuclear weapons in Korea was reported. Arkins and Fieldhouse estimate the current number of nuclear weapons is 151: sixty aircraft bombs, forty 8-inch artillery shells, thirty 155mm artillery shells, and twenty-one atomic demolition munitions (ADMs, or land mines). It is reported that Kunsan Air Base is the storage location for U.S. nuclear weapons. The United States has already withdrawn warheads for Honest John surface-to-surface missiles, Nike-Hercules surface-to-air missiles, and other sys-

tems. For further details, see William Arkins and Richard Fieldhouse, *Nuclear Battlefields* (Cambridge, MA: Ballinger Publishing Co., 1985), pp. 120–21 and 231; Peter Hayes, *Pacific Powderkeg: American Nuclear Dilemmas in Korea* (Lexington, MA: Lexington Books, 1991), p. 102; U.S. House Appropriations Committee, *Military Construction Appropriations for 1987*, Pt. 5 (Washington, DC, 1986), p.216. On the other hand, there are more than one thousand nuclear weapons of all kinds, means of their delivery, and even neutron bombs in South Korea, according to the Foreign Ministry of the DPRK; see *The Pyongyang Times*, March 10, 1990. For deployment of U.S. troops and nuclear arms in South Korea, a U.S. nuclear forward base, in the eyes of North Korea, see *The Pyongyang Times* November 11, 1989.

2. Arkins and Fieldhouse, *Nuclear Battlefields*, p.120.

3. Stephen Goose, "The Military Situation on the Korean Peninsula," in John Sullivan and Roberta Foss, eds., *Two Koreas—One Future?* (Lanham, MD: University Press of America, 1987), pp.76–77.

4. *Dong-A Annual,* Dong-S Yongam (Seoul, 1987), p.87.

5. Goose, "The Military Situation," p.77.

6. Ibid., p.80.

7. "Mission Accomplished in Korea: Bringing U.S. Troops Home," *The Defense Monitor*, Vol. 19, No. 2, 1990, p.8.

8. See Ralph N. Clough, *Deterrence and Defense in Korea: The Role of U.S. Forces* (Washington, DC: The Brookings Institution, 1976).

9. See Tae-Hwan Kwak, "ROK National Security in the 1990s," *Korean Journal of International Studies*, Vol. 19, No. 3, 1988, pp.389–414; also see Tae-Hwan Kwak, "Korea–U.S. Security Relations in the 1990s: A Creative Adjustment," *The Korean Journal of Defense Analysis*, Vol. 1, No. 2 (Winter 1989), pp.143–66.

10. Tae-Hwan Kwak, "Military Capabilities of South and North Korea: A Comparative Study," *Asian Perspective*, Vol. 14, No. 1, Spring-Summer 1990, pp.113–43.

11. *Korea Herald*, July 8, 1988.

12. *Korea and World Affairs*, Vol. 12, No. 4, Winter 1988, p.842.

13. For further details, see ibid., pp.870–76.

14. For further details, see *Rodong Shinmun*, June 2, 1990.

15. *New York Times*, February 15, 1990; *Los Angeles Times*, February 16, 1990; *Washington Post*, February 24, 1990; *Newsreview*, February 3 and 10, 1990.

16. For further details, see *A Strategic Framework for the Asian Pacific Rim: Looking Toward the 21st Century* (Washington, DC: Department of Defense, April 18, 1990).

17. Ibid., pp.15–17.

18. Ibid., p.15.

19. For further details, see *Korea Herald*, November 16 and 17, 1990.

20. Ibid., March 25, 1991.

21. The author argued for the first time that the U.S. troop withdrawal issue should be used as a political bargaining chip in negotiations with North Korea in 1983; see "How to Deal with the Stalemated Inter-Korean Dialogue: The Non-Zero Sum Formula," paper presented at the Fifth Joint Conference of the Korean Political Science Association and the Association of Korean Political Scientists in North America, August 8–10, 1983, Seoul, Korea. This idea was accepted by the South at the March 14, 1990 hearing before the Foreign Affairs and National Unification Committee, ROK National Assembly; see *Korea Times Los Angeles*, March 15, 1990.

22. *The Pyongyang Times*, March 10, 1990.

23. For further details, see *The Pyongyang Times*, June 9, 1990; for Korean text, see *Rodong Shinmun*, June 2, 1990.

24. For a "Block-Building Model of Korean Political Integration," see Kwak, *In Search for Peace and Unification on the Korean Peninsula*, ch. 6.

25. *The Pyongyang Times*, March 10, 1990.

26. For further details of current U.S. policy toward North Korea, see *Korea: North-South Nuclear Issues*, hearing before the Subcommittee of Asian and Pacific Affairs, U.S. House Committee on Foreign Affairs, July 25, 1990 (Washington, DC: U.S. Government Printing Office, 1991). For further details of North Korea's nuclear capability, see Andrew Mack, "North Korea and the Bomb," *Foreign Policy*, No. 83 (Summer 1991), pp.87–104; *The Arms Control Reporter*, April 1991; and Charles Lane, "A Knock on the Nuclear Door?: North Korea Insists It Isn't Building Atomic Weapons, But the Evidence is Compelling," *Newsweek*, April 29, 1991.

27. The DPRK Foreign Ministry issued a May 27, 1991 statement regarding its application for separate U.N. membership in which it announced that, "the DPRK Government has no alternative but to enter the United Nations at the present moment as a step to overcome the temporary difficulties caused by the south Korean authorities." For further details, see *The Pyongyang Times*, June 1, 1991. For Korean text, see *Rodong Shinmun*, May 29, 1991.

Economic Frictions and Alliance Cohesion in Northeast Asia

Edward A. Olsen

The Northeast Asian security situation remains dominated as the 1990s begin by the two alliances that have guided the region since the late 1940s. As the decade progresses, however, these alliances may be altered significantly by economic factors. Alliances exist between Japan and the United States and South Korea and the United States. The American connection constitutes the linchpin for these two regional allies, which have virtually nothing to do with each other militarily.[1] Together these parallel security relationships, with the United States as a nexus, formed a bulwark against perceived communist threats from the Soviet Union and North Korea during the long Cold War.

The two regional allies also benefitted enormously in economic terms from the strategic mandate the United States imposed upon itself at the end of the Second World War. Prospering under American political, economic, and strategic protection, both Japan and South Korea evolved from the 1950s to the 1980s into leaders of the world economy. This was, of course, most true of Japan, but by the late 1980s and early 1990s, the Republic of Korea (ROK) also became a world class economic player. From their earliest days, therefore, the U.S.–Japan and U.S.–ROK security relationships incorporated an

227

economic component. This is emphatically not a new factor in regional strategic calculations, but it is one which has changed enormously over the years.

If one were to step back to around 1955 and, with the assistance of a remarkably accurate crystal ball, predict that Japan someday would rank right behind the United States as an economic power, that South Korea would rank alongside several European powers economically, and that these Asian capitalist success stories would be part of the cause of the failure of Marxism-Leninism to prevail in the Cold War (assuming anyone would believe such a forecast in the 1950s), one might logically expect to hear nothing but praise in reaction to these prospective events. There is, in fact, enormous self-congratulation occurring as of 1990–91, as the victors in the Cold War savor their economic accomplishments and geopolitical successes.[2] There is also, however, much second guessing about the unforeseen consequences of these developments.

In a situation replete with ironies, the United States and its two Northeast Asian allies face the post-Cold War era burdened by two problems that were utterly unanticipated in the 1950s. Now that a successful global U.S. strategy has helped to bring prosperity to Japan and the ROK and each faces a sharply ameliorated threat environment because of changes in the Soviet Union brought about by that same strategy, the United States and its two regional allies are having enormous problems adjusting to the new pecking order between the three of them, and between the United States and the former Soviet Union in the region.

Years of festering economic frictions between the United States and Japan and the United States and South Korea, which long have jeopardized alliance cohesion, are now being compounded by a dramatically altered security environment. Accordingly, this analysis shall examine three interrelated issues: (1) the origin and the nature of U.S. trade frictions with Japan and South Korea that affect the two bilateral security relationships; (2) the nature of the post-Cold War security environment that the United States, Japan, and South Korea confront in Northeast Asia; and (3) the ways in which the United States' national security planning strategy and economic policies may interact in the post-Cold War years.

Linkages Between Trade and Security

Despite occasional charges in Northeast Asia, especially from radical elements in South Korea, that U.S. post-Second World War security policy was always motivated by economic imperialism, nothing could be further from the truth.[3] Had U.S. officials desired a security strategy designed to create American economic hegemony in East Asia, the overwhelming power of the United States in the late 1940s would have enabled those officials to fashion such a strategy. It would have been simple to enunciate such goals and to foster client states in Japan, Korea, Taiwan, and various Southeast Asian countries. There was a vacuum left by Western and Japanese colonialism throughout the Far East that Americans could have filled had they wanted to. The United States had the option of imposing American economic and military hegemony in the region. Who would have been able to block the United States? In time, perhaps regional opposition would have arisen, but at that point in early postwar history the United States easily could have reshaped Asia to suit venal American purposes. In fact, it did nothing of that sort. Nonetheless, economics and defense were linked within American strategy from the outset.

American ambitions in very early postwar Asia were largely limited to helping to put the region back on its feet, controlling Japan, wiping out the legacy of Japanese imperialism, keeping its prewar promise of independence to the Philippines, and to use its newfound clout in Asia to induce European colonial powers to follow the American example by liberating their colonies. Early U.S. goals may have been naive, but they were high-minded and emphatically not imperialist. The advent of tensions between the United States and Soviet Union that evolved into the Cold War quickly influenced the United States' agenda in Asia too. The Cold War's roots in Europe put a twist on that confrontation that endured until its formal end in the late 1980s. In fact, the European focus of the Cold War era was so profound that it persisted beyond the Cold War and influences Asian remnants of that period into the 1990s.

As the American strategy for coping with a communist challenge for leadership of the Western world developed in the late 1940s, and became solidified during the 1950s, it had derivative effects globally. Other regions were treated consciously or by default as adjuncts for which corollary policies had to be devised. This was the context in which U.S. security policy in Asia emerged. Much of the high-mindedness of U.S. ambitions in Asia was retained, but it was modified in varying degrees by the exigencies of the Cold War. Asia was still to be put back on its feet, but instead of being in pursuit of rather vague humanitarian reasons, a concrete geopolitical goal became tangible. Asian stability and self-reliance became U.S. goals as part of the process of containment of communism within Eurasia's "heartland" and the prevention of Soviet intervention around the continent's rim.

Accordingly, U.S. "control" of Japan assumed new proportions because it quickly became evident that the strongest potential fulcrum for basing a U.S. strategy in the Pacific against a Soviet threat would be Japan, which—despite being a defeated and bitter enemy—retained human skills that no other country in the region possessed. Despite lingering American ambiguity about Japan and desires that countries such as China and the Philippines should be the central actors in postwar U.S.–Asian relations, no country—other than Japan—had the extant human resources, and none could be manipulated as readily as Japan. While Americans remained committed to wiping out the legacy of Japanese imperialism in the form of encouraging national sovereignty within the region, the United States also adjusted rather quickly to the necessity of dealing with people in Korea, China (especially Taiwan), and Southeast Asia who had absorbed Westernized modern skills and values in large part through colonial or wartime Japanese intermediaries.

All those policy shifts were relatively incremental. The more dramatic shift had to do with U.S. attitudes toward decolonization. Washington kept its word vis-à-vis the Philippines. It was granted independence rapidly. Its long overdue new status was, however, clouded by two factors. The Republic of the Philippines was poorly positioned to play the central role in the Asian theater of the emerging Cold War. It lacked the level of human skills Japan possessed and was not near the front lines of the Asian Cold War as it emerged in Korea. This meant that the Philippines did not receive the primacy in U.S. postwar policy that it might otherwise have received.

Compounding this situation, the United States' development of rear-area bases in the Philippines (i.e. Subic and Clark) had the unintended effect of making these bases disproportionately important for a Philippines economy that otherwise lagged in the region. That, in turn, reinforced the dependence of the Filipinos upon the United States and created an atmosphere of neo-colonialism.[4] So, even as the United States tried to set the pace for Southeast Asian decolonialization, it inadvertently set a slow and ambiguous pace. That poor precedent was exacerbated by the United States' emphasis on European affairs in the Cold War. This emphasis led to American acceptance of European colonial arguments that Britain, France, and Holland could not follow the United States' example and jettison their Asian colonies without risking instability in both Asia and those portions of Europe that proclaimed an economic need for colonies. Consequently, American sensitivity to Cold War pressures compelled the United States to waffle on its anti-colonialist desires for Asia.

A major result of all these Cold War-generated factors was the creation of a more concrete sense of purpose behind U.S. policy in Asia. In contrast to the initial postwar policies that had a stop-gap quality about them and lacked a long-range vision, the Cold War fostered a framework upon which U.S. policy in Asia was draped. For better or worse, this framework was discretely military. More relevantly, there was scant evidence that U.S. economic ambitions played a major role in determining U.S. policy. To be sure, economic considerations were factored into the strategic calculations, but primarily in a supportive role. There was no serious thought given to the desirability of using U.S. military means to foster a thriving economic entity in the Asian region that eventually would be ripe for American plucking. It was the other way around: Americans sought to use economic instruments (aid, trade, technology transfer, etc.) as means to create levels of prosperity that would not only make Asian states resistant to Soviet inducements and/or threats but also make those states capable of contributing to their own defense and that of the region. Thus, the linkage between economics and security was clearly dominated by the latter. The long-term goal was American-led regional strategic supremacy over the Soviet Union and any states in its camp of the Cold War, not any economic vision.

As the Cold War matured, many seemingly permanent organizational structures also evolved. Central among them were the various security treaties between the United States and regional actors. Unlike the European theater where the United States also played the central strategic role but with one eye on the economic benefits to the United States that would eventually spin off from the Marshall Plan, in Asia the United States played a uniquely powerful central military role and scarcely imagined that that role would directly benefit the United States economy at home. It was no accident that the United States did not devise a multifaceted Asian equivalent of the Marshall Plan. U.S. officials thought primarily in military-strategic terms, and when those terms spilled over into the economic realm the spillover was in terms of long-term burden-sharing potentials and reduced costs to the United States.

Throughout the 1960s and 1970s, when East Asian economic success stories were becoming too obvious to be legitimately overshadowed by long-standing U.S. strategic priorities, the beginning of a major inconsistency in U.S. policymaking was evident. Despite the fact that economic relations between the United States and several Asian states, especially Japan, were achieving intrinsic importance on a global scale, the region continued to be treated primarily as a military theater of the Cold War. This emphasis was important because it enabled American officials to justify (or rationalize, depending upon one's perspective) the reasons why the United States should continue to accept the economic costs of being the geopolitical leader of the Western camp of the Asian Cold War. Therefore, Americans were told to tolerate the inequities of keeping U.S. markets open to quasi-mercantilist Asian competitors, to accept exaggerated Asian free trade rhetoric as though it represented reality, and to not grumble about the levels of Asian defense spending or unwillingness to contribute to regional collective security. Those Americans who considered these costs to be onerous were counseled not to rock the boat for fear the United States' leadership position would be diminished, its access to bases in the region would be reduced, and valuable allies might be alienated.[5]

During the late 1970s and the 1980s, the illogic of preserving American leadership at significant costs to U.S. economic interests grew. The 1980s also marked two other major phenomena. The Cold War reintensified during the first Reagan administration to a level that it drove the Soviet Union to, and past, the economic breaking point. In short, communism proved unable to sustain the Cold War as well as capitalism. At the same time as the U.S.-led camp was winning the Cold War, however, the pecking order within the "camp" was being altered dramatically. Paul Kennedy's controversial book, *The Rise and Fall of Great Powers*, suggested that any great power's strength is predicated on a complex of underlying factors that are subject to attrition and/or dissipation.[6] Whether it was because of such "declinist" factors or the simple recognition that the once-manifest comparative preeminence of the United States within the Western camp was being partially eclipsed by the successes of many others within that camp, there could be no denying that evolutionary change was afoot.[7]

The key to understanding this transformation was to grasp the correct nature of the linkage between the diverse elements of national power. Depending upon the level of analysis encountered, linkage could be a useful or an obtuse approach. No one denied that there were links between economics and security. Encouraging trade and investment long had been keys to propping up U.S. strategy in the Pacific. Similarly, as technological levels and cash reserves increased in Asia, it became obvious that the United States sought and, to some extent, relied on each. In Asia, too, there was clear recognition that the linkage between economics and security was real. Japan's comprehensive security doctrine is largely predicated on those linkages, seeing security as based upon prosperity-induced peace and stability.[8] Other Asian states were less explicit, but they too accepted the linkage.[9] Despite this virtually universal recognition and acceptance of linkages between economics and security, it remained an extraordinarily sensitive subject. Washington, Tokyo, and Seoul consciously tried to steer away from the concept of linkages because of its inherent utility for critics of either set of relationships.

The best examples of such caution are seen on the trade and investment fronts where American critics of Tokyo and Seoul's policies toward (and Japanese and Korean societies' receptivity regarding) U.S. competition have tried to use U.S. security commitments in Northeast Asia as leverage to extract concessions on these economic fronts.[10] Conversely, other American critics who were unhappy with Japanese and South Korean levels of contributions to their own defense or to common security concerns (in the region or externally, such as in the Persian Gulf) sought to use their dependence upon American economic goodwill as leverage to induce enhanced security cooperation.[11] Though less common, Japanese and Korean nationalist critics of U.S. bases in their countries and of U.S. pressures on each country for economic concessions have periodically raised the argument that Tokyo and Seoul should use the U.S. desire to maintain American military facilities on their soil as economic leverage against Washington.[12] As a consequence of the sensitivity of all three governments to any proposed use of defense versus trade/investment linkages for political leverage purposes, Tokyo, Seoul, and Washington are adamant that each country's economic policy and defense policy must not be permitted to contaminate the others.

They, therefore, strive mightily to exclude trade and/or investment leverage considerations from any discussion of defense policy alternatives. Security policy draws special attention, evidently because it is considered particularly vulnerable in light of American officials' preference for focusing on the maintenance of allegedly "smooth" Asian security ties rather than dwelling on troublesome economic issues. This vulnerability is exacerbated by the American public's frustrations with unsatisfactory Asian defense burden sharing when juxtaposed to Asian economic competitiveness. The principle of separate security and economic tracks is maintained when contentious economic issues are raised. This seems partially because of a desire for consistency, but mainly for fear that already serious U.S. bilateral economic frictions with Japan and Korea will only be exacerbated, either by comparing them to relatively good defense ties or by allowing economic tensions to spread like a disease to security issues. The net result is a persistent reluctance to deal with these two unequivocally linked policy issues in tandem.

This artificial division of emphases became increasingly illusory during the Reagan years. Nonetheless, it was perpetuated for the sake of assuring alliance cohesion. Few were willing to risk openly raising this contentious issue for fear that alliances in Asia might crack precisely at a point when the strategic adversary and its regional cohorts were on the geopolitcal ropes.[13] The irony in this situation was that most supporters of the Reagan defense build-up, which proved to be the straw that broke the Soviet camel's back, stressed the ways in which Moscow was being stretched to the economic limits by hefting unbearable defense responsibilities. In short, the Reagan strategy that pushed the Soviet system beyond the breaking point and ultimately ended the Cold War clearly used linkage leverage against the United States' adversary. Japan

234

and South Korea constituted key parts of that linkage. This created a contradiction. While using economics-security linkage with one hand and in one context, they denied its existence with the other hand in another context. This made little sense then, and makes still less sense now that the Cold War has been formally ended.

Post-Cold War Security in Northeast Asia

The perpetuation of an inconsistent analytical approach to U.S. policy in Asia is made possible by several factors. In addition to the persistence of anxieties about contaminating the two areas of U.S. policy, which Washington fears would weaken the U.S. posture in Asia economically and militarily, there also are doubts about whether the Cold War in Asia is really over in the same sense that it is in Europe. These doubts are expressed in the willingness of American strategists to retain old ways of thinking vis-à-vis Asia even as they display remarkably innovative thinking regarding Europe.

Since the fall of the Berlin Wall, the dissolution of the Warsaw Pact, the unification of Germany, the spread of democratic and market-oriented thinking to former East bloc states, and the collapse of the former Soviet Union's ability to sustain what President Reagan once labeled an "evil empire," American policymakers have been playing catch up. Diplomatically, militarily, and economically, the United States has been adjusting to a new global reality. The world has become a far less dangerous place for the United States in terms of any superpower threat. Precisely what military unipolarity, mixed with economic and political multipolarity, will mean in the long run for U.S. policymakers remains to be seen. The world probably will not settle into whatever new patterns are to emerge for several years, perhaps not until well into the twenty-first century. Be that as it may, U.S. policymakers cannot wait for trends in world affairs to become crystal clear. They must be, and have been, ready to adapt to unforeseen contingencies wherever they emerge.

In a very restricted sense, Washington's response to the Persian Gulf crisis in the form of "Desert Shield/Storm" was contingency-based. It was not a true indicator of future policy, however, because in that instance the United States adapted old strategies, designed for use in Cold War Eurasia, to a regional application in the Middle East. Concurrent with all that hasty activity, however, the United States also quietly spawned a new national security strategy specifically designed for the new era. Though largely ignored by the American and allied publics during the Persian Gulf war, the new strategy—alternatively known so far as "the president's strategy," "Powell's strategy," or "the reconstitution strategy"—is decidedly different.[14] It assumes there will not be a major war with any superpower on short notice (i.e., a few days, weeks, or months). Instead it assumes the United States will have many months, probably a couple of years, warning of any such renewed threat. Therefore, the United States has been, and is (as of this writing), en route to creating a new planning strategy that sees fewer and less dangerous threats, but wants to have the flexibility of maintaining smaller active and reserve forces. These smaller forces will nonetheless be capable of coping with threats that might emerge but that cannot be readily identified for planning purposes. If this sounds vague, that is because it *is* vague; intentionally. As Chairman of the Joint Chiefs of Staff Powell said, "Think hard about it: I'm running out of demons. I'm running out of villains. I'm down to Castro and Kim Il-sung."[15] On another occasion General Powell elaborated when asked about the source of a likely war without a major Soviet threat, "Haven't the foggiest. I don't know. That's the whole point. We don't know like we used to know."[16]

On balance, this new strategic approach is a sound one globally. Regarding the Asia–Pacific region, however, it is not quite in harmony with the post-Cold War era. Most of the changes announced in response to the new strategy have affected the Euro-Atlantic regions, including their extensions into the Mediterranean and the Middle East. In all these areas it is easy to see why the successors to the Soviet Union are a less credible threat. On the Far Eastern end of Eurasia, however, common wisdom still holds that Russia remains a relatively credible military threat. When evidence is cited that Russian forces in the Far East are also shrinking, American leaders tend to perceive this shrinkage in Cold War terms as proof that these forces are only getting "leaner and meaner."[17] Consequently some outposts of the Cold War are considered alive and well in Asia. This is especially true in Northeast Asia, where the divided Korean peninsula and the former Soviet Union's nuclear "bastion of the bear" in the Sea of

Okhotsk are routinely noted as reasons why the United States and its two regional allies cannot afford to let down their guard.

This posture is increasingly untenable. One must ask why Moscow's economic system, which is so weak and inept that it can no longer support a credible short-term military threat against Western Europe, should be perceived simultaneously as strong enough to project and sustain "lean and mean" forces in the furthest-flung reaches of Eastern and Southeastern Eurasia? If Moscow can no longer cope militarily in Europe against NATO, a region where its interests are demonstrably greater than in Asia, why should it be any more capable of coping in Asia? The answer clearly is that the successors to the Soviet Union are no more dangerous in Asia than they are in Europe, and probably are much less threatening. When that basic contradiction in existing U.S. threat perceptions is compounded by the collapse of the Soviet Union into smaller states and the probability that any reforms likely to emerge in those countries will take many years to become effective, if they ever do, contemporary apprehension about lingering Cold War-vintage scenarios in Northeast and Southeast Asia must be treated as even more illogical. Despite this argument, U.S. security policy in the Western Pacific remains far less subject to change than its counterparts in the Atlantic and contiguous areas.

The reasons for American reluctance to change are clearly put forth.[18] In Korea, the United States faces a genuine pocket of Cold War-vintage anachronisms in the form of the Kim Il Sung regime. The North Koreans do pose a genuine continuing threat, but the scale of that threat is being exaggerated by two factors. The diminishment of the Soviet global threat does not make the North Korean regional threat seem any less severe, even if it does not change much (in either direction) in objective terms. In short, even without a huge and menacing Soviet bear sniffing around the door, an aging North Korean tiger still gives reason for concern. That concern tends to be magnified in the eyes of the beholder, in this case U.S. Army personnel. Having lost major commands in Europe and facing severe force reductions, they are motivated to perpetuate their last major long-term overseas command in what approximates a front line, semi-combat milieu. For some Americans, retaining the status quo in Korea has become part of an intraservice turf battle over a smaller U.S. Department of Defense budget, sharply reduced staff, and relative roles within a U.S. Pacific Command which is likely to be in flux.

Despite such factors, inter-Korean tensions are being ameliorated and there is a real chance that the divided Korean nation will be reconciled during the 1990s. By the start of the twenty-first century, there is an excellent chance that Korean tensions will be sufficiently reduced to warrant far more significant cuts in U.S. forces in Korea than have already been announced by the Bush-Cheney-Powell team. Remaining U.S. security tasks in Korea almost certainly can be transferred rapidly to ROK forces and their commanders over the next decade. Regardless of such positive prospects, however, reluctant U.S. Army officials are joined in their go-slow approach by many South Korean defense officials who want to retain a U.S. trip-wire and backstop strategy as an insurance policy against the failure of a seemingly optimistic future to actually materialize. When put solely in strategic terms, their arguments are strongest. There are enough latent uncertainties in and around Korea to warrant substantial caution as shifts in U.S.–ROK responsibilities are carried out.

Other factors must be added to the calculations regarding Korea, however, before judgment is passed on the wisdom of existing U.S.–ROK plans for post-Cold War security. Seoul seems increasingly motivated by a strategic mind-set that is akin to Tokyo's approach to comprehensive security. The ROK is exploring its geopolitical options, diversifying its interdependence with new international actors on its horizon (i.e., Russia and the People's Republic of China), and broadening its contacts with Western economies by strengthening ties with Europe, Latin America, and Japan. This is a sound approach that deserves praise by Americans, but the United States also ought to pay close attention to the other lesson South Korea has learned from Japan about security and its costs. Seoul increasingly emulates Tokyo when it comes to responding to U.S. pressures for burden sharing and measuring the costs versus benefits of its security and economic ties with the United States. Seoul, too, is anxious that it not assume too much too soon when it comes to self-defense. The longer South Korea can keep the United States committed to and involved in the defense of the ROK against a North Korean assault, the better it is for both Seoul's sense of security and the health of its wallet. In this context, South Korea in the 1980s and 1990s has become a less cooperative ally and tends to drag its feet strategically in ways that help assure the United States will persist in its existing defense policies.

In the South Korean situation, a fairly plausible case can be made for retaining existing U.S. commitments, though not a truly persuasive one. In the case of Japan, on the other hand, the equivalent argument has become increasingly unpersuasive. Tokyo has been a reluctant partner in an American strategy for Asia since Japan regained its postwar independence partially on condition that it become the cornerstone of U.S. strategy for the Asia–Pacific region. Throughout the long years of the Cold War, Tokyo was an ambiguous participant on the United States' side. Japan clearly wanted to be an integral part of the West economically because that was where Japanese postwar national interests were firmly embedded. Defeat in the Second World War was a traumatic watershed event for Japan that put it unequivocally on a new route in world affairs. Thanks in large part to U.S. leadership, Japan was able to become integrated into a Western world order from which prewar imperial rivalries had excluded it. While there was virtual unanimity within Japanese leadership circles on the wisdom of that facet of Japan's post-Second World War foreign policy, there was much less certainty about the trade-offs Tokyo would be compelled to accept by becoming a security "partner" of the United States.

At a minimum this arrangement was perceived to be a one-sided partnership in which Japan would have little voice. More importantly, the threats ostensibly perceived by the two partners in pursuit of allegedly common interests struck the huge majority of Japanese as being skewed toward American perceptions of a global Soviet threat. Most Japanese saw the Cold War as an "American war," not really their own affair. Notwithstanding profound Japanese distrust of Russians that long predated the Cold War and persists into the 1990s when the Cold War is over, most Japanese never saw the Soviet threat to their country in Cold War terms that are analogous to American or South Korean images of the Soviet Union or North Korea, respectively. This Japanese attitude that the Cold War globally and in neighboring Korea was somebody else's business is a classically xenophobic example of a tendency among the Japanese to not want to be contaminated by the *gaijin*'s problems. In other words, it was another case of *kaigan-no kasai* (a fire on a distant shore).

Against this background Japan's foreign and defense policies throughout the Cold War were predicated on an emphasis upon economics that was the mirror opposite of the United States' military-oriented focus on a strategic framework. Whereas Americans simultaneously counted their strategic blessings and grew frustrated over the economic costs inflicted on the United States in the name of protecting vaunted but reluctant allies, the Japanese adopted roughly opposite attitudes. The Japanese zeroed in on the economic benefits that participation in the Western alliance network afforded to Japan in terms of U.S. market access, on American help as an intermediary smoothing the way for Japanese economic expansion worldwide, on its diplomatic status as a key cog in the global machine assembled by the United States in the Cold War, and on the latitude permitted Japan to stress its economic roles in broadly defined "security" while hewing to a pacifist course in its limited self-defense that was mandated by its U.S.-sanctioned postwar constitution.

Both sides in the U.S.–Japan alliance understood that these arrangements gave Japan enormous economic advantages and acted as a de facto subsidy for Japan's military security. That was intentional because it would foster Japanese and regional prosperity, which was seen by Americans as essential for the kind of U.S.-led peace and stability Washington desired in Asia in order to keep the Soviets at bay. Despite the great advantages to Japan, some Japanese remained suspicious that Japan was gratuitously endangered by being an unequal partner of the United States. Many Japanese did not want to be a Cold War target because of U.S. bases on their territory. This produced a sense of ambiguity about the United States among many Japanese and a pronounced reluctance to share burdens as defined by Americans and to fit needs determined by Americans. Borrowing from the American pre-revolutionary war experience, many Japanese resented U.S. policies which amounted to "taxation without representation."

An odd thing happened as the Cold War thawed elsewhere. Japanese who had, at best, been reluctant cold warriors ironically became the most cautious among the United States' important security partners regarding their acceptance of rapid international change in the late 1980s and early 1990s. Whether compared to Germany, France, Great Britain, or others in Europe, not to speak of the highly adaptable South Korean responsiveness to changes in the Soviet Union, Tokyo was—comparatively—a stick in the mud. The Japanese reluctance to be flexible vis-à-vis the Soviet Union can be seen in bilateral Japan–Russian Republic contacts that remain relatively frigid, in Japan's trepidation about the changes occurring in relations between the two Koreas and Russia, and in Japan's hypercaution when called upon to back U.S. and Western European efforts to draw Russia further into the free market system. Some of this caution can be chalked up to innate Japanese societal conservatism. Some of it is traceable to Russo–Japanese enmity that long predated the Cold War and may long outlive any remnants of the Cold War.

There is another troubling factor, however, which is directly related to the issue of the impact of economic factors on alliance cohesion. The Japanese have grown accustomed to the cost-effective ways in which Japan's economically-oriented foreign policy and the United States' militarily-oriented foreign policy interact in Asia. Tokyo likes the role it plays and clearly does not want Americans to visualize Asian security in ways that might sanction a radically different U.S. strategy for the Western Pacific. As a Foreign Ministry official, Takenaka Shigeo, said in *Gaiko Forum,* "The policy which Japan ought to take must be a policy which will foster sound U.S. internationalism. It must be a policy which will give self-confidence to the American people that the United States can manage with internationalism."[19] In short, Japan in the 1990s is coming to terms very reluctantly with the ways in which the end of the Cold War might remove the anticommunist ideological incentives for the United States to remain committed to Western Pacific security. Tokyo appears nervous that post-Cold War Washington will abandon its fixation with military security and broaden its horizons to include a greater emphasis on economic issues in a manner that might contaminate alliance cohesiveness.

As of this writing (in early 1992), Tokyo is extraordinarily pleased that Washington has chosen to stress a need for the United States to remain a military presence in Japan's backyard for the sake of regional stability and in order to retain the United States' dominant strategic voice. Though many Japanese sense that the United States may, indeed, have the feet of clay that Paul Kennedy described, they want the United States to try to be the foundation of the international system for as long as possible. There are two key reasons for this desire on Japan's part: (1) it is highly cost-effective for Japan; and (2) Tokyo does not want regional or global circumstances to change in ways that might tend to thrust leadership upon the Japanese, who do not desire it and would not know what to do with a leadership role if it were forced upon them by default.[20] As a consequence the Japanese are very nervous about, and conversely strong supporters of, perpetuating existing U.S.–Japan security arrangements.

Their long-standing ambiguity about the rationality of Japan's participation in the Cold War is being replaced by another form of ambiguity about coexisting in the post-Cold War era. Ironically, this new ambiguity has put Japan in a position of clinging to the remnants of its theater of the Cold War (in which it never was a true believer) in order to retain American commitments. Japan now wants to keep the United States involved, relishes the propensity of American leaders to perpetuate what Assistant Secretary of State Richard Solomon called a U.S. "balancing wheel" in the Asia–Pacific region, and will do whatever it can to keep the United States militarily active in the region.[21] In sum, so that Japan's prosperity and security is preserved, Tokyo is becoming far more active than it was in the past as a proponent of the value of regional military security. Logically (if perversely from the point of view of American critics of past Japanese reluctant security policy), Tokyo still emphasizes what Japan can do economically and that this division of labor should satisfy Americans as they support a continued U.S. military central role in the Asia–Pacific region. Increasingly it is joined in that policy position by South Korea. Despite the ways in which the Cold War has either ended, is ending (i.e., in Korea), or is irrelevant (i.e., regarding certain Japan–Russian disputes), the United States listens carefully to Tokyo and Seoul, retains much of its Cold War-vintage strategy in the Pacific, and has been remarkably slow to apply its new planning strategy to the Asia–Pacific region.

Prospects for U.S. Strategy in Asia

There is a real chance, perhaps a high probability, that little will change in U.S. strategy toward Asia because of the inertia of seemingly successful policy, the vested interests of the U.S. civilian and military bureaucracy in retaining the structural status quo, and the great skill of Asians (especially Japanese and Koreans) in convincing Americans to stay the course militarily even if the costs economically are high. This analysis could end with that prognosis as its conclusion. To do so would make some American and Asian decision-makers much happier, but it would do an injustice to U.S. national interests. The end of the Cold War is a profound process, and it is almost unimaginable that it will not compel major changes in U.S. strategy worldwide, certainly including Northeast Asia. The most essential question that must be asked about post-Cold War Northeast Asian security will be "where's the threat?" If by "post-Cold War" one assumes a resolution of the Korean situation and acceptance by Americans that outstanding Japan–Russian tensions are *not* "Cold War" issues, then one is hard-pressed to discern a regional threat to U.S. national interests in the Western Pacific that emanates from external sources. If the United States and Russia can cooperate and develop amiable relations bilaterally and with regard to regions such as Europe and the Middle East, there is no intrinsic reason why the Asia–Pacific region need be any different. There are reasons why U.S. military, economic, and diplomatic policy toward Asia also should be reconstructed in the context of the post-Cold War realities of drastically reduced superpower tensions. At a minimum one can envision the new U.S. planning strategy being fully applied in the Pacific, with consequent dramatic changes in roles and missions for U.S. forces, altered command structures, and an overall shift from a U.S.-centered international security system to a new regional security focus which will be as Asian-focused as Europe will be European-focused.[22] While this does not mean an American withdrawal from either region or the revival of American isolationism, it does portend a sharply reduced U.S. role in overseas regions and the reemergence of the United States as a more normal player in world affairs.[23]

Something of that sort seems to be in the cards, though the unique strengths enjoyed by the United States as a unipolar superpower, and the hubris of the American people as they wield U.S. power, no doubt will temper the process of adjustment. Compounding the likelihood of such prospective alternative roles is the reality of changing patterns of wealth in the world. Though many analysts denigrate the declinist approach to assessing U.S. relative power, there can be no denying that—for all its armed assets and renewed confidence in the wake of the Persian Gulf War—the United States economy is not remotely what it used to be compared to all those allies in Europe and Asia that prospered under the protection of a U.S.-led Cold War world order. The United States may not be in "decline," but it is being relatively eclipsed by ascendant powers such as Germany and Japan.[24] In that context, and in the absence of the Cold War verities upon which the U.S. national security state was predicated after the Second World War, the post-Cold War pressures on virtually all American political fronts will be enormous throughout the 1990s. Americans across the political spectrum will be compelled to husband U.S. national wealth and not fritter it away on the defense of allies who either do not require defense from reduced (or eliminated) "threats" or are perfectly capable of paying for and providing their own defenses. In these terms, the economic frictions that have been nibbling away at alliance cohesion throughout the 1960s, 1970s, 1980s, and early 1990s seem likely to take even larger bites, as Americans ask themselves and their government why U.S. strategy should require unacceptably high economic sacrifices.

If the GATT-based world trade system remains intact, the impact of economic frictions upon U.S. alliances should be manageable and felt over a protracted period, during which adjustments can be made by all parties. Should the Cold War interdependent economic order be replaced by a system of trading blocs in Europe, North America, and Asia as many now fear, the impact on U.S. strategy likely would be as profound, perhaps more profound, than the end of the Cold War. While one can imagine the inertia and momentum of Cold War-vintage policies and structures outliving their real utility well into the post-Cold War era, it is very difficult, probably impossible, to discern reasons why the United States would remain as committed to the defense of explicitly rival trading blocs. One need not have recourse to hackneyed notions that the United States needs "demons" to sustain a national security state to understand that American leaders are not so naive that they will continue to defend economic rivals perpetually, particularly not if those rivals form themselves into coalition blocs that treat the United States and its neighbors as economic adversaries.

Regardless of the shape of the global trading order, it is a virtual certainty that the United States will face increased economic competition in the foreseeable future and probably well beyond. In that context, economic relations with allies seem equally certain to assume levels of importance that will not permit

Washington to perpetuate an excessive emphasis on security policy at the expense of sound national economic policy. None of this augers well for smoother alliance cohesion. Unless these allies become far more forthcoming in terms of economic concessions and defense burden sharing that matches the post-Cold War context, the American need to stress economic policy is likely to prove disruptive to harmonious security policy. This principle applies worldwide, but it is likely to be enforced with special enthusiasm in Northeast Asia, a region which is seen widely by Americans as a key source of the new economic challenges confronting the United States in the post-Cold War era.

Notes

1. The notion of a triangular Japan–ROK–U.S. security relationship is routinely denounced by North Korea as an imperialist plot. Nevertheless, the first trilateral security meeting did not occur until after the formal end of the Cold War and was held on June 23–24, 1991 to discuss coping with changes in the Soviet Union and North Korea. For coverage of that meeting, see *The Korea Herald,* June 22, 1991, p. 1.

2. For a survey of Asian and American reactions to the end of the Cold War and its meaning for Asia, see the *Far Eastern Economic Review (FEER),* December 13, 1990, pp. 25–32 and March 7, 1991, pp. 8–12.

3. South Koreans, in particular, perceive the United States as guided by motives described by American dependency theorists who primarily focused on Latin America. South Korean leftists, with sympathy from the Japanese left, believe American security policy is aimed at carving out an economic zone of influence in Northeast Asia that constitutes a kind of economic imperialism and colonialism. American complaints about Japanese and South Korean economic aggressiveness do not deter them from their quaint beliefs.

4. Filipinos whose criticism of American policy in Asia echoes that of the South Korean radicals are on much firmer logical ground. The legacy of prewar American colonialism thrives in the Philippines in terms of physical infrastructure, mutual attitudes, and excessive reliance on the United States. It is made more profound by the persistence of Spanish-era colonial legacies in Philippine society, which further distort the American role. The removal of U.S. bases in the Philippines promises to eliminate a key source of such pseudocolonial dependence.

5. In addition to the author's previous writings, see the many writings of Chalmers Johnson, Donald Hellmann, Clyde Prestowitz, Doug Bandow, Paul Kennedy, and other critics.

6. Paul Kennedy, *The Rise and Fall of Great Powers: Economic Change and Military Conflict from 1500 to 2000* (New York: Random House, 1987).

7. Nonetheless, a counter-declinist school emerged. See, for example, Henry R. Nau, *The Myth of America's Decline: Leading the World Economy into the 1990s* (Oxford: Oxford University Press, 1990).

8. For a survey of that doctrine, see Robert W. Barnett, *Beyond War: Japan's Concept of Comprehensive National Security* (Washington, DC: Pergamon-Brassey's Press, 1984).

9. The best example is the Republic of Korea. See the author's "Korean Security: Is Japan's 'Comprehensive Security' Model a Viable Alternative?" in Doug Bandow and Ted Galen Carpenter, editors, *U.S.- Korean Security Relations* (New York: Transaction Publications, 1992).

10. The best examples are found in Clyde Prestowitz, *Trading Places: How We Allowed Japan to Take the Lead* (New York: Basic Books, Inc., 1988); and C. Prestowitz, R. Morse, and A. Tonelson, editors, *Powernomics: Economics and Strategy after the Cold War* (Washington, DC: Economic Strategy Institute, 1991).

11. Congressional critics of Japan's Persian Gulf War performance relied heavily on this leverage.

12. The most explicit example was Maeda Hisao, "So Who's Getting the 'Free Ride'?", *Japan Times Weekly,* November 29, 1981, p. 21. See also Korean critics of U.S. bases in South Korea who want the United States to pay rent for them as it allegedly did in the Philippines.

13. The author did so midway through the Reagan years in his *U.S.- Japan Strategic Reciprocity* (Stanford: Hoover Institution Press, 1985).

14. For a scholarly assessment of that new strategy, see James J. Tritten and Paul Stockton, editors, *Reconstituting Defense: Problems in the New United States National Security Strategy* (New York: Praeger Publishers, 1992).

15. *Newsweek,* April 22, 1991, p. 19.

16. *The Washington Post* (Weekly), May 27–June 2, 1991, p. 8.

17. For an analysis of this treatment, see *FEER,* June 21, 1991, pp. 23–27.

18. An excellent example of this caution is presented in an interview of General Robert Ris Cassi, Commander of U.S. Forces in Korea, in *FEER,* May 2, 1991, pp. 18–19.

19. Quoted in *The Washington Post* (Weekly), February 25–March 3, 1991, p. 25.

20. For insights into Japan's reluctance, see Donald Hellmann and John H. Makin, editors, *Sharing World Leadership: A New Era for America and Japan* (Washington, DC: American Enterprise Institute, 1989).

21. *The Christian Science Monitor,* November 6, 1991, p. 6.

22. The author addressed these prospects in greater detail in his "A New American Strategy in Asia?" in Tritten and Stockton, *Reconstituting Defense.*

23. For a more favorable examination of those alternatives, see Ted Galen Carpenter, editor, *Collective Defense or Strategic Independence?: Alternative Strategies for the Future* (Lexington, MA: Lexington Books and the Cato Institute, 1989).

24. For a particularly harsh treatment of the Japanese challenge to the United States, see the unauthorized draft version of the Rochester Institute of Technology's contract analysis for the CIA, *Japan: 2000,* and coverage of it in: *FEER,* June 27, 1991, p. 15; *The Washington Post,* June 8, 1991, p. A5 and June 12, 1991, p. A31; and *The Japan Digest,* June 20, 1991, p. 5.

The United States' Economic Interdependence with Japan and the Republic of Korea*

Robert W. Beckstead

The focus of relations between the United States and Japan and the Republic of Korea has been directed towards both national security and economics. The economic dimension has emphasized the importance of fostering favorable trade relations. The United States has entered into mutual cooperation and security treaties with both Japan and the Republic of Korea. At the same time, the United States has been their number one trading partner for decades. In turn Japan is well situated as the number two trading partner with the United States, and the Republic of Korea has risen steadily to become the seventh most important trading partner. Thus, these three countries have become progressively more interdependent, particularly in regard to access to goods and services as well as preserving national security.

In principle and practice it is through trade that nations become tied together for their mutual betterment. This is so because trade allows participating nations to have access to resources, technologies, goods, and services that they may not oth-

*The paper represents the views of the author and does not necessarily reflect the official opinion of the Industrial College of the Armed Forces, the National Defense University, the Department of Defense, or the U.S. Government.

erwise have. Therefore, trade and economic well-being go hand in hand and nations which restrict trade activity do so at an economic cost.

Especially since the end of the Vietnam War, relations between the United States, Japan, and the Republic of Korea have experienced heightened levels of confrontation on trade matters. The United States viewed the export growth policies of these two nations with accompanying restrictions on imports as the major cause of its staggering trade deficits. Pure and simple, the situation reflected unfair trade practices on the part of Japan and the Republic of Korea. In fact, the mammoth U.S. trade deficits with Japan as well as the rapid escalation in trade deficits with the Republic of Korea and other Pacific Rim countries during the 1980s were responsible in large measure for the passage of the U.S. Omnibus Trade and Competitiveness Act in 1988 along with its Super 301 provision in which unfair trade practices were specifically addressed.

This chapter is organized to first address the issues surrounding nations adopting trade protectionism in contrast to free trade policies. Second, comparisons are made about the general economic growth of the United States, Japan, and the Republic of Korea during the decade of the 1980s along with a discussion of other indicators of economic activity. Third, an analysis is given of the nature and direction that direct foreign investment has taken among the three nations. Fourth, an analysis is rendered of the economic interdependence of the three countries by addressing the composition and characteristics of commodities traded between the United States and Japan and the United States and the Republic of Korea. Lastly, conclusions are drawn from the analysis.

Protectionism versus Free Trade

There is a natural tendency for nations to position themselves in the most favorable status relative to trade relations. In this light, mercantilism followed much later by neo-mercantilism expressed specific ways in which this favorable trade relation could be established and maintained. Nations should incorporate export-led economic policies and target industries to be developed that would be competitive in international markets. At the same time, protection from foreign competition should naturally be provided for the newly emerging industries and additional trade barriers should likewise be raised to ensure that a trade surplus is possible. Such policies have patterns resembling a beggar-my-neighbor policy—a nation wishes to profit at the expense of all others. Should such policies be pursued, trading partners may simply counter with their own restrictions, resulting in a worsening trade condition for all.

Adam Smith attacked protectionism in his *Wealth of Nations*, in which he argued that free trade would allow nations to specialize in producing those things where they were most efficient. Specialization and efficiency lead to greater productivity and well-being. Later David Ricardo brought to the attention of the world how all nations could benefit through trade even though some nations could produce everything more efficiently than other nations. His analysis centered on the concept of "comparative advantage." Ricardo noted that regardless of how efficient a nation was in producing goods and services, it was unlikely that production was equally efficient among all goods and services. So, a country could increase its production and productivity by concentrating on producing those goods and services where the greatest efficiencies existed and relying upon foreign sources to supply remaining needs.

The power of the free trade argument and its proponents have driven trade policy among the principal trading nations of the world for over 150 years with the stark exception of the 1930s. Nations such as England followed by Germany at the end of the nineteenth century and then the United States after World War II have been the strong advocates of free trade. For example, to avoid the basic pitfalls of protectionism that strangled international trade during the 1930s, an international economic conference of Allied nations was held in late 1944 at Bretton Woods, New Hampshire. Out of this conference came an agreement that established the foundation for promoting "free trade" or "freer trade" practices among participating nations.

The United States has carried the torch of free trade and endorsed the trade liberalization movement in the world since World War II. This has been accomplished through numerous negotiation rounds held in relation to forming a broader General Agreement on Tariffs and Trade (GATT). The Kennedy Rounds started trade barriers for goods to move in a sharply downward direction; and the Tokyo Rounds addressed reducing indirect trade barriers (e.g. government bureaucratic actions). The Uruguay Rounds are presently "on hold" because the major trading nations have failed to reach agreement on issues dealing with services, investment, and particularly agricultural trade barriers. It is anticipated, however, that future negotiations will produce further tariff reductions simply because that which has been accomplished over thirty-five years could quickly become unraveled with serious economic consequences befalling all trading nations.

As would be expected, the reductions of trade barriers have been uneven among trading nations partially because nations are at different stages of economic development and also because nations protect infant industries from competition of mature industries found in other nations. Eventually, the asymmetry of trade policy among nations, where developing countries exhibited greater protectionist trends when compared to developed nations, brought the United States to endorse a "free and fair" trade policy and tipped the country toward a reciprocal trade position. This new trade policy still advocates free trade practices by encouraging trading partners to adopt more import liberalization policies and to resist protectionist measures to cope with trade imbalances. At the same time, the United States is committed to responding in a reciprocal way to legitimate concerns raised by its industrial and political leaders about unfair trade practices of other countries.

General Economic Growth

The decade of the 1980s witnessed significant changes in economic relations among the United States, Japan, and the Republic of Korea. The United States made adjustments to the rapid escalation of oil prices in the 1970s and returned to the nation's peacetime average economic growth rate of 2.6 percent. What was different about the economic growth that occurred was the role played by the foreign sector of the economy. The growth and decline of the foreign sector exceeded that of changes in gross national product. In other words, the foreign sector became a much more important player in the economic health of the nation. The United States had in fact become significantly affected by the nature of the economically interdependent world. Likewise, Japan and the Republic of Korea experienced major economic growth, 4.4 and 8.4 percent respectively, which in turn was driven by investment and export growth, even though the growth rates of both countries were off slightly from the long-term trends. Growth of consumption has nearly always lagged behind the rates of expansion witnessed for the aggregate economy in Japan and the Republic of Korea. With a shift in the United States trade liberalization policy at the end of 1988, trading partners were encouraged to rely upon domestic demand as the engine of economic progress. Since this time, the Republic of Korea has experienced consumption growing at a faster rate than gross national product.

The plague of high inflation rates of the 1970s was substantially reduced in the 1980s (see table 10.1). In contrast to the United States where wage increases remained below the inflation rate, both Japan and the Republic of Korea found that wage increases exceeded the overall inflationary rate. Thus, wages contributed significantly to inflation in those countries. This was particularly true in the case of the Republic of Korea where wage rates had been held down by government policy in order to provide a competitive cost position in international trade. The competitive advantage has been adversely affected by the successive double digit wage increases, 20 percent or more per year since 1987, given to laborers in the Korean workplace. Also, the expansion in the world economy brought about employment opportunities that resulted in unemployment rates falling, or in some cases, remaining about the same during the 1980s.

The decade of the 1980s witnessed the United States moving from an international creditor to a debtor nation (see table 10.1). Trade relations with countries on the western rim of the Pacific contributed significantly to this condition, especially Japan and to a much lesser extent the Republic of Korea. By 1987 the current account and trade deficits peaked at $162 billion and $160 billion respectively; however, in 1990 the position of the United States had improved somewhat with the current account deficit at nearly $97 billion and the trade deficit registered about $106 billion. Trade relations with Japan accounted for about 40 percent of the total trade deficit and only 4 percent in the case of the Republic of Korea. During the same period, Japan's current account and trade balance grew rapidly in the first half of the 1980s and peaked in 1987 with surpluses of $87 billion and $96 billion respectively; but by 1990 the surpluses in the current account had dropped by nearly 60 percent from the peak year and the trade account decreased by about 35 percent. The Republic of Korea started the decade of the 1980s with deficits in both the current and trade accounts (see table 10.1). By 1988 the current and trade balances peaked with surpluses of $14.2 billion and $11.4 billion respectively. In 1990 surpluses had now turned to deficits of $2.2 billion in the current account while trade balances still registered surpluses but at a reduced level of $2 billion.

The intensely competitive activity that took place during the decade brought about significant changes in the overall trade balances. The United States started the 1980s with a combined deficit trade balance with Japan and the Republic of Korea of $7.2 billion. By 1986, this combined deficit had surged over eight times to $58.8 billion. This explosion in trade deficit heightened American awareness of its decline in international competitiveness and brought about federal government action to curb unfair trading practices of trading partners. It also highlighted the need for shoring up the competitiveness of American industry. In partial response to these developments, the combined deficits were reduced 41 percent to $40.4 billion by 1990. On the other hand, Japan's trade surpluses with the United States and the Republic of Korea grew from $10.3 billion in 1980 to a peak of $57.3 billion in 1987, an increase of 456 percent in only six years. However, by 1990 the combined surplus had fallen 23 percent to $43.9 billion. In the case of the Republic of Korea, its generated surpluses with the United States provided a source of funding to cover deficits incurred with Japan. Korea had a combined trade deficit of $3.1 billion in 1980. By 1984 a slight combined surplus was experienced and by 1988 that surplus had grown to $4.7 billion. The effects of domestic economic problems, resulting in some loss of competitiveness, found the growth rate in exports declining; and even with the introduction of an import liberalization policy, there was a decline in the rate of growth in imports as well. Consequently, there was a sharp decline in trade surpluses with the United States but a small rise in deficits with Japan. This condition created a deficit in the combined trade balance of $3.5 billion in 1990.

Certainly, there has not been a single cause and effect relation to the economic well-being of these three trading countries.

Table 10.1 • United States, Japan, and Republic of Korea Economic Growth and Other Industries

	United States			Japan			Republic of Korea		
	1980	1985	1990	1980	1985	1990	1980	1985	1990
Growth Rates									
Real GNP	− 0.2	3.6	0.9	4.5	4.9	5.7	− 3.7	7.0	9.1
Consumption	− 0.2	4.7	1.0	0.8	2.7	3.6	0.3	6.3	10.0
Fixed Investment	− 7.9	5.3	0.2	7.7	12.7	13.4	− 11.4	4.7	21.7
Exports	9.0	− 1.2	6.2	18.7	5.6	7.8	47.0	4.5	4.8
Prices, Wages and Unemployment									
Consumer Prices %	13.5	3.6	5.4	7.8	2.0	3.1	28.7	3.1	8.6
Nominal Wages %	6.9	2.1	3.5	6.0	5.0	4.7	22.7	9.9	21.1
Unemployment %	7.0	7.1	5.4	2.0	2.6	2.3	5.2	4.0	2.5
Current Account Balance US$B	1.5	− 122.3	− 96.8	− 7.0	49.2	35.8	− 1.3	− 0.9	− 2.2
Trade Balance, US$B	− 19.3	− 122.1	− 105.5	6.7	46.0	63.5	− 4.4	0.0**	2.0

**Less than $0.05 Billion

Sources: U.S. Department of Commerce, Japan, Economic Planning Agency, and Republic of Korea Economic Planning Board.

Nevertheless, the United States has been the heavy player in trade relations, adding substance to the adage, "when the United States sneezes, the world catches cold." It is a fact that the United States is the major consumer of goods and services produced in Japan and the Republic of Korea. Over the decade of the 1980s, the United States has been characterized as "a nation on a consuming binge, having lost its motivation to save." The consuming public found the products produced in Japan and Korea of excellent quality and very price competitive. It should then come as no surprise that the United States chalked up huge trade deficits with these two countries. Actually, the trade deficits were not confined to these two countries but existed with most trading nations around the world.

Direct Foreign Investment

A significant part of an export growth policy for economic development is acquiring capital for establishing an economic infrastructure and creating industrial enterprises. In most cases, countries are short of internal capital at the beginning of their industrial development or reconstruction. This was so with Japan after World War II and the Republic of Korea after the Korean War. The United States played a very important role in supplying such needed capital to them for rebuilding their economies from the devastations of war. The successes experienced in their economic recovery and subsequent "economic miracle" serve as a testament to the wise use of these funds and the creativeness of their people.

During the decade of the 1980s, corporate America continued to plow capital into these two countries. According to data released by the U.S. Department of Commerce, the total stock of American direct foreign investment in Japan increased at an annual rate of 13.6 percent and reached $21 billion in 1990. Only ten percent of the Japan figure has been invested in the Republic of Korea. In fact, the stock of American direct foreign investment in Korea remained nearly constant during the first half of the decade but after the Korean government eased its foreign investment-related regulations, the stock of capital tripled during the last half of the 1980s. Japanese foreign direct investment in

Korea has generally led that of the United States and by 1990 amounted to $3.7 billion.

Over half of the total stock of U.S. direct foreign investment in Japan was in manufacturing industries in 1990, with a concentration in non-electrical machinery, chemicals, and transportation. Other industries that have attracted capital are wholesale trade and petroleum. The finance and insurance industry came into more prominence during the latter part of the 1980s. The Republic of Korea has attracted American capital mostly in the manufacturing and banking industries; the two industries account for over 80 percent of the total stock of investment. Within the manufacturing industrial category, electrical machinery, transportation, chemical, and food industries received over 80 percent of the investment.

Much has been made of foreign direct investment in the United States in recent years. During the first 135 years of the nation's existence, there was a heavy reliance upon foreign capital for economic development from which the nation greatly benefitted. Today, Japan ranks second to the United Kingdom in the size of foreign direct investment in the United States. The total stock of investment in 1990 was nearly $84 billion. During the 1980s the increase in the flow of Japanese capital to the United States averaged 34 percent per year. A broad array of industries attracted Japanese capital, but wholesale and retail trade received slightly over one-third of the total, followed by banking and finance at 20 percent, real estate at 19 percent, and manufacturing at 18 percent. In contrast to Japan, the flow of capital to the United States from the Republic of Korea has fluctuated greatly. During some years, the total stock of capital increases because of new investment and retained earnings. In other years, payment of debt and repatriating profits reduce the overall stock of capital. Korean direct foreign investment peaked in 1988 at $505 million, which reflects the mounting surpluses in its current account balances. The investment has been mostly in wholesale and retail trade and real estate with little going into manufacturing.

The flow of capital between these three countries increases the degree of economic interdependence; but even more, it represents a shared belief in the future economic growth and prosperity of each of the trading partners. It is also a recognition of the skills and abilities of their people to be productive and innovative as well as having ability to be effective managers of their resources.

Economic Interdependence

The dynamics of trade relations were notable during the decade of the 1980s. This was particularly true during the period 1983 to 1988 for which data are available. This period began at a time when economic activity was picking up worldwide from a recession and freer trade policies were being more widely adopted. This is also the period when the Uruguay Rounds of the GATT were underway, which emphasized the importance of providing greater access to agricultural goods, service categories, and protection of intellectual property rights. During this same period, the United States' commodity trade activity around the world as measured by the total amount of American exports and imports increased at an average annual rate of 10 percent.

It is readily acknowledged that international commodity trade transactions reflect the production capabilities and consumer preferences of the trading nations as well as the willingness of such countries to engage in commercial transactions. In a way, these transactions register a level of economic interdependence. In order to facilitate commercial transactions, it is necessary to establish business enterprises that produce, promote, sell, and service the merchandise. Commercial and financial enterprises become a part of the local economy and as such establish the foundation for economic interdependence.

The extent of the nations' economic interdependence can be assessed by the mere volume of commodities traded and its relationship to the trade that occurs elsewhere. The breadth in the kinds of commodities traded can, likewise, be an indicator of interdependence. Along with interdependencies, it is possible for nations to develop actual dependencies in particular kinds of commodities. The degree of dependency can be revealed in a free market environment by trade imbalances or the ratio of imports to exports between countries. It is possible to overstate the degree of dependency if one of the trading partners merely imposed some barriers to trade in order to tip the imbalance in its favor. The degree of dependency on any one nation also reflects the availability of the commodities from other sources in sufficient quantities to meet requirements.

In a free market condition, the nature of trade imbalances describes a nation's relative dependency either upon foreign markets for its goods or on access to wanted merchandise produced abroad. A ratio of the value of imports divided by exports measures the relative significance of the trade imbalances. When the ratio is greater than one, the coefficient notes the extent to which a nation is dependent upon foreign merchandise. If the ratio is less than one, it notes the degree to which a nation is dependent upon foreign markets for its produce. By comparing ratios as measured in a bilateral relationship to the ratios experienced worldwide, it is also possible to gauge the relative importance this bilateral trade has to overall trade relations. In addition to the consideration of evaluating the trade ratios, the degree to which a nation relies upon a few countries for marketing its produce or obtaining its merchandise requirements is also considered. The broader the trading base, the greater the accessibility of commodities and the options for trade.

The degree of economic interdependence that exists between the United States, Japan, and the Republic of Korea is based upon the nature of commodity trade transactions between them in the form of commodity flows. The following is a discussion about the general composition of the commodities traded followed by an analysis of commodity trade between the United States and Japan and the United States and the Republic of Korea.

Composition of Commodity Trade

Commodity trade is categorized by the Organization for Economic Cooperation and Development (OECD) into ten industry classifications or transactions (see table 10.2). As noted in table 10.2, the worldwide commodity trade of the United States between 1983 and 1988 was concentrated in four major industrial groups: machinery and transport equipment; miscellaneous manufactured articles; manufactured goods; and mineral fuels, lubricants and related materials. These four categories averaged over 75 percent of all export and import transactions during the period. The largest proportion, 42 percent, was in the machinery and transport equipment industries which produce office machines and ADP equipment, telecommunications and sound recording apparatus, electrical machinery, and road vehicles.

The nature of commodity trade between the United States and Japan had some similarities as well as differences from the distribution of transactions worldwide. For instance, the largest proportion of trade was in machinery and transport equipment; however, these transactions constituted nearly 64 percent of the total as compared to 42 percent worldwide. This significant concentration in commodity trade was due mainly to transactions in office machines and ADP equipment and road vehicles. All of the rest of the commodity categories received smaller proportions of transactions than were found worldwide (see table 10.2). Food and live animals replaced mineral fuels, lubricants and related materials in worldwide trade and were the fourth most important commodities traded with Japan. The top four commodity categories in U.S.–Japan trade amounted to nearly 87 percent of the total trade.

The distribution of commodity trade between the United States and the Republic of Korea was centered in machinery and transport equipment, miscellaneous manufactured articles, and manufactured goods. These categories represented nearly 80 percent of all commodity trade between the two countries (see table 10.2). For years commodity trade has emphasized articles of apparel and clothing accessories and footwear. In more recent years the trade has broadened to include telecommunication and sound recording apparatus, electrical machinery, iron and steel, and manufactures of metals. The broadening of merchandise traded between the two countries only testifies to the significant progress the Republic of Korea has made in becoming a modern industrialized economy.

United States–Japan Trade

The importance of trade between the United States and Japan can not be overstated; the two economies are interlinked. During the period of 1983 through 1988, total exports and imports experienced an average annual rate of increase of nearly 15 percent and was 45 percent higher than the United States' worldwide trade increase. For the same period, trade between the United States and Japan averaged $98.5 billion annually and represented over 16 percent of the United States' total world trade.

Table 10.2 • Composition of Total U.S. World, Japan, and Republic of Korea Commodity Trade*

Major Categories	Average Percentage for Year 1983–88		
	World	Japan	Republic of Korea
Food and Live Animals	7.0	5.3	4.4
Beverages and Tobacco	1.2	0.6	0.2
Crude Materials, Inedible, Except Fuels	5.0	4.9	8.7
Mineral Fuels, Lubricants and Related Materials	10.1	1.7	1.6
Animal and Vegetable Oils, Fat and Waxes	0.4	0.1	0.2
Chemicals and Related Products	6.6	4.9	4.6
Manufactured Goods	11.5	9.2	12.5
Machinery and Transport Equipment	42.4	63.8	36.1
Miscellaneous Manufactured Articles	12.2	8.5	31.0
Commodities Transactions	3.6	1.0	0.7
Total Commodities	100.0	100.0	100.0

*Includes U.S. exports plus imports

Source: Calculations made from data found in the OECD, *Foreign Trade By Commodities*, 1990.

Fundamentally, trade represents a flow of merchandise along a two-way path and when in balance, the value of a country's exports equals its imports. For many years, trade between the United States and Japan has registered a continuous imbalance in favor of Japan. The United States' trade deficit with Japan during the decade of the 1980s grew at an average rate of 17 percent per year, and $360 billion of trade deficits were accumulated during that period. Trade with Japan accounted for 40 percent of the total deficit incurred during the decade. This situation prompted outcries in the United States of unfair trade competition and created demands for reciprocal treatment.

During the 1983–88 time period, the trade deficit for all commodities averaged $53 billion per year (see table 10.3). These deficits resulted as a consequence of commodity trade of machinery and transport equipment, manufactured goods, miscellaneous manufactured articles, and commodities transactions where net deficits totaled an annual average of $66.2 billion. These deficits were partially offset by surpluses of $13.2 billion incurred in commodity trade among the remaining categories. The categories with the largest surpluses were in crude materials, food and live animals, and mineral fuels, lubricants and related materials (see table 10.3).

The import-to-export ratio for all commodities traded with Japan was 2.9 and conveys that imports from Japan exceeded United States exports by nearly 200 percent. The trade of machinery and transport equipment demonstrated once again the significant imbalance that has occurred with a ratio of 8.8. This was followed with ratios of 4.8 and 3.3 for manufactured goods and miscellaneous manufactured articles respectively (see table 10.3). At the other end of the spectrum, Japan had a weighty reliance upon the United States in chemicals and related products, food and live animals, and crude materials where trade ratios were 0.5 or less.

When the trade ratios are compared with the world trade ratios, it becomes evident that the pattern of trade flows with Japan is greatly different from the world average. For example, the world ratio for all commodities of 1.6 was 45 percent less than that experienced with Japan. Furthermore, in those incidences where the U.S. exports were greater than imports from Japan, the ratios were much below the world norm. In fact, in world trade, the United States had a heavy reliance upon the world for mineral

Table 10.3 • U.S. Commodity Trade with Japan
(*Average for 1983–88, Billions of Dollars*)

	Total (Exports plus Imports)	Net (Exports less Imports)	Ratio (Imports divided by Exports)	World Ratio (Imports divided by Exports)	U.S.–Japan Trade as a Percentage of U.S. World Trade
All Commodities	98.5	− 53.0	2.9	1.6	16.4
Food and Live Animals	5.2	4.3	0.1	1.0	12.3
Beverages and Tobacco	0.6	0.5	0.1	1.3	8.2
Crude Materials, Inedible, Except Fuels	4.8	4.5	0.0*	0.6	15.2
Mineral Fuels, Lubricants and Related Materials	1.7	1.5	0.1	5.8	2.8
Animal and Vegetable Oils, Fat and Waxes	0.1	0.0*	0.2	0.5	3.4
Chemicals and Related Products	4.8	2.4	0.5	0.6	12.4
Manufactured Goods	9.1	− 5.7	4.8	3.1	13.4
Machinery and Transport Equipment	62.8	− 55.7	8.8	1.5	24.8
Miscellaneous Manufactured Articles	8.4	− 4.4	3.3	3.1	11.5
Commodities Transactions	1.0	− 0.4	2.7	0.8	4.6

*less than 0.05

Source: Calculations made from data found in the OECD, *Foreign Trade Commodities*, 1990.

fuels, lubricants and related materials but registered a trade surplus with Japan. At the same time, the U.S. dependence on Japan for manufactured goods and machinery and transport equipment is considerably greater than with the world at large (see table 10.3).

When one analyzes more specifically the commodities that comprise the three most important categories of trade, important insights are revealed. Those commodities with the largest ratios were road vehicles with 98.3, iron and steel with 49.3, telecommunications and sound recording apparatus with 34.2, and photo apparatus, optical goods, watches and clocks with 11.7 (see table 10.4). Each of the industries producing these commodities has had an impact on the industrial structure of America and has caused changes in industry to occur in order for them to become more competitive. It is also interesting to note that in office machines and ADP equipment as well as professional and scientific instruments, the United States had surpluses in worldwide trade or ratios of 0.9 and 0.5 but experienced trade deficits with Japan of 4.7 and 1.2 ratios respectively.

Although Japan is the number two nation in trade relations with the United States, a closer look at respective industrial commodities traded will further highlight their relative significance. Bilateral trade with Japan amounted to one-fourth of all U.S. trade in the world in machinery and transport equipment (see table 10.4). By looking at its subcategories, telecommunications and sound recording apparatus accounted for 45 percent, road vehicles 32 percent, and office machines and ADP equipment 27 percent. Among commodities included in miscellaneous manufactured articles, photo apparatus, optical goods, watches and clocks constituted 35 percent of like commodities in world trade. The major commodities in the manufactured goods category where concentrated trade flows occurred were iron and steel with 24 percent and manufacturers of metals with nearly 17 percent.

There is indeed an enormous economic interdependence between the United States and Japan and each would have difficulty finding alternative sources of suppliers and markets for traded commodities both in quality and volume. It therefore becomes apparent that both nations need to work strenuously to develop harmonious economic relations for continued prosperity.

Table 10.4 • U.S. Commodity Trade with Japan
(Average for 1983–88, Billions of Dollars)

	Total (Exports plus Imports)	Net (Exports less Imports)	Ratio (Imports divided by Exports)	World Ratio (Imports divided by Exports)	U.S.–Japan Trade as a Percentage of U.S. World Trade
Manufactured Goods	9.1	− 5.7	4.8	3.1	13.4
Iron and Steel	2.8	− 2.7	49.3	7.6	24.3
Manufacturers of Metal	1.7	− 1.3	8.1	2.3	16.6
Machinery and Transport Equipment	62.8	− 55.7	8.8	1.5	24.8
Office Machines and ADP Equipment	8.4	− 5.5	4.7	0.9	26.8
Telecommunications and Sound Recording Apparatus	10.4	− 9.7	34.2	4.1	44.6
Electrical Machinery	6.8	− 4.7	5.5	1.4	17.7
Road Vehicles	25.7	− 25.1	98.3	3.1	31.9
Miscellaneous Manufactured Articles	8.4	− 4.4	3.3	3.1	11.5
Professional and Scientific Instruments	2.0	− 0.1	1.2	0.5	17.4
Photo Apparatus, Optical Goods, Watches and Clocks	2.3	− 1.9	11.7	2.9	34.6
All Commodities	98.5	− 53.0	2.9	1.6	16.4

Source: Calculations made from data found in OECD, *Foreign Trade By Commodities*, 1990.

United States–Republic of Korea Trade

As the Republic of Korea has developed economically into a modern industrial state, trade with the United States has broadened as well as intensified. From 1983 through 1988, the total commodity trade, exports plus imports, grew at an average rate of 18.4 percent per year and represented an 82 percent increase in growth rate over that witnessed in total U.S. worldwide trade. Trade relations have always been extremely important for the Republic of Korea—one third of its exports and nearly one fourth of its imports are tied to the United States.

Prior to the 1980s the United States consistently operated with a trade surplus with the Republic of Korea, but during the decade of the 1980s, trade conditions changed dramatically. During the decade, the United States accumulated trade deficits amounting to $42 billion and an average of 4 percent of the United States trade deficits originated with the Republic of Korea. It was not the amount of the trade deficit that provoked concern in the United States as much as it was the strength of the swing from a surplus to deficit trade relationship. There was no return in sight to the former status under existing rules of trade. An import liberalization policy and implementation were viewed as critical on the part of the Republic of Korea in order to move trade flows toward a more balanced condition.

Commodity trade between the two countries from 1983 through 1988 was predominantly centered in machinery and transport equipment, miscellaneous manufactured articles, and manufactured goods. These three categories accounted for 80 percent of commodities traded. The composition of goods traded followed very closely with those industries triggered by the Korean government to lead in its export growth policy. It was these same commodities that registered an average trade deficit for the United States of $9.7 billion per year (see table 10.5). Surpluses of $3.2 billion partially offset the deficits and came from crude materials, food and live animals, chemicals and related products, and animal and vegetable oils, fats and waxes.

The trade ratio for all commodities was 1.9 and reflects the degree of deficit trade balance. That is, the United States imported an average of 90 percent more than it exported to the Republic of Korea. The most striking trade ratio was 19.1 found in miscellaneous articles followed by 5.2 in manufactured goods (see table

Table 10.5 • U.S. Commodity Trade with the Republic of Korea
(Average for 1983–88, Billions of Dollars)

	Total (Exports plus Imports)	Net (Exports less Imports)	Ratio (Imports divided by Exports)	World Ratio (Imports divided by Exports)	U.S.–ROK Trade as a Percentage of U.S. World Trade
All Commodities	20.0	−6.5	1.9	1.6	3.3
Food and Live Animals	0.9	0.5	0.3	1.0	2.1
Beverages and Tobacco	0.0*	−0.0*	4.2	1.3	0.4
Crude Materials, Inedible, Except Fuels	1.8	1.7	0.0*	0.6	5.5
Mineral Fuels, Lubricants and Related Materials	0.3	0.3	0.1	5.8	0.6
Animal and Vegetable Oils, Fat and Waxes	0.0*	0.0*	0.1	0.5	1.9
Chemicals and Related Products	0.9	0.7	0.1	0.6	2.3
Manufactured Goods	2.5	−1.6	5.2	3.1	3.7
Machinery and Transport Equipment	7.3	−2.5	2.0	1.5	2.8
Miscellaneous Manufactured Articles	6.2	−5.6	19.1	3.1	8.5
Commodities Transactions	0.1	−0.0*	1.4	0.8	0.7

*less than 0.05

Source: Calculations made from data found in the OECD, *Foreign Trade Commodities*, 1990.

10.5). The ratio of 4.2 in beverages and tobacco noted the trade imbalance but the volume of trade is very small. The Republic of Korea has a significant reliance upon the United States in the commodities found in the categories of crude materials, chemicals and related products, and food and live animals, where 90 percent or more of the trade originated in the United States.

Historically, articles of apparel and clothing accessories have been the leading export of the Republic of Korea and its trade ratio measured 733.4 for the 1983–88 period (see table 10.6). For footwear all trade originated in the Republic of Korea. The introduction of apparel and clothing accessories along with footwear commodities have seriously affected industries producing like products in the United States, causing them to advocate government protection. The commodities of iron and steel and road vehicles have also penetrated the American market and had trade ratios of 21.4 and 11.0 respectively. In addition, the trade ratios showed that among those commodities where the United States experienced either surpluses or deficits, it had larger surpluses or deficits in trade with the Republic of Korea than it did worldwide. Exceptions did occur in the commodities of food and live animals and in mineral fuels, lubricants and related materials. In the former, world trade was in balance but registered a strong surplus in bilateral trade. The latter experienced deficits in world trade but surpluses in bilateral trade with the Republic of Korea (see table 10.5).

The rapid rise of the Republic of Korea as an important trading partner attests to its emergence as a modern industrial state that can effectively compete in the international marketplace. Its size, relative to the world trade of the United States, is small compared to that of Japan, but still important. The bilateral trade was 3.3 percent of the United States world trade. Categories of commodities such as miscellaneous manufactured articles, crude materials, and manufactured goods exceeded the all commodity percentage. Specifically, footwear accounted for 21.9 percent, articles of apparel and clothing accessories—14.7 percent, telecommunication and sound recording apparatus—7.4 percent, manufacturers of metal—6.3 percent, iron and steel— 5.8 percent, and electrical machinery—5.7 percent (see table 10.6).

Certainly, the industrial strategy launched by the Republic of Korea of blending light and heavy industry formation has

268

Table 10.6 • U.S. Commodity Trade with the Republic of Korea (*Average for 1983–88, Billions of Dollars*)

	Total (Exports plus Imports)	Net (Exports less Imports)	Ratio (Imports divided by Exports)	World Ratio (Imports divided by Exports)	U.S.–ROK Trade as a Percentage of U.S. World Trade
Manufactured Goods	2.5	−1.6	5.2	3.1	3.7
Iron and Steel	0.7	−0.6	21.4	7.6	5.8
Manufacturers of Metal	0.7	−0.6	8.1	2.3	6.3
Machinery and Transport Equipment	7.3	−2.5	2.0	1.5	2.8
Office Machines and ADP Equipment	0.8	−0.3	1.8	0.9	2.5
Telecommunications and Sound Recording Apparatus	1.7	−1.4	8.1	4.1	7.4
Electrical Machinery	2.2	−0.7	2.0	1.4	5.7
Road Vehicles	1.1	−1.0	11.0	3.1	1.2
Miscellaneous Manufactured Articles	6.2	−5.6	19.1	3.1	8.5
Articles of Apparel and Clothing Accessories	2.7	−2.7	733.4	17.7	14.7
Footwear	1.5	−1.5	∞	42.0	21.9
All Commodities	20.0	−6.5	1.9	1.6	3.3

Source: Calculations made from data found in OECD, *Foreign Trade By Commodities*, 1990.

proven to be highly successful. The Republic of Korea has made gigantic strides in world competition in a relatively short period of time and has developed a very competitive economy by developing and exercising its comparative advantages.

Conclusions

The multilateral trade system launched by the Bretton Woods Conference set in place the means for industrialized and developing nations to grow and develop economically, albeit at different rates. The system assisted Japan in revitalizing its economy from the ashes of war to become a major player in international trade and finance. Also, the Republic of Korea was able to tailor an industrialization plan within the scope of the international economic system and break the poverty cycle to become a newly industrialized country. Along these paths of accomplishments, the United States played a dominant role by providing technology, investment capital, and markets for goods and services. In all of this, the stage was set for a strong and meaningful economic interdependency.

The decade of the 1980s witnessed an intense degree of economic interaction and competition. These were accompanied by increased political tension on all sides, which first led to confrontations and later to negotiations. These negotiations established a framework for addressing mutual economic issues. It is evident that tensions should not be allowed to rise to a point where trade relations are sorely affected. The consequences of allowing such to happen would be that all economies would suffer economic decline, costly industrial restructuring, lower levels of efficiency, and national instability.

The temptation of surrendering to trade protectionism lurks just below the surface. Nations should resist such temptations. The United States provides the most important market for Japanese and Korean commodities. No alternative markets exist for their commodities now or in the near future. It is critical for maintaining mutual prosperity that the United States provide open access to its markets and render support for an open trading system in the world.

One of the most dramatic developments occurring in the 1980s was that the United States ran such huge trade deficits.

Trade deficits were with trading partners around the globe. This situation tended to focus attention on the size of bilateral trade deficits and Japan and the Republic of Korea, along with some other countries, came under serious scrutiny. However, with foreign markets opening up and American businesses now focusing more on international competition and markets, the country is positioned to return to viewing trade deficits with a multilateral perspective and move away from bilateral confrontation.

Even though the United States changed from a creditor to a debtor nation in the 1980s, its stock of direct foreign investment continued to grow at a slower rate. The United States still remains the largest holder of foreign investment in the world. Japan has advanced on the world scene as a major source of investment capital and has moved into second place in direct foreign investment in the United States. This situation should not be viewed with great alarm, for the foreign capital provides funds for investment that domestic savings could not provide. After all, investment creates jobs and increases income and economic well-being. However, if reliance upon foreign capital is perceived as a problem, the solution lies in reducing the growth in private consumption and/or government consumption.

The commodity trade flows revealed the nature of the economic interdependence. Simply stated, Japan and the Republic of Korea have strong reliance upon the United States for its markets and for such commodities as food and live animals, beverages and tobacco, crude materials, mineral fuels, lubricants and related materials, animal and vegetable oils, fats and waxes, and lastly chemicals and related products. At the same time, the United States has dependencies for manufactured goods, machinery and transport equipment, and miscellaneous manufactured articles. For a highly developed country such as the United States to be in such a position is indeed unusual. It is for this reason that some advocate an economic policy in which the United States emphasizes developing industrial competitiveness at the higher end of the value-added scale of economic activity in contrast to the lower end of the scale. Raising the level of confrontation over lifting trade barriers on agricultural products, crude materials and mineral fuels that constitute only 13 percent of commodity trade with Japan and the Republic of Korea seems counterproductive from this perspective. Even if all the barriers were lifted on such commodities, it would not reduce the size of the trade deficit appreciably. The real payoff in reducing trade deficits will occur when American manufacturing industries enhance their efficiency and productivity. The competitiveness of American industry has improved and will get even better when given proper incentives.

Two of the most important allies of the United States are Japan and the Republic of Korea. Economic interdependence is firmly in place and the breadth of trade relations with the two countries has brought economic growth and prosperity. Although economic conflicts will occur, a healthy relationship will be maintained because it is in the mutual interest of all that it does.

American Themes Regarding Japan: The Persian Gulf Case

R. Christopher Perry

As of the middle of the 1980s, both Americans and Japanese viewed overall relations between their two nations as friendly; moreover, they saw their personal attitudes toward the other nation that way.[1] Nevertheless, in recent years, unsettling and at times hostile themes traceable to the early 1980s have received media coverage in several contexts. As a result, one problem for those hoping for smooth relations between the United States and Japan has been a notably dramatic representation of what that nation means to America's citizens. Without being exhaustive at this point, Japan has been portrayed as the home of selective and clever players with ruthless and scornful attitudes; America has received—in American as well as Japanese circles—an equally exotic casting as a home of ignorant, pampered, and slothful people, unfit for a recognizable continuation of a government, an economy, or an authentic cultural existence.[2] Naturally this sort of compound mythos breeds backlash, legislation, and other headaches.

During late 1990 and early 1991 there was a great deal being written in the mainstream U.S. press about Japan,[3] with only a small percentage of articles—other than those discussing Persian Gulf affairs—directly having to do with long-term future issues such as international security arrangements.[4] Even in the presentation of short-term topics, elements of tone, diction, and journal-

273

istic format (as well as actual messages) can offer a glimpse of the role(s) and voice(s) the daily press chooses to undertake. This article will examine the "images" (using the term in a cognitive sense) available through print media no less than in photos, cartoons, etc. that continue to be highlighted, with particular reference to various mainstream messages dealing with the Persian Gulf crisis.[5]

A brief word on some assumptions: America's "thinking Establishment" consists of those who dip into, utilize, or "live in" the dominant modes and messages of the culture. No less than other mythmakers, America's "thinking Establishment" members enjoy and profit from the mediated discussion of dramatic issues. Certainly the leading Establishment newspapers, which exemplify and practice opinion-making and reality-making skills to a high degree, have a variety of formats which allow, singly and collectively, for an esoteric and multilayered form of drama. Editorials, op-ed pieces, news analyses, regular opinion columns and feature columns, and features in specialized sections are all represented in what follows.[6]

Japan, Leading U.S. Media, and the Persian Gulf

Even in the general press, a range of images about Japan can be invoked. Certainly social and economic affairs during 1990–91 involved a great many images of Japan, of America, and of relations between the two. Most of these images are (arguably) somewhat tangential to the discussion of security arrangements and the goodwill needed to bring them into being. However, one should note the resilient images that are a legacy of Japan's and America's experiences before and during World War II.[7] Certainly this time period contained little article-length material that waved the bloody shirt of Japanese imperial conquest during World War II, although there is occasional reference to this theme as part of larger stories on current Japanese success in the United States. One story, however, did indicate that the Japanese are now being told about specific atrocities that might frame a picture of historical guilt.[8] Watchers of the Hiroshima commemorations in late summer 1991 know the Japanese are acknowledging that

274

Americans were not the only violators of morality during that time.

Of similarly lasting impact may well be the upsurge in Japan-bashing that emerged during the U.S.-led Desert Shield and Desert Storm operations. Perhaps the best way to start this discussion is to observe that a "fine line" between criticism and bashing was possible, at least at first. One Desert Shield-era theme that extended an international approach, without taking it so far as to amount to "bashing," asserted that Japan should take more of an internationalistic "role." As early as October 1990, the *New York Times*'s heavily internationalistic columnist Flora Lewis, after aligning herself against "Japan-bashing" in one portion of an op-ed piece, unsheathed her sagacity to the extent of telling the Japanese to "think harder."[9] A similar theme appeared toward the end of another of her pieces, later that month.[10] Still later in the same month the *Times*'s main editorialists thought to include Germany in their analysis,[11] and later they added other allies (and other burdens).[12] People not identified as internationalists had reason to concur.[13] Yet Lewis and others would come to see that "thinking" was indeed occurring among the Japanese, with politically wrenching portent for them.[14]

Things took a different turn in December of the year. First, Japanese leaders were heard to be joining the Monday morning quarterback crowd with advice for the United States on its handling of the conflict.[15] Fair's fair, perhaps, but then Japan signalled a cutback of its military spending generally,[16] setting off a series of advances and retreats that were easily as complex as those on any battlefield—or, for that matter, as the openings and closures on the trade front.

An advance was announced on December 20, 1990—"Japan to Share More of U.S. Troop Cost."[17] But the *Wall Street Journal*—less relentlessly internationalist than the *Times*—answered with a "Washington insight" news analysis (not on the editorial or op-ed page), entitled "Japan and Germany Shirk Gulf Duties with Nary a Peep from the White House." The piece was possibly devastating in its revelations that Japan's aid was more in loan than grant form, that Germany's aid was largely "cast-off gear from the defunct East German army," and that the actual aid was "flowing like molasses." A leading internationalist member of the House of Representatives, Charles Schumer, was influenced by these data to predict tough times for already strained trade relations.[18]

Perhaps because Desert Shield had not yet become Desert Storm, the commentary did not heat up greatly during early January. Looking only at the newspapers monitored for this study, the materials were slim: a single editorial, appearing January 8 in the *Chicago Tribune*, did call on Japan to speed up its Persian Gulf aid efforts. The message was combined with a call for Japan to exercise a more appropriate "role," and did not get into historically-based or otherwise extreme bashing.[19] The *Wall Street Journal* was less restrained on January 11, raising in its lengthy front-page feature story the question of what "Americans Ask." Only at the very end of the lengthy article was a defense of Japan heard. This placement was particularly unfair because the defense offered was novel and somewhat persuasive: Japan was emphasizing the provision of goods, which tend by their nature to be slow-arriving, rather than the provision of money.[20]

The *Chicago Tribune*'s chief Japan correspondent from 1984–91, Ronald Yates, appears to have weighed in only on the eve of the war, with a piece entitled "Risk of War Doesn't Faze Japanese." Interestingly, the column-long article simply reported Japanese attitudes; it avoided moralizing about Japan's "role" until nearly the very end, and then only through quotations from a Japanese academic.[21] Characteristically, the *Wall Street Journal* of two days later played the same basic story with a more biting headline. The *Journal* also utilized a news-pages comment-format (titled "Foreign Insight") to get its author's bold compilation off of the *Journal*'s occasionally off-putting opinion pages.[22]

Japan then temporized again; the *Journal* on January 21 was thus obliged to include a report in the straight news pages with the title, "Japan Is Studying Added Aid for Forces Aligned Against Iraq."[23] The *New York Times*'s "personal computers" column was the location for a story noting that Japan was sending $21 million worth of advanced computing equipment to the troops.[24]

Yet January 25 brought another disparaging *Chicago Tribune* editorial concerning the then-existing monetary and other contributions of Japan and Germany. The editorial closed, "It's not enough. They owe us."[25] Certainly Japan had ceased to be the sole target; on the next day the *New York Times* homed in strictly on Germany. The title of its lead editorial, "Germany's Ostrich-Politik," signalled the "role" that was earnestly being urged upon this leading financial power. The *Times*'s editorial invoked proud and not-so-proud German historical lessons, its responsibility "for helping Saddam Hussein build his war machine," and so forth.[26] But on January 27, the *Times* placed Japan (only) under the microscope of the Sunday "Week in Review" section. In a piece that contained a dashed "zinger" in its title ("Japan Counts the Costs of Gulf Action—or Inaction"), the *Times* made a clever strategist's attempt both to promote insecurity and to turn that insecurity into a decision that would cast Japan in the desired "role."[27]

Events continued; after all, there was a war going on. On February 1, Japan announced the compromise it had worked out: more money would be spent, but not for lethal purposes. In the U.S. press the moral aspect of Japan's dilemma was largely ignored, perhaps because it was inconvenient to Gulf intervention. An interesting story about the influence of Japan's Clean Government Party was mentioned but somewhat buried in the *New York Times*'s report on the story.[28] The *Chicago Tribune*'s editorialist seemed to greet the latest news, in all its conflicted subtlety, with a "let's lecture them anyway" attitude.[29] More coolly, the *New York Times* on Sunday, February 3, opened its "Week in Review" op-ed page with a U.S. policy writer's critique of a near-unilateral (Washington-monopolized) global policy financed by all—but the Sunday-punching headline-writer gave it the title, "Germany and Japan—Dragging Their Boots."[30]

On the same Sunday, the *Chicago Tribune* led its business section with a story about the impressive performance of Japanese technology on the Gulf-area battlefield. But the headline was "Japan *Claims* Big Role in U.S. Weapons Success" (emphasis supplied). Nowhere in the lengthy piece is there any reason to believe the cynical implication that the article concerns a "claim" rather than a reality, and nowhere in the story is there any reason to doubt the substance, whether as "claim" or fact.[31]

War-related bashing moved from headline to story as the *Washington Post* weighed in with another "modern role" piece on Japan alone—trade policy, the Persian Gulf, lack of GATT magic, no "vision thing," lack of intellectual originality at its universities, you name it.[32] The *Wall Street Journal* had an op-ed analyst who looked askance at the Japanese constitutional "excuse," preferring his image of the nation as "the world's biggest free rider."[33]

More astutely, and relevantly, the *Chicago Tribune*'s Japan correspondent (Yates) reminded readers that all the interim steps in the Japanese political process hadn't really led to much aid, and that there was little reason to think that the most recent ones would.[34] Specifically and importantly, he described the bitter scene in the Japanese parliament over the matter, and summarized the antiwar nature of the latest Japanese opinion poll results. A sourced quotation about a more mature "role" followed, but the reality of a government on the verge of defeat and resignation quickly took up the remainder of the story.[35] Two days later, the *Times* was astute in an internationalist sort of way, doing a personality profile of an heroic Prime Minister Kaifu as he battled these forces—complete with a large and stoic in-the-chamber photo of the prime minister, on the article's continuation page.[36] The *Chicago Tribune*, often less tendentious than the *New York Times*, paused on February 10 with a thoroughly apolitical story on Crown Prince Narushito's love life and (lack of an) upcoming marriage.[37]

The *Wall Street Journal* seemed to set up a Japan–Germany contrast when on February 11 it played up data showing that public opinion in Germany was turning in favor of the war effort and a more global "role." Balancing information regarding large and continuing German antiwar groups and the like was presented only much later in the piece, and Chancellor Kohl was allowed the last quotation, urging Germans to live up to their global "responsibilities."[38] From different sources, the *Chicago Tribune* ran a similar story on February 12, likewise leaning heavily to the change-in-opinion line.[39]

Also on February 11, a *Times* piece appearing on the front page of the business section noted the "pressure" on Japan to buy U.S. jets. To some in the U.S. Congress, the high-minded call for Japan's bearing the burden apparently had become a matter of how many Boeing Awacs units, and when.[40]

On February 19, the *Wall Street Journal*, perhaps becoming leery of the credibility of the Japanese Gulf aid announcements, printed a *short* notice that Japanese parliamentary leaders appeared to have backing for more war appropriations.[41] The *Times* managed a laconic (which is to say, an insufficiently ironic) presentation of Prime Minister Kaifu's phone call to U.S. President Bush supporting an Iraqi withdrawal ultimatum a full five hours before the deadline![42] The *Washington Post* (National Weekly

Edition) had a longer piece that started at but moved beyond lecturing Japan about its "role." The article also advised the United States to maintain a military presence in Asia.[43]

Congressional concerns (called "fears") about allied war payments—especially the matter of actually securing them—were featured in a domestic-beat *Times* piece. The use of "fears" here as elsewhere when a powerful party has or doesn't have plans to which a less-powerful party is not privy puts the focus on the lack of certain knowledge of future harms by those voicing objections. Scorn for this lack of knowledge is of course inappropriate in many situations, most notably those involving the future, concerning which no one has knowledge. Nevertheless, in doing this "fears"-framing, the news outlet shifts focus from the source of slow payments.[44]

The *New York Times* was also found putting the best face on Japan's desire not to be seen as rushing in too quickly to grab postwar reconstruction contracts in Kuwait. The *Times* thus shifted some of the focus away from the irony of a less-than-vigorous combatant's being in position to win postwar construction and construction-related contracts at the devastated site of the war.[45] A week later, the *Wall Street Journal* did a similarly sympathetic mind-reading piece about/for the Japanese.[46] But a *Chicago Tribune* headline writer cut to the bottom line: "Japan Still May See Kuwait Bonanza."[47] (The accompanying story mixed bottom-line and "diplomatic" emphases.)

Early March found another topic of wartime tension and irony, this time located in the United States. A series of U.S.–Japanese scholarly exchanges, to be financed and controlled in some measure from the Japanese end, became a source of controversy. Circling the internationalist wagons, the *New York Times*'s reporter and an internal-headline writer suggested that the Gulf War may have played a part in souring the American view of Japanese motives.[48]

Another laconic piece in the *Wall Street Journal* reported on March 7 that the upper house of the Japanese national legislature had passed the $9 billion Gulf aid package.[49] Treatment in the *Chicago Tribune* was a bit lengthier, but pedestrian in its placement of items. Excellent "role" quotations from Japanese sources were relegated to a latter but not a culminating portion; unconvincing "crystal ball" material got the choice spots.[50]

By March 9 the *Chicago Tribune* had unburdened itself to offer editorial congratulations to Germany and Japan for "pledges, at least." The editorial also took the opportunity to lecture the Japanese on the inadvisability of quibbling with the United States over terms of disbursement, arguing, in effect, that those isolationists out there are even tougher cops than we are.[51]

About this time there were pieces concerning Japanese "American-bashing" sentiment that linked the war and trade. This was part of a larger ferment that impacted trade discussions, and will be summarized shortly. The Gulf War also allowed for another sort of American-bashing by the Japanese. Basically, many Japanese commentators saw the war as foolish, a pathetic attempt to assert power via weapons rather than commerce.[52] Overall, some jokesters in Japan were calling the United States "a nice place to own, but you wouldn't want to live there."[53]

Perhaps the big "post-gulf" noise in the U.S. press, including as it often does some polls and other soundings of American mass opinion, concerned popular attitudes after the war—attitudes that conformed to official American preferences during its conduct. Israel, Egypt, and the U.N. were examples of entities which had "gained respect" in American eyes; Japan, by contrast, suffered a drop.[54] But how much did all of this mean? It is perhaps noteworthy that in a March 29 dispatch one of the *New York Times*'s Tokyo correspondents could redirect his attention from the Gulf War to a political contest in Tokyo:

> The Persian Gulf war is over, trade frictions with the United States are in a lull, the Japanese economy is running smoothly, as always; what better subject of gossip for residents of this crowded, noisy capital than the sloppiest political brawl in anyone's memory?[55]

Still, such lightheartedness was in the distinct minority. Postwar stories concerning both trade-related and more general events in Japan–U.S. relations continued to mention the Gulf War as a source of bad feelings.[56] And further ironies exist; a maverick's victory in the Tokyo election, which the *Times* seemed determined to take so light-heartedly, was summarized by a CUNY professor as a rebuff to, among other things, "President Bush's humiliating treatment of Japan in the Persian Gulf crisis."[57]

One interesting postwar development was that Japan continued to debate sending a postwar contingent of four minesweepers to the Gulf. When the minesweepers were sent, some of the U.S. media expressed approval,[58] but Prime Minister Kaifu had to reassure countries (like Singapore) for whom the minesweepers raised old fears of Japanese militarism.[59]

Squabbles over the terms and occasions for Japanese Gulf War payments also continued, and one account of them rightly asked if this was the way to get the "New World Order" off the ground.[60] Japan's eventual concessions on one such issue[61] seemed politically timed in a late spring of trade disputes, but perhaps there were more disputes and more American postures and thrusts because of the Gulf! Certainly the prewar tendency toward inherently overbearing "role" pontifications was exacerbated by the Persian Gulf conflict; for example, regular *New York Times* international columnist Flora Lewis spoke of "dithering [Japanese] passivity on all but trade" and of a nation "in a sense immature, avoiding asking itself what it should do but asking what others, perhaps unfairly, expect of it."[62]

Other sources were less condescending. Some took Japan deadly seriously, predicting an actual shooting war in the future. (This development—amid the overall topic of justified American-bashing—inspired Mike Royko to an excellent run of wit.[63]) Another line, attributed to the most vocal of several Japan-bashing Europeans, French Prime Minister Edith Cresson, was that Japan had already matured; indeed, that it was so "controlling and manipulative" in nature as not to be trusted. One article discussing this also noted several aspects in the structure of the European Community that made its picking-apart by the Japanese that much easier.[64]

Gulf Aftermath Among Other Themes: The Case of Trade

As the Gulf conflict approached its conclusion, it didn't take long for U.S.–Japan trade conflict to heat up, with the Gulf as one subtext. Still, the Gulf was a minor theme, as the following review of trade-related messages in mid-1991 will attest.

For those who would imagine that mainstream Americans would be exposed only to articles about Japanese war vacillation and what it shows about the need for Japan to take a larger "role," it is important to note that one quite different trade–Gulf War

281

linkage piece, written from a Japanese perspective, was generated as early as mid-March. An "opinion in Japan" review that was something akin to an American-bashing piece (including but not confined to a bashing of the U.S. government) appeared March 14 in the *Wall Street Journal*. The compound idea of the piece, captured in one phrase ("man-eating tiger"), was that the Japanese did not think the United States would be a gracious Gulf victor, given that: (1) the United States had been pretty bloodthirsty throughout the conflict; and (2) it had been and likely would be equally bloodthirsty in trade-related matters. The patriotic fervor among the American people was also connected with this perception. One suggested remedy reported in the same piece was for Japan to build more trade ties to Asia, and fewer to the United States; quoted with some favor in this connection was a former Malaysian foreign minister who scored the Gulf-era United States for "materialistic values of absolute secularism, racism, sexism, imperialism."[65]

Similar review and stock-taking, also centered on the interface between economic and military-related "post-gulf" policies, appeared at about the same time in the *Washington Post*[66] and in an op-ed piece in the *Wall Street Journal*.[67] In the *Post* piece, both gratitude and criticism were voiced concerning the United States as the "new number one" power. Additionally, some comment elicited from Japanese sources focused on what niches Japan might fill in a U.S.-led international order. The *Wall Street Journal* column, written by the editor of the *Japan Digest*, a daily summary of news about Japan for U.S. readers, focused on the justification for Japanese resentment of shabby post-gulf treatment, and on noncooperative trade rumblings that could grow from the resentment.

In the immediate post-Gulf War aftermath, U.S.–Japan trade events buzzed into gear quite afresh, but Gulf-related themes were usually absent in these events' discussion. A general narrative of commentary along the trade front during these days, originally drafted for other purposes, is inserted at this point by way of demonstration. In reviewing what follows, the reader may well be struck by the nuances of fact and interpretation that are possible—that, indeed, have been developed—in the trade-oriented, leading U.S. press. It may well be that even broad security concerns become somewhat "walled off" from these narratives.

To begin the discussion of "post-Gulf" trade-related events: in mid-March 1991, a U.S. Rice Council display in Tokyo earned its exhibitors threats of arrest before the Council was forced to withdraw. The *New York Times* was quick to tie this incident to others (particularly involving the attempts to revive multilateral trade negotiations), to play the story up, and to subhead an assertion of "embarrassment."[68]

Another event, this time with a longer shelf life, first engaged the *Times* during late March and concerned Japan's importation of rare sea turtles. Among the outlets surveyed for this report, the *Times* was clearly the leader (and yet, later, the leading backpedaler and temporizer) among those who publicized some strong U.S. trade moves and Japanese acquiescence regarding turtle shell imports and related commerce.[69] Initial expressions in this area of concern progressed handily into the business of moralizing about those who would do "anything to make a buck." Still, this message rings more hollow when coming from a media adjunct of a highly competitive New York financial Establishment, especially when later articles opined or implied that there was a traditional shell-stripping industry involved and that "the environment" was tough to harmonize with the imperatives of "trade."[70]

So long as Japan contributes to world trade and security, the *Times* seems readier than most to handle "damage control" chores. While this report does not focus as much as it could on inter-outlet variations, one U.S. summary of other nations' trade barriers that was reported on March 29 did receive different bannering and treatment in New York than in Chicago. Japan was "single[d] out" in the *Chicago Tribune*'s headline, and its text focused on the "barriers" themselves. The occasion, a mandated annual report on trade barriers, would in a formal sense arise independently of any ferment over the Gulf conflict, sea turtles, or other issues. Needless to say, the issuance of such a report is not a blue-ribbon occasion in the free trade press. In the *Times*'s story, all sorts of diminishing terms such as "complaints" were used, as was the presentation of attenuating foci such as holding administration spokespersons to remedies promoting free trade. Further, the *Times*'s trade correspondent Clyde Farnsworth took the occasion to discuss (and to attempt, with little success, to tie in) several quite unrelated items culled from the Bush administration's free trade agenda.[71] By further contrast, the *Wall Street Journal* did its lumping together of the trade barriers report (minimally featured) with a reporting on a large number of specific U.S.–Japan matters, less organized about a theme. By still further contrast, the *Journal* editor's lead and headline called it all part of a case of U.S. Japan-bashing.[72]

Combined themes were present in a *Chicago Tribune* editorial of April 2, which managed to bring up the rice exhibit (in connection with the political "coddling" of Japan's rice farmers), the Persian Gulf, and American business protests; and to close with a "role" message suggesting that Japan should take more of a lead in world affairs, enduring the assiduous stewardship and the sacrifice that this implies.[73] When Japan is selfish and making money, the "role" theme quickly emerges; for example, there was a lead story from the *New York Times* when Japan in its role of creditor balked at being part of a debt-forgiveness regime following the Gulf War. In the article's initial paragraphs, the *Times* managed to phrase the issue in a businesslike and internationalistic way that was favorable to Japan; namely, to ask how much "politics" should enter into these decisions. Matters of compassion were raised much later, immediately after the *Times* noted a "high level of emotion" over the issue.[74]

In spring 1991, stories about unfair pricing manipulations appeared. The Commerce Department first found this "dumping" among Japanese word processor manufacturers.[75] Later the topic was mini-vans.[76] Additionally, the exclusion of American firms from Japanese public works construction projects raised the possibility of sanctions, albeit amid tough and continuing negotiations and media-fanned concerns about the rigidity and "symbolic" nature of the U.S. position.[77]

Problems in talks over computer chips and dumping were wedded in a brief and downbeat piece the *Times* seemed to be sweeping under the rug in late April 1991.[78] Yet the *Times* doesn't downplay everything; in fact, in trying to set the climate for the non-invocation of "Super 301" sanctions by the United States (over construction, chips, etc.), it buried the Japanese-subsidiary subsidization aspect of a story on Japanese financing of American exports, thus turning the lead and the title into a public relations morsel for Japan,[79] one that was gulped down—hook, line, and sinker—in a *Chicago Tribune* editorial.[80]

But the *Times* did not hold the monopoly on reporting the story, and other segments of American business marshalled their own forces. A news conference featuring an appearance by leading U.S. Senator Lloyd Bentsen (D., Texas) dramatized the U.S. Commerce Department accusations in early May 1991 that Japanese semiconductor makers were preferring Japanese to American manufacturers in the distribution of the newest equipment, indeed withholding technology from the latter. This combined occasion and worthwhile story were recognized by the *Wall Street Journal*, which filed a story with no misleading (titles or) leads,[81] and also filed a story on the Japanese firms' denials (unsurprisingly, the *Times* did cover the denial story, identifying Bentsen but not Commerce as the origin of the complaint and referring instead to "several reports from the United States").[82]

Japanese investment patterns in U.S. high technology firms were examined in a brief *Wall Street Journal* article in mid-May. The article was based on a study done by a think tank (the Economic Strategy Institute), and that study included proposed legislation.[83] By predictable contrast, the *Times*'s next story featured statesmanlike quotations on why a new agreement on the pricing of Japanese computer chips was still "elusive." Included in the article was a bland passage stating that dumping had "generally" been "reduced."[84]

As the late-May 1991 deadline for sanctions invocation neared, Japanese business interests, speaking through their powerful Keidanren organization, began counterattacking by pointing out various American shortcomings—and the *Chicago Tribune* lapped it up.[85] Notable in the *Tribune* piece were extended quotations from Keidanren Vice President Akio Morita, chairman of Sony Corp. Another free trade big gun trotted out the very next day in the pages of the *Tribune* was U.S. Ambassador to Japan and former BankAmerica CEO Michael Armacost.[86] Never think that the Establishment doesn't have a stable of useful heroes for legislative and other audiences—even if America's youth never name them in opinion polls!

Japan also attempted to leak any favorable intentions on other fronts. Some concessions on sea turtles (reported elsewhere in the current summary) were real; some were a product of favorable reporting. Rice market concessions to occur in June were leaked in mid-to-late May.[87]

At this crucial juncture, the *New York Times* also dusted off an earlier story about the failure of a U.S. launch of a Japanese communications satellite as an example of lousy American know-how and the need for Japan to avoid concessions that threaten its autonomy.[88] In addition, Japan "sweetened the pot" in the matter of Gulf aid.[89]

A May 22 article in the *Wall Street Journal* reported that U.S. and Japanese negotiators had announced they were close to a target-oriented, multifaceted approach to progress in the computer chip area, but with sanctions possible after a year's experience.[90] Strangely, the *Times* ran a story a day later that focused on little of substance—opting, rather, to discuss nasty things said by each side about the other.[91]

Reenter the construction talks: a dispatch that ran in the *Wall Street Journal* on May 24 spoke of the deadline and its likely invocation and of a threatened Japanese retaliation against previous American participations.[92] Other construction pieces followed (see previous construction footnote), followed by the *Times*'s attempt (on June 2) to tie up this story and several others in a bow. Consider the following language:

> TOKYO, June 1—In a sudden reversal to avoid another important trade conflict with the United States, Japan acceded today to American demands that it allow foreign companies to bid on a variety of big construction jobs. In return, Tokyo wants Washington to abandon sanctions against some of Japan's biggest construction companies.

Three paragraphs later:

> The reversal seemed likely to ease tensions at a time of intensified trade battles over everything from semiconductors and mini-vans to agricultural products, and broad cultural and political restraints on trade.[93]

The article continued with an optimistic forecast covering semiconductors and rice but not automobiles ("continue to be an irritant"), before moving on to the possible internal politics of the construction concession, and finally, the details of it.[94] As it turns out, the forecast was prophetic with regard to a semiconductors accord, but the story on that was terribly sanguine, given the withdrawal by the United States of a claim to be authorized to impose sanctions quickly (as the Reagan administration did in 1987, under the American interpretation of a secret or "unpublished"[95] letter of understanding).[96]

Soon thereafter, the *Wall Street Journal* contained another optimistic article, this time concerning rice imports for Japan, which squared with the line the *Times* had set forth.[97] Further material on mini-vans—from the *Journal* as well as the *Times*—continued to bury the gravamen of the Big Three's complaint in the irony of their excellent mini-van sales figures.[98] And a *Times* "foreign affairs" columnist totally bought into the Japanese position in the ongoing "Structural Impediments Initiative" talks.[99] So the anti-bash spin was in full swing, and a long piece of this sort in the *Washington Post* also made mention of the large number of talks that had recently been completed.[100] But these are weekly certitudes; by June 28 we had news that the U.S. Commerce Secretary was investigating the high price of U.S. auto parts in Japan.[101]

In short, the Gulf War was but one of several themes in the complex U.S.–Japan trade constellation of early to mid-1991, as reported in leading trade-concerned U.S. print media. Whether to play the "role" card may well have been a concern, however, as there seems to have been pragmatic progress even during this highly charged period. Certainly complementary and opposing themes emerged within even the dramatic casting of things; whether any of them were wholly fair is another question.

Concluding Remarks/Recommendations

While this review shows that there are several stories that can be traced to bygone days, new wrinkles and topics have also appeared. "Mixed" reviews/prognoses are one example of newer things; in addition, "mixed" truths can also be found at the policy level.

Certainly this is true in specific areas; for example, the theme of Japanese "role" may look like an overbearing negative imposed by the United States, but then one spots stories about increased Japanese global bank lending,[102] possible Japanese rethinking of the decades-old Arab League boycott of Israel,[103] "lavish" charitable contributions in the United States by Japanese businesses,[104] or "sweat charity" assistance by Japanese executives in New York City,[105] and one suspects a genuine new-role quest by Japan itself. One can only hope American internationalists will appreciate and commend these developments in a non-condescending way![106]

If we accept images of Japanese altruism, it would be wise to look further and accept that nation as something other than a yen-bearer. Consider, for example, that a repeatedly voiced Japanese concern is its desire to become a permanent member of the United Nations Security Council. In considering this request, a good starting point is Japan's credible and unappreciated recent history of pacifism, and its continuing pleas in that domain; these could serve the U.N. in good stead,[107] Articles 53 and 107 of the U.N. Charter to the contrary notwithstanding.[108] Certainly the Japanese have every right to contend for top positions in the International Monetary Fund and other organizations, as well.[109]

A general sort of recommendation which this review suggests is that lively interpretative interchanges, like Japanese–American trade negotiations, should always enter a new round—and, again like trade negotiations, do seem to occasionally accomplish something. One route regarding "interpretation and beyond" might well be to abandon many disingenuous and now tiresome sorts of authority-based "objective" framing—involving "painful truths," assertions of inevitability,[110] formulaic acceptance of comments by "analysts," and the like—and instead go directly to an honest and vulnerable advocacy of policy alternatives, with these supported by clearly identified premises and other materials as needed. There is very little advocacy writing of this sort in the sources reviewed above; one exception was a couple of writings advocating a liberal policy on technology transfer.[111]

One final aspect of the year's stories and columns, an aspect often commented on and yet perhaps unsystematically captured by this largely literal-minded report, is the degree to which news media outlets have their own agendas, such that "Japan," for example, is really a shorthand for other concerns. The major concern of this sort tends to be internationalism, and in those eyes the threat is also readily observable to nationalism.

Other values and concerns may intrude in their own fashion; for example, the *Wall Street Journal* and other publications may choose to use "Japan" as a model for efficiency *in general*, or to pillory Japan for behaving slowly, after all, in this or that government-controlled area,[112] to need to deregulate for abstract "marketplace" reasons,[113] and so on. Japan might also become an arena of conflict, a fought-for belle of the ball, in clashes between the most established (currently commercial-bank-related) entities and their geographical and product adversaries.[114] Whatever the case, Japan is still such a sufficiently delicate topic that writers should not dismiss lightly the consequences of playing fast and loose with the truth.

Lest this exhortation seem vague and idealistic, one particular fear is that in their Japan-related themes and shadings the leading media are trying to create an image of "we happy few against the Philistine world." In the process, the danger always is that American internationalists will cut themselves off from domestic sources of support. And criticism breeds criticism; the possibility might be enhanced that Japan will come to say, "Oh Eastern U.S.A., the world is all wrong but thee and me, and I'm not so sure about thee." This is especially the case if the Eastern press is as free with advice and proposed "reforms" for Japan as it was in 1991.

A final thought: Much of what one recommends for the leading "media of record" in the United States involves assumptions about their relationships with a given object of comment. Both the *New York Times* and the *Wall Street Journal* appear to have something like three full-time correspondents stationed in Japan; it is likely that Japanese matters will be portrayed in some richness regardless of editorial tendencies in Tokyo and back in New York. It is even possible that the writers and/or editors have fears that they have met an adversary whose ability to generate intermediate "pseudo-events" and pressures matches their own. If this is so, and if the more internationalist among these media think *and* fear that U.S. national survival is therefore at stake, it makes additional sense for them not to degrade countervailing resources in the U.S. "political" world.

Notes

1. See Adam Clymer, "The United States and Japan: Polling Two Unmatched Sets of Opinion on World War Two and on Today's Trade Conflicts," paper presented at the 1986 Annual Meeting of the American Political Science Association, Washington, DC, August 29, 1986, p.3

(regarding attitudes in 1985); p.5 (regarding a 1986 follow-up, which did include a slight decline in positive ratings). It is of additional interest that much of Clymer's work during the 1980s, and again recently, has been for the *New York Times*.

2. Two of the more respectable sources are William G. Ouchi, *Theory Z* (New York: Avon, 1982), and Robert B. Reich, *The Next American Frontier* (New York: Times Books, 1983). Even this sort of book tended to cast a blind eye to the environmental and gender-based problems of Japanese methods, to say nothing of the emphasis on worker manipulation. See Jules Cohn, "They Go to Bars After Work, Too," *The Nation*, August 8–15, 1981, pp. 117–19. Indeed, much of the literature was quite uncritically approving of a "Japanese perspective." See, for example, Jim Powell, *The Gnomes of Tokyo: The Positive Impact of Foreign Investment in North America* (New York: American Management Association, 1989).

3. Essentially, this review is concerned with leading U.S. daily print media, primarily because (1) print is associated with a large volume of information and with permanence; and (2) those who seriously follow public affairs do so on a daily as well as a weekly basis. A case could also be made for this focus in terms of the comparatively high cumulative quality of the leading daily press, at least as compared with its weekly counterpart, but this reason seems less important for present purposes.

This is not to say that television's "sound bites" do not have an impact of their own, and that this impact is not of a wounding nature, at times, to the Japanese.

4. One exception was a short op-ed piece by Jonathan D. Pollack and James A. Winnefield, which ran in the *Chicago Tribune*, November 27, 1990, section 1, page 15 (subsequent *Tribune* citations have section and page information simply in the form "1:15"). Titled "Japan's Security Is Vital to U.S.," the piece argued that Japan could not be released from U.S. arrangements to cut its own security deals elsewhere, because this would have devastating strategic consequences for the U.S.

5. The author clipped and photocopied all pieces on the paper's subject which fell to him by means of his subscriptions to the *New York Times*, the *Wall Street Journal*, the *Chicago Tribune*, and the *Washington Post National Weekly Edition*. Other sources to which the author subscribes were also consulted, especially if they contained material not available elsewhere. Errors in the study's "sampling" are random.

All in all the period from October 1, 1990 through July 1, 1991 yielded 486 stories on Japan. Most were beyond the scope of the editor's project in this volume. They dealt with social and economic issues, and many dealt with trade-related matters. A good many stories tracked major Japanese financial and business interests. Some of the notions and side-comments essayed in the present writing apply with greater force to the other topics. An extended writing is available from the Center for Governmental Services, Indiana State University (inquire of Dr. M. K. Mohapatra, Center Director).

6. Letters to the editor are also important, and some were included in the present study. These letters are subject to editorial manipulation through placement, headlines, juxtaposition with other letters, and other tactics. Still, their actual text often provides useful correctives.

7. See Karel van Wolferen, "Why Militarism Still Haunts Japan," *New York Times*, December 12, 1990, p. A19. See also his *The Enigma of Japanese Power* (New York: Knopf, 1989), chapter 13.

8. Ronald E. Yates, "Film of Japan Wartime Horrors Stuns Viewers, Unmasks History," *Chicago Tribune*, May 12, 1991, 1:4.

9. Flora Lewis, "Japan's Past Weighs," *New York Times*, October 3, 1990, p. A19.

10. See Flora Lewis, "Ms. Doi's Advantage," *New York Times*, October 10, 1990, p. A15.

11. "Bonn and Tokyo as Global Police," *New York Times*, October 22, 1990, p. A14.

12. "Share More Than the Gulf Burden," *New York Times*, December 11, 1990, p. A18 (editorial).

13. Robert Kuttner, "Thanks for Sharing," *New Republic*, December 31, 1990 (available to subscribers December 17, 1990), pp. 17–18.

14. "Plan to Send Japanese Forces to Mideast Falters Amid Strong Domestic Opposition," *Wall Street Journal*, November 2, 1990, p. A10; David E. Sanger, "Why the Japanese Find It So Difficult to Unsheath [sic] Swords," *New York Times*, November 4, 1990, section 4, p. 2.

15. "Japanese Leaders See Support for U.S. Stand in Gulf Ebbing," *New York Times*, December 11, 1990, p. A9.

16. "Japan Is Moving to Scale Back Military Spending," *New York Times*, December 16, 1990, p.8.

17. "Japan to Share More of U.S. Troop Cost," *New York Times*, December 21, 1990, p. A3.

18. The analysis piece was written by Walter S. Mossberg; it appeared December 24, 1990, p. 4.

19. "Japan's Actions and Its Words," *Chicago Tribune*, January 8, 1991, 1:12 (editorial).

20. "Americans Ask Why Germany, Japan Bear So Little of Gulf Cost," *Wall Street Journal*, January 11, 1991, p. A1 + .

21. *Chicago Tribune*, January 15, 1991, 1:8.

22. Urban C. Lehner, "Tokyo's 'Full Support' for U.S. in Gulf Is Limited by Japanese Public's Apathy," *Wall Street Journal*, January 17, 1991, p. A8.

23. *Wall Street Journal*, January 21, 1991, p. A4. See also Ronald

E. Yates, "Japan Expected to Up Gulf Aid by $5 Billion," *Chicago Tribune*, January 21, 1991, 1:4. See also "Germany, Japan Promise More Aid for Gulf Effort," *Wall Street Journal*, January 23, 1991, p. A3.

24. Peter H. Lewis, "Special Order for Gulf Sends Powerful PC's," *New York Times*, January 22, 1991, p. B8.

25. "Too Soon to Tax for War . . ." *Chicago Tribune*, January 25, 1991, 1:12 (editorial). The editorial drew a response from the Consul General of Japan, Takeshi Nakamura; this ran as the lead "letter to the editor"—a slot which the *Tribune* calls "Voice of the People." "Japan Bearing Its Share in Gulf Crisis," February 1, 1991, 1:12.

26. *New York Times*, January 26, 1991, p. 18 (editorial).

27. "Japan Counts the Costs of Gulf Action—or Inaction," *New York Times*, January 27, 1991, 4:2.

28. Steven R. Weisman, "Japan's Premier Backs a Compromise on Aid for the Gulf War," *New York Times*, February 2, 1991, p. 6. The Clean Government Party got lengthier treatment later; see Steven R. Weisman, "Japanese Party Gets Big Gulf Role," *New York Times*, February 27, 1991, p. A5.

29. "Japan, Germany and the Gulf," *Chicago Tribune*, February 2, 1991, 1:12.

30. Walter Russell Mead, "Germany and Japan—Dragging Their Boots," *New York Times*, February 3, 1991, 4:19. A writer for the *New Republic* similarly reproached the U.S., but reached that conclusion only after several paragraphs of Japan-bashing. John B. Judis, "Burden Shirking," *New Republic*, March 4, 1991 (available to subscribers on February 18, 1991), pp. 21–22.

31. "Japan Claims Big Role in U.S. Weapons Success," *Chicago Tribune*, February 3, 1991, 7:1+ . Even the "claim" language, it should be noted, was insufficient Americanism for one letter-writer. See Jack M. Heeren, "Don't Discount American Ingenuity," *Chicago Tribune*, March 2, 1991, 1:10 (letter in "Voice of the People" slot arguing that because of procurement rules, international leading-edge technology is not to be found in American weapons systems, and that American abilities are such that international technologies are not needed).

32. Paul Blustein, "Economic Garbo: Japan Is a Star Who Vants to Be Alone," *Washington Post National Weekly Edition*, February 4–10, 1991, p.9. See also James Walsh, "Good Riddance to Arms," *Time*, February 11, 1991, p. 39.

33. Donald Hellmann, "Japan's Bogus Constitutional Excuses in the Gulf," *Wall Street Journal*, February 6, 1991, p. A12. But see Kyoko Inoue, "Respect the Japanese Constitution," *Chicago Tribune*, February 20, 1991, 1:12 (letter in "Voice of the People" slot); Bob Greene, "A Japanese Youth Comes in Peace," *Chicago Tribune*, April 15, 1991, 2:1 (opinion column).

34. Ronald E. Yates, "Aid from Japan Is No Sure Thing," *Chicago Tribune*, February 6, 1991, 1:1 + . Material summarized to this point is at 1:1.

35. Ibid., 1:5.

36. Steven R. Weisman, "Test for Japan's Leader: Kaifu Faces Growing Difficulty in Building a Consensus on Tokyo's Role in Gulf War," *New York Times*, February 8, 1991, p. A1 + .

37. Ronald E. Yates, "Japan's Heir Watchers Are Growing Nervous." *Chicago Tribune*, February 10, 1991, 1:21 + .

38. Frederick Kempe, "Germans' Support for U.S., After Time, Grows Resolute," *Wall Street Journal*, February 11, 1991, p. A8.

39. Naomi Morris, "German Public Opinion Pulls a Switch, Now Supports Coalition," *Chicago Tribune*, February 12, 1991, 1:10.

40. Clyde H. Farnsworth, "Pressure on Japan to Buy Jets," *New York Times*, February 11, 1991, p. C1 + .

41. "Japanese Ruling Party Gets Gulf Pledge Backing," *Wall Street Journal*, February 19, 1991, p. A12.

42. "Firmness in Europe, Egypt and Japan," *New York Times*, February 24, 1991, p. 12.

43. Paul Blustein, "In Japan, Seeing the War on a Five-Inch Screen," *Washington Post National Weekly Edition*, February 25 to March 3, 1991, p. 25.

44. Adam Clymer, "Senators Fear Allies Will Renege on War Payments," *New York Times*, February 27, 1991, p. A11.

45. "Japan Is Wary of Kuwait Role," *New York Times*, February 28, 1991, p. A11.

46. Urban C. Lehner, "Japan Considers Taking the Initiative on Middle East Reconstruction Plans," *Wall Street Journal*, March 5, 1991, p. A10. See also "The Superpower That Isn't There," *Time*, March 11, 1991, p. 43 (strictures may persist concerning Japanese construction, but not financing, of the projects).

47. Ronald E. Yates, "Japan Still May See Kuwait Bonanza," *Chicago Tribune*, March 10, 1991, 7:3.

48. Steven R. Weisman, "Furor in Japan over U.S. Funding Program," *New York Times*, March 3, 1991, p. 14. See also "Dispatch Case," *Chronicle of Higher Education*, April 17, 1991, p. A41.

49. "Japan's Gulf Aid Budget Approved by Lawmakers," p. A8.

50. Ronald E. Yates, "Japan Approves $9 Billion in Gulf Aid," *Chicago Tribune*, March 7, 1991, 1:9.

51. "The Allies Deliver—in Pledges, at Least," *Chicago Tribune*, March 9, 1991, 1:12 (editorial).

52. See Yates, "Rising Friction Tests . . ." p. 1:6.

53. Ibid.

54. Richard Morin, "The Winners in the War: Bush, Republicans

and the U.N.,'' *Washington Post National Weekly Edition*, March 18–24, 1991, p.38.

55. Steven R. Weisman, "Who's Not Fit to Be Governor? Just Look at This," *New York Times*, March 29, 1991, p. A5. See also Ronald E. Yates, "Vote May Depose 'Emperor' After Reign of 12 Years," *Chicago Tribune*, April 5, 1991, 1:5. It is interesting that the New York paper presents Tokyo "politics" as a diverting sideshow (and, in the world of political economy, it seems to be moving that way, with New York's help); while Chicago—in the Yates story, at least—focuses on the Tokyo political story as an object lesson in abhorrent cronyism, further criticized as much worse than that of Richard J. Daley's old Chicago machine.

56. See Christopher J. Chipello, "Kaifu Seeks Better U.S.–Japan Ties in Talks with Bush," *Wall Street Journal*, April 3, 1991, p.A16.

57. Yoshi Tsurumi, "Tokyo Voters Sent a Message to Washington," *New York Times*, April 25, 1991, p. A14 (letter to the editor).

58. See "Japanese Minesweepers May Be Sent to Persian Gulf," *Wall Street Journal*, April 17, 1991, p. A12; "Japan, Gorbachev and the Gulf," *Chicago Tribune*, April 25, 1991, 1:10 (an approving editorial that rather bluntly raised the "role" question); Steven R. Weisman, "Japan Flotilla Will Go to Gulf," *New York Times*, April 25, 1991, p. A6 (a short treatment that noted extensive blow-by-blow coverage in the Japanese press); Christopher J. Chipello, "Japan, by Sending Minesweepers to Gulf, Takes Step Toward Broader World Role," *Wall Street Journal*, April 25, 1991, p. A10 (a bit lengthier and more multifaceted than the *Times*, leading with the "role" question); Ronald E. Yates, "6 Japanese Ships Head for Persian Gulf Duty," *Chicago Tribune*, April 26, 1991, 1:5 (a short article, but the *Tribune* did write a favorable—if muddled and perhaps qualified—editorial, noted above).

59. Ronald E. Yates, "Japan Expanding Asia Role: Neighbors Wary in Face of Past Militarism," *Chicago Tribune*, June 17, 1991, 1:1 + .

60. Jim Hoagland, "A Dispute over Small Change with Japan," *Washington Post National Weekly Edition*, April 29–May 5, 1991, p. 29. See also "Japan Says No Money for War," *Tribune-Star* (Terre Haute, Ind.), May 19, 1991, p. B9 (regarding money not to be paid because of a change in the value of the yen).

61. See James Sterngold, "Japanese to Pay More in Gulf Aid," *New York Times*, May 22, 1991, p.A4.

62. Flora Lewis, "The Great Game of 'Gai-atsu'," *New York Times*, May 1, 1991, p. A17. See also Barry Hillenbrand, "In Search of a Triumph," *Time*, April 8, 1991, p. 42 (subtitle speaks of "Tokyo's dithering on the Gulf war").

63. Mike Royko, "2-Way Bashin' Could Start War," *Indianapolis News*, June 20, 1991, p. A3.

64. William Drozdiak, "The Land of the Rising Resentment,"

Washington Post National Weekly Edition, June 24–30, 1991, p. 16. See also, e.g., David E. Sanger, "Japan's Newest Bete Noire Is French Prime Minister," *New York Times*, June 1, 1991, p. 20. Note that Cresson, an excellent and veteran adversary of financial capitalism, was also pilloried in the U.S. press during 1991 for reasons having nothing to do with Japan.

65. Urban C. Lehner, "More Japanese See a 'Fearsome' U.S. After Gulf Victory," *Wall Street Journal*, March 14, 1991, p. A15.

66. T. R. Reid, "We're Number Two! We're Number Two!" *Washington Post National Weekly Edition*, March 18–24, 1991, p. 21.

67. Ayako Doi, "$13 Billion Should Buy Japan a Little Respect," *Wall Street Journal*, March 20, 1991, p. A24.

68. David E. Sanger, "Japan Shuts U.S. Rice Exhibition," *New York Times*, March 18, 1991, p. C1 + .

69. Keith Schneider, "U.S. Moves to Punish the Japanese for Trade in Sea Turtles," *New York Times*, March 21, 1991, p. A9. "U.S., Japan in Tiff About Sea Turtles," *Indianapolis News*, May 4, 1991, p. A-2 (discussing, among other things, Vice President Quayle's role in the negotiations); Keith Bradsher, "U.S. Ready to Penalize Japan Over Endangered Sea Turtles," *New York Times*, May 17, 1991, p. A1 + .

But see "Japan Agrees to Gradual Ban on Imports of Turtle Shells," *New York Times*, May 18, 1991, p. 15 + (President Bush's postponing of sanctions played as secondary to Japanese agreement on eventual ban on turtle shell imports); "Bush: Japanese Pledge to End Turtle Trade," *Chicago Tribune*, May 19, 1991, 1:12; "Japan, Backing Down, Plans Ban on Rare Turtle Import," *New York Times*, June 20, 1991, p. C4.

70. As one of the last of several stories, see David E. Sanger, "Japan, Backing Down, Plans Ban on Rare Turtle Import," *New York Times*, June 20, 1991, p. C4.

71. Compare "U.S. Singles Out China, Japan for Trade Barriers," *Chicago Tribune*, March 30, 1991, 2:9; with Clyde H. Farnsworth, "U.S. Shifts Complaints on Trade," *New York Times*, March 30, 1991, p. 15 + .

72. Peter Truell and Eduardo Lachica, "Japan-Bashing Over Trade, Fueled by Tokyo's Foot-Dragging on War Funds, Is on Rise in U.S." *Wall Street Journal*, April 1, 1991, p. A12.

73. "Japan's Offensive Rice Fight." *Chicago Tribune*, April 2, 1991, 1:12 (editorial).

74. James Sterngold, "Japan Retreating on Foreign Loans," *New York Times*, April 14, 1991, p. 1 + (Initial focus on p. 1; "emotion" etc. on p. 7). See also Marcus W. Brauchli, "Japan Warns It May Limit Loans to Poland," *Wall Street Journal*, April 17, 1991, p. A12.

75. Eduardo Lachica, " 'Dumping' Duties Sought on Japan's Word Processors," *Wall Street Journal*, April 17, 1991, p. A9.

76. Jim Mateja, "Big 3 Charge Japan Dumping Mini-Vans," *Chicago Tribune*, June 1, 1991, 2:12 (note: Mateja is an automotive section writer); "Gephardt View on Cars," *New York Times*, June 3, 1991, p. C6; compare with Paul Ingrassia and Eduardo Lachica, "U.S. Car Makers Charge Japanese with Dumping," *Wall Street Journal*, June 3, 1991, p. A3 + .

77. Clyde H. Farnsworth, "U.S. Trade Panel Asks Sanctions on Japanese," *New York Times*, April 18, 1991, p. C2; Ronald E. Yates, "U.S. Builders Hammer Away at Japan," *Chicago Tribune*, April 28, 1991, 7:3 + ; Yates, "Japan Warns U.S. Against Sanctions," *Chicago Tribune*, April 30, 1991, 3:1 + ; Keith Bradsher, "Progress in U.S.–Japan Building Pact," *New York Times*, May 10, 1991, p. C2; David E. Sanger, "U.S.–Japan Talks at Impasse on Access to Building Jobs," *New York Times*, June 1, 1991, p. 17 + ; Sanger, "Japan to Allow Foreigners to Bid on Construction Jobs," *New York Times*, June 2, 1991, p. 13; Keith Bradsher, "Japan Splits the Difference on Building Contracts," *New York Times*, June 3, 1991, p. C2.

The criticism (in the *Times*) continued even after the deal was struck; Keith Bradsher did a column on the threat-oriented nature of the U.S. side of the bargaining, contrasting it with the style of the chips negotiations—which also, however, had a deadline involved, and this deadline was beaten by two months only at the expense of utter ambiguity about what, if any, useful sanctions the U.S. might now have at its disposal. See Bradsher, "Talking Deals: The Big Contrasts in 2 Japan Pacts," *New York Times*, June 6, 1991, p. C2; compare with Bradsher, "Chip Pact Set by U.S. and Japan," *New York Times*, June 4, 1991, p. C1 + (on sanctions point).

78. "U.S.–Japan Talks on Chips," *New York Times*, April 29, 1991, p. C8 (Reuters dispatch).

79. Clyde H. Farnsworth, "U.S., Japan Reach Pact on Exports," *New York Times*, May 3, 1991, p. C1 + .

80. "Tokyo Extends a Hand to U.S. Exports," *Chicago Tribune*, May 10, 1991, 1:12 (editorial).

81. Eduardo Lachica and Jim Bartimo, "U.S. Claims Japanese Firms Withhold Equipment from American Chip Makers," *Wall Street Journal*, May 6, 1991, p. B4.

82. "Sematech Bias Charges Are Denied By Japanese Semiconductor Firms," *Wall Street Journal*, May 9, 1991, p. B4; "Japan Defense on Chip Issue," *New York Times*, May 9, 1991, p. C5.

83. Eduardo Lachica, "Japanese Firms the Most Active Investors in U.S. High-Tech Concerns, Study Says," *Wall Street Journal*, May 14, 1991, p. B4.

84. Andrew Pollack, "A Semiconductor Agreement with Japan Is Still Elusive," *New York Times*, May 14, 1991, p. C2.

85. Ronald E. Yates, "Japanese Lash Back at U.S. Reform Demands," *Chicago Tribune*, May 16, 1991, 3:1 + ; Ted Z. Manuel, "Trade Debates," *Chicago Tribune*, June 3, 1991, 1:14 (letter to the editor).

86. John N. Maclean, "U.S. Ambassador Stresses Good Will Toward Japan," *Chicago Tribune*, May 17, 1991, 3:3.

87. "Japan May Open Rice Market," *Tribune-Star* (Terre Haute, Ind.), May 21, 1991, p. B12. (from *Journal of Commerce*).

88. David E. Sanger, "Japan Again Faults West's Skills," *New York Times*, May 22, 1991, p. C1 + .

89. James Sterngold, "Japanese to Pay More in Gulf Aid," *New York Times*, May 22, 1991, p. A4.

90. Jacob M. Schlesinger and Christopher J. Chipello, "U.S., Japan Close to Chip Trade Pact Setting Targets, Not Quotas, for Sales," *Wall Street Journal*, May 22, 1991, p. A2.

91. James Sterngold, "U.S. and Japan Give Out Economic 'Report Cards'," *New York Times*, May 23, 1991, p. C2.

92. Christopher J. Chipello, "U.S., Japan Failing in Talks to Expand Construction Trade," *Wall Street Journal*, May 24, 1991, p. A8.

93. David Sanger, "Japan to Allow Foreigners to Bid on Construction Jobs," *New York Times*, June 2, 1991, p. 13.

94. Ibid.

95. Jacob M. Schlesinger, "New U.S. Semiconductor Pact Irks Some Japanese Companies," *Wall Street Journal*, June 6, 1991, p. A14.

96. See Keith Bradsher, "Chip Pact Set by U.S. and Japan," *New York Times*, June 4, 1991, p. C1 + ; Bradsher, "New U.S.–Japan Chip Pact Approved," *New York Times*, June 5, 1991, p. C11. See also "U.S., Japan Extend Computer Chip Pact," *Chicago Tribune*, June 5, 1991, 3:3.

97. Christopher J. Chipello, "Slowly but Surely, Japanese Objections to Foreign Rice Are Falling by Wayside," *Wall Street Journal*, June 10, 1991, p. A6.

98. See Bradley A. Stertz, "Chrysler's Minivans Regain Momentum, Propelled by Price Cutting and Air Bags," *Wall Street Journal*, June 20, 1991, p. B1 + (continuation page information: loaded models from Japan sell at prices just above those of "stripped" U.S. models; this is a problem because it depresses sales of top-end domestics, which traditionally carry larger margins). See also a brief note in the *Times* the next day in which a Japanese reply of "absurd" is buttressed by market share figures researched by the publication, followed at the very end by the allegation of the amount the Japanese prices to American dealers are below fair value. "U.S. Inquiry on Mini-Vans," *New York Times*, June 21, 1991, p. C16.

For comparison with Stertz (first portion of this note) regarding Chrysler's overall prognosis, and for a much fuller appreciation of what

Japan is doing to the U.S. auto market, see Kevin L. Kearns, "Is Japan About to Do In the Big Three?" *Washington Post National Weekly Edition*, June 24–30, 1991, p. 23 (commentary).

99. Leslie H. Gelb, "Whining, Excuses, Hysteria," *New York Times*, June 23, 1991, p. 15.

100. T. R. Reid, "America's Love-Hate Relationship with Japan," *Washington Post National Weekly Edition*, June 24–30, 1991, p. 24.

101. Eduardo Lachica, "U.S. to Push Japan to Open Market for Auto Parts," *Wall Street Journal*, June 28, 1991, p. A9.

102. "Global Bank Lending Up," *New York Times*, February 14, 1991, p. C17.

103. Jonathan Karp, "Japan Easing Stance on Trade with Israel," *Chicago Tribune*, April 28, 1991, 7:7A.

104. Suzanne Alexander, "Japanese Firms Embark on a Program of Lavish Giving to American Charities," *Wall Street Journal*, May 23, 1991, p. B1 + .

105. Kathleen Teltsch, "Sweat Charity Tapping a New Source in U.S.: Japanese Companies," *New York Times*, May 2, 1991, p. B12.

106. In the wake of bruising trade negotiations and the Gulf War, even leading internationalist politicians on the Japanese side were quoted as being without flexibility on a number of perceptions that had been bruited about. See Marcus W. Brauchli and Clay Chandler, "Finance Chief Hashimoto Urges Japan to Abandon Rigid Policies," *Wall Street Journal*, June 12, 1991, p. A11.

107. See Ronald E. Yates, "Japan to Nations: Cut Arms Sales," *Chicago Tribune*, May 28, 1991, 1:4.

108. Ronald E. Yates, "Japan Pushes for UN Security Council Membership," *Chicago Tribune*, June 17, 1991, 1:8 (concerning charter, low signing rate for human rights declarations, Gulf War performance as barriers to approval of U.N.–related requests).

109. See Brauchli and Chandler, "Finance Chief Hashimoto Urges Japan" (on IMF-related thoughts of Japanese notable, Ryutaro Hashimoto).

110. Such assertions are not limited to U.S. publications. One *Chicago Tribune* writer acted as a reviewer for several articles in *Business Tokyo*, a publication by Japanese business for an American audience, and some of what he found goes like this:

[The magazine] is an insight to Japanese thinking about themselves and the U.S. There are stories about Japan, but there are also a great number explaining how to work with Japanese, what happens when the Japanese buy a U.S. company, and how the Japanese view U.S. antitrust efforts.

"Is there cause to worry about the economic implications of Japan's global agenda?" asks an article in the May issue that lists the 100 largest

Japanese investors in the U.S. The answer comes from an official of the Bank of Tokyo, who says the investment in the U.S. simply reflects economic realities.

"To expect the flow to be reversed is like expecting someone to swim against the current," *Business Tokyo* quotes Bank of Tokyo Vice President Kenji Yoshizawa.

Stephen Franklin, "A Glossy Look at How Tokyo Views U.S.–Japanese Ties," *Chicago Tribune*, April 28, 1991, 7:3 (review article).

111. Jerome B. Weisner, "Technology Transcends the Borders of Nations," *New York Times*, January 8, 1991, p. A12 (letter to the editor); Robert B. Reich, "Barring Foreign Access to Fruits of U.S. Science Is Nonsensical," *Chronicle of Higher Education*, March 20, 1991, p. A52 ("Point of View" column).

112. See Christopher J. Chipello, "Mr. Ogawa's Tale: How Sweet Potatoes Grounded an Airport," *Wall Street Journal*, April 12, 1991, p. A1 + ; see also Clay Chandler, "Japan Moves to Ease Controls On Banks, Securities Firms; Bureaucracy to Benefit," *Wall Street Journal*, June 21, 1991, p. C1 + .

113. See "Shocked in Tokyo," *Wall Street Journal*, June 26, 1991, p. A10 (editorial on Nomura stock scandal; first paragraph includes the following: "Heavy regulation is just asking for foul play in markets").

114. See the nature of commentary on a 1991 story about a rival entity, American Express. Kurt Eichenwald, "American Express–Japan Bank Talks," *New York Times*, April 23, 1991, p. C19; also, a personality-profile commentary on a bureaucratic loss by Japanese commercial bankers trying to do what American commercial bankers are trying to do by way of deregulation. Also see James Sterngold, "A Japanese-Style 'Old Boy' Network," *New York Times*, June 7, 1991, p. C1 + ; and the *Journal's* predictable spin on the same subject: Chandler, "Japan Moves to Ease Control," p. C1 + .

Resultant biases can be subtle, yet no less significant. Two stories on the poor fortune of Japanese securities firms, at least in any form that was apparent by mid-May 1991, are instructive. The *New York Times*, perhaps considering the impending rivalry between these firms and deregulated commercial banks from all over the globe, bannered the misfortunes of the largest firms; the *Wall Street Journal*, on the other hand, correctly bannered what the *Times* had internally reported, namely, that it was an industry-wide low report. Compare James Sterngold, "Japan's Top Securities Firms Report Big Drop in Profits," *New York Times*, May 17, 1991, p. C1; with Marcus W. Brauchli, "Securities Firms in Japan Report Earnings Plunge," *Wall Street Journal*, May 17, 1991, p. C11.

ABOUT THE CONTRIBUTORS

David Arase, Assistant Professor of Government at Pomona College, received an M.A. in International Relations from the Johns Hopkins School of Advanced International Studies and a Ph.D. in Political Science from the University of California at Berkeley. He has written several articles and book chapters on Japanese foreign policy. He is currently working on a book manuscript dealing with Japanese foreign aid. His research interests include the international relations of East Asia as well as Japanese foreign policy.

Robert W. Beckstead is the J. Carlton Ward Jr. Distinguished Professor at the Industrial College of the Armed Forces of the National Defense University. He received his B.S. in Economics and M.B.A. from the University of Utah and his Ph.D. in Economics from the University of Illinois. He is co-author of *Defense Economic Issues: Some Implications of Managing Defense Resources* and is preparing a manuscript for publication entitled *A United States International Logistics Strategy: An Economic Perspective.* He has written numerous articles on international economic issues.

Stephen Blank has been a National Security Affairs Analyst at the Strategic Studies Institute, U.S. Army War College, since 1989. Prior to that appointment he was Associate Professor of Soviet Studies at the Center for Aerospace Doctrine, Research, and Education at the Air University, Maxwell Air Force Base. He received his M.A. and Ph.D. in Russian History from the University of Chicago. He has published numerous articles on Soviet military and foreign policies, notably in the Third World, and is the author of a forthcoming study of the Soviet Commissariat of Nationali-

301

ties. He is the editor of books on Soviet foreign policies in Latin America and on the future of the Soviet military.

Tae-Hwan Kwak is Professor of International Relations at Eastern Kentucky University and a specialist on East Asian affairs, international politics, and foreign policy. He received his Ph.D. from Claremont. He is the author and co-editor of numerous books, the most recent of which are *Forty Years of U.S.–Korean Relations* and *The Korean–American Community: Present and Future*. He has published more than 120 articles in scholarly journals and has contributed to more than fifteen books in English, Japanese, and Korean. He is a member of the editorial boards of *Asian Perspective, Korean Journal of International Studies,* and *Pacific Focus*. His research interests include international security issues, South–North Korean conflict behavior, and the four major powers' policies toward the two Koreas.

Edward A. Olsen is Professor of National Security Affairs at the Naval Postgraduate School, Monterey, California. A specialist in Northeast Asian affairs, he received his B.A. from the University of California of Los Angeles, M.A. from University of California at Berkeley, and Ph.D. from American University. He is the author of four books, three monographs, forty book chapters, and over eighty articles. His most recent books are *U.S. Policy and the Two Koreas* and *Bei-nichi boei keizai rinku ron (Japan–U.S. Defense Economics Link Theory)*. His current research focuses on U.S.–Asian relations in the post-Cold War era.

R. Christopher Perry (Ph.D., University of Minnesota) is an Associate Professor of Political Science at Indiana State University. His research most related to the concerns of this volume has to do with patterns of discourse in American national-scale and big-city print media. Articles and conference papers in this vein have discussed the "rhetoric of inevitability" and the creation of heroes, adversaries, and pressures for policy action. One current project is entitled, "1991's 'Bank Reform' in the Mind of the *New York Times* and *Washington Post*: a Summary and Critique."

Robert H. Puckett is Professor of Political Science at Indiana State University. A specialist on American foreign policy, he received his B.A. from De Pauw University and his M.A. and Ph.D. from the University of Chicago. He is the author of *America Faces the World: Isolationist Ideology in American Foreign Policy* and numerous articles on U.S. foreign policy issues. His current research focuses on Japan and global security.

Sheldon W. Simon is Professor of Political Science and faculty associate of the Center for Asian Studies at Arizona State University. He received his Ph.D. from the University of Minnesota and is the author or editor of six books and over seventy scholarly articles and book chapters. His most recent book is *The Future of Asian Pacific Security Collaboration.* His research interests focus on Asian security.

Martin E. Weinstein is Professor of Japanese Studies and International Politics at the University of Illinois. He completed his doctorate at Columbia University and studied Japanese at Yale and Columbia. He served as Special Assistant to Ambassadors James Hodgson and Mike Mansfield in Tokyo. His most recent book is *The Human Face of Japan's Leadership: Twelve Portraits.* His previous publications include *Japan's Postwar Defense Policy, Northeast Asian Security after Vietnam,* and *Japan: The Risen Sun,* as well as numerous articles on Japanese foreign policy and U.S.–Japanese relations.

Jimmy W. Wheeler, Director of International and Asia–Pacific Studies at the Hudson Institute, completed his undergraduate studies at the University of Missouri and his doctoral studies at Rutgers University. He is an economist specializing in public policy analysis and corporate planning. His most recent publications include *The Taiwan Relations Act: A Decade of Implementation* and *Beyond Recrimination: Perspectives on U.S.–Taiwan Trade Tensions* (with Perry Wood). He has authored, co-authored, or acted as project director or principal investigator of over twelve publications. His current research studies include Asia/Pacific economic cooperation, multinational military cooperation in the 1990s, and U.S. military basing in the Asia–Pacific region.

Robert S. Wood is Dean of the Center for Naval Warfare Studies and Special Academic Advisor to the President of the Naval War College. He also holds the Chester W. Nimitz Chair of National Security and Foreign Affairs. He received a B.A. in HIstory from Stanford University and his M.A. and Ph.D. degrees in Political Science from Harvard University. He has served as a consultant to the Department of Defense, Federal Executive Institute, and the National Security Council, and is author of the forthcoming studies, *America the Vincible: Foreign Policy Challenges in the Nineties* and *France in the World Community.* He has also contributed, authored, co-authored, or edited seventeen other books and numerous articles on public affairs, executive development, international politics, and national security policy.

INDEX

DATE DUE